Wastelands

Wastelands

RECYCLED COMMODITIES AND
THE PERPETUAL DISPLACEMENT OF
ASHKALI AND ROMANI SCAVENGERS

Eirik Saethre

UNIVERSITY OF CALIFORNIA PRESS

University of California Press
Oakland, California

Library of Congress Cataloging-in-Publication Data

Names: Saethre, Eirik, author.
Title: Wastelands : recycled commodities and the perpetual displacement
 of Ashkali and Romani Scavengers / Eirik Saethre.
Description: Oakland, California : University of California Press, [2020] |
 Includes bibliographical references and index.
Identifiers: LCCN 2020017886 (print) | LCCN 2020017887 (ebook) |
 ISBN 9780520368491 (hardback) | ISBN 9780520368514
 (paperback) | ISBN 9780520976139 (ebook)
Subjects: LCSH: Romanies—Serbia—History. | Refugees—Serbia—
 Belgrade. | Dumpster diving—Serbia—Belgrade.
Classification: LCC DX269 .S24 2020 (print) | LCC DX269 (ebook) |
 DDCE 305.8914/9704971—dc23
LC record available at https://lccn.loc.gov/2020017886
LC ebook record available at https://lccn.loc.gov/2020017887

29 28 27 26 25 24 23 22 21 20
10 9 8 7 6 5 4 3 2 1

Contents

Acknowledgments

Foremost, I am an extremely grateful for the overwhelming help and patience of Polje's Ashkali and Romani residents. They invited me into their homes, taught a very awkward American how to scavenge, trusted me with their stories, and never stopped looking after me.

I must also thank those individuals who generously supported me and my research in Belgrade. Slobodan Stanković worked tirelessly as my research assistant. His remarkable insights, feedback, and linguistic skills played an enormous role in the success of this project. I could not have done it without him. I must credit Goran Ševo, my longtime friend and fellow Australian National University alum, for first encouraging me to work in Belgrade. Later, he supplied invaluable advice and logistical help, which made this research possible. Bojan Žikić coordinated my time in the Department of Ethnology and Anthropology at the University of Belgrade and commented on an early draft of this book. Our discussions of Serbia and Serbian anthropology grounded my thinking and writing. Biljana Sikimić kindly shared her expertise regarding Serbia's diverse Romani population and introduced me to academic networks in Belgrade. Finally, I must acknowledge the financial assistance of the Fulbright Scholar Program and the support of the United States Embassy in Serbia.

I also received tremendous help from my friends and colleagues in the United States. From the very beginning, Ruth Anderson contributed her boundless encouragement, knowledge, and editing skills. Ian Hancock graciously provided advice prior to my departure for Belgrade and then upon my return. I would also like to thank Carol Silverman and Melissa Caldwell, who offered insightful and valuable comments on the manuscript. At the University of Hawaiʻi at Mānoa, I am grateful for the unceasing support and guidance of Christine Beaule, Jan Brunson, Alexander Mawyer, and Christian Peterson.

Introduction

THE OTHER WORLD

Polje was a space unto itself. An informal Romani settlement on the edge of Belgrade, it was home to approximately two hundred Ashkali and Roma living in small one-room shacks. Piles of trash lined the narrow lane that served as the main thoroughfare. Water was obtained from nearby fire hydrants while electricity was siphoned from streetlights. Completely concealed by a series of small berms, Polje was situated between two contrasting geographies. On one side, gray concrete high-rise buildings punctuated an urban landscape, and on the other, bucolic green fields stretched to the horizon. If Polje seemed out of place, so too did its inhabitants. Every resident was a migrant, refugee, or displaced person. A site of temporary asylum, the settlement was largely divorced from the realm beyond its borders. A teenage resident, Deon, aptly described Polje as "the other world."[1] But the settlement was also an Other world, where the exiled sought to build their lives before they were inevitably dislodged once more.

Characterized as unhygienic, a squatter camp, and a slum, Polje was one of an estimated 583 "substandard" Romani settlements that pervaded Serbia.[2] Serbs decried the blight caused by these settlements while the government prioritized their destruction. Polje's residents were continually under threat; their homes would never be secure. In addition, informal

1

Romani settlements were socially, materially, economically, and legally isolated from the rest of the nation. The most substantive link between Polje's inhabitants and the world outside its borders was the trash. In the urban sprawl just beyond the settlement lay a realm of discarded commodities that could be converted into food, housing, and cash. In so doing, Ashkali and Roma sought to turn garbage into success. Like everyone else in Polje, this is what drew Bekim to the settlement.

Although he was twenty-four years old, Bekim stood just over five feet tall and weighed barely ninety pounds, a result of being malnourished for most of his life. Given his slight build, Bekim had difficulty finding clothes that fit. Because he refused to wear boy's sizes, he was constantly pulling up his pants in an effort to keep them from falling off. But this did not bother Bekim, who often joked about his wardrobe malfunctions. However, his humor belied a history of loss and dislocation. He came to Serbia as a child when his family fled the Kosovo War. Arriving in Belgrade, they first lived in Zgrade, and then, after it was destroyed by the Serbian government, Polje. Despite residing in Serbia for almost two decades, Bekim still lacked identity documents. As a result he was unable to work legally, open a bank account, or access state health care. Barred from the formal economy, Bekim earned money recycling paper and metal he found in dumpsters. This work was filthy, physically debilitating, and barely provided enough income to support his family. Married at sixteen, Bekim had fathered eight children, four of whom died in infancy. His wife, Fatime, was pregnant again and he fervently hoped this child would live.

Late one night as Bekim and I visited a nearby supermarket for food, his incessant struggle for survival was vividly illustrated. Walking out of the settlement, we entered a busy street lined with bright lights and tall buildings. As Bekim contemplated the proliferation of stores along our route, he asked if I had visited the nearby mall. He had never been inside and was curious what it was like. Even though it was not far from his home, the mall was a place Bekim would probably never go. People like him, he said, could get into trouble if they went to malls. Bekim knew the areas he should avoid. Suddenly, his stomach started to rumble. There had not been much food for dinner and Bekim only ate a fraction of it, wanting to ensure that his children had enough. Thinking about his last meal, Bekim casually commented that another one of his molars had fallen out. This was the second in as many weeks and a little more than half of his teeth remained. Stoically, Bekim added that at least it had been painless. He expected to begin losing his incisors soon, which were already black with decay.

Before long, we crossed an empty parking lot and arrived at the front of a large supermarket. Its windows were dark and the building appeared deserted. As I expected, it had closed an hour earlier. We had not come to shop. Wanting to avoid harassment, Polje's residents assiduously avoided purchasing food at supermarkets. Nevertheless, these large stores were an important source of sustenance for Bekim's family. Skirting around the side of the building, we made our way to a row of dumpsters in the rear. With Bekim starting at one end and me at the other, we meticulously combed through their contents. This is where we hoped to obtain our next meal. We were searching for any rotten fruits and vegetables that the supermarket had discarded at closing. While Serbs expressed disgust at eating food found in dumpsters, it was an accepted part of everyday life in the Other world. Molding tomatoes were not trash; they were nourishment. But despite our efforts the dumpsters yielded nothing. Fortunately, two other supermarkets were not far away. Perhaps, Bekim mused, we would have better luck there.

As we began walking, Bekim suggested that we buy a soda from a nearby convenience store. Although the door was locked, a clerk was conducting transactions through an open window. She fetched candy and snacks from inside the premises but allowed customers to choose their own beverages from an exterior refrigerator. For security, it could only be opened once the clerk disengaged a magnetic seal. However, when Bekim asked her to unlock the refrigerator, as she had done for the Serbs in line before us, the clerk refused. Instead, she summoned a coworker to fetch the bottle. Bekim paid in silence but as soon as we were out of earshot, he vented his anger. She treated us like thieving *cigani*, he said. Although *cigan* is routinely translated as Gypsy, these words have different origins.[3] Furthermore, the former is far more pejorative and pervades Serbian speech. While Lady Gaga sings about loving the "Gypsy life," Serbs discuss the dirty, lazy, and dishonest *cigani* who pervade their city. Given these stereotypes, Bekim was accustomed to regularly enduring interactions like the one at the convenience store.

Strolling two blocks more, we found ourselves in front of another supermarket. This time, Bekim paused. A group of young Serbian men was loitering not far away. Bekim knew that like the clerk, they regarded him as a *cigan*. *Cigan* was not only an insult; it inspired violence. Especially at night, *cigani* were chased and assaulted. Bekim had been forced to run for his life on several occasions and he did not want to repeat the experience now. A few scraps of food, he whispered, were not worth broken bones. Turning around, he guided me to yet another set of dumpsters. Once again, several men were standing nearby. Urging me to walk faster as we made our retreat, Bekim repeatedly glanced over his shoulder to ensure we were not followed. At this point he decided to return home, remarking that it was simply too dangerous to stay out any longer.

As we entered Polje, I was reminded just how separate the settlement was. Leaving the main thoroughfare, we turned down an inconspicuous lane. In the distance lay only darkness. Walking further, we left the city behind. The streetlights grew fainter, the din of traffic disappeared, and the air became colder. Soon we were enveloped by the night and unable to see anything but the narrow road we were traversing. Then, through the blackness, a scattering of faint lights began appearing in the distance. Suddenly, we entered the settlement, surrounded by shacks, trash, and silence. Bekim and I were home.

Sitting down outside his shack, I thought about our experiences that night. Bekim, a refugee, had spent an hour trying to feed his family by rummaging through dumpsters for rotten vegetables. During this brief time his alienness seemed to be omnipresent: he was fearful to enter a mall, treated as a thief, and risked being beaten. He returned to his home, a shack in a trash-strewn, segregated settlement, with nothing more than a bottle of soda. And this settlement, Bekim's shelter from the dangerous streets, was continually threatened with demolition. He could lose what little he had in a matter of days. Seeing my expression, Bekim asked what I was thinking. I replied that I was contemplating our evening. Bekim nodded. Yes, he said, it had been an incredibly boring night.

Boring was a word commonly used to describe people's lives in Polje. For Bekim, there was nothing exceptional about scavenging for food, avoiding assault, or facing eviction. Hunger, segregation, racism, and marginalization were so entrenched that they were not just the norm, they were tedious. This response was born out of the world of the settlements and the trash that sustained them. Polje and the people who called it home were so fundamentally estranged from Serbian society and from the Serbian state that the Other world became their only world. There was simply no alternative way to be. But if life in the settlements was boring, it was not without hope. The potential for a better existence lay in the dumpsters. Banned from the world beyond Polje, Ashkali and Roma looked to its detritus for their survival and prosperity. To understand these precarious spaces of displacement where trash is ubiquitous and transformative—these wastelands—this book follows Bekim and his neighbors as they scavenge life.

VISIBLE INVISIBILITY

Four years before that night with Bekim, I arrived in Belgrade to explore the feasibility of conducting anthropological research in informal Romani settlements. During that initial trip I quickly became aware of how Roma were both exceptionally visible and relentlessly hidden. Every day I saw Roma. When I walked to the grocery store or to the tram stop, I observed Roma sorting through dumpsters, begging at traffic lights, and pedaling three-wheeled bicycles called *trokolice*. As I sat in my apartment, I regularly heard the clop, clop, clop of horses' hooves on the asphalt before catching a glimpse of a Rom driving a cart laden with scrap metal. Scavenging, coupled with their noticeably dark skin and black hair, marked Roma as Other. Their difference was obvious but also unremarkable. My Serbian neighbors were accustomed to passing Roma on the street and standing next to them at convenience stores. Yet despite the ubiquity and visibility of Roma, they were in many ways just as much of a mystery to my neighbors as they were to me. When I asked where the Romani horsemen were from or how many settlements were in the vicinity, Serbs could not answer. They passed the same Romani individuals every day but knew nothing about their everyday lives. Echoing Deon, one woman replied, "*cigani* live in their own world." This book explores the alternating contexts of visibility and invisibility to understand the complex relationships that occur between Roma and Serbs, between Roma and the state, and between Roma and a global economy of trash.

Serbs saw little reason to know the particulars of Romani lives because *cigani* were assumed to be a homogeneous and eternal underclass. *Cigani* would always be poor and dirty, I was told. They lived in shacks and remained unemployed because that was their preferred lifestyle. One man was adamant that although *cigani* blamed the Serbian government for their poverty, it was their own fault. In their hearts, he said, *cigani* were different. Overhearing this conversation, a young woman volunteered that when she was a child, her parents told her *cigani* would kidnap her. To this day she was still terrified. *Cigani* were deceitful, she added, predicting they would only talk to me for money and would never be my friends. Others were concerned that I would be robbed or assaulted while visiting Romani settlements. One man believed that my informants would encourage me to steal manhole covers or electrical wires. Once the police discovered these crimes, he continued, they would send me to prison while the instigators remained free. Although most comments focused on the inherent laziness and criminality of Roma, a few stressed their carefree attitude. One woman remarked that *cigani* always smiled and laughed even though they could not feed themselves. These Serbian narratives were a patchwork of uncertainties, emotions, and moral equivalencies that exerted considerable power but were ultimately, and necessarily, based in ignorance.

Stereotypes of Roma were not confined to Belgrade. For hundreds of years, representations of Gypsies have circulated through Europe and North America.[4] Authors including Shakespeare (*Othello*), Cervantes (*La gitanilla*), Austen (*Emma*), Hugo (*Hunchback of Notre Dame*), Lawrence (*The Virgin and the Gipsy*), and King (*Thinner*) have written about Roma while painters such as Hals (*The Gypsy Girl*), Caravaggio (*The Fortune Teller*), Manet (*Gypsy with a Cigarette*), and van Gogh (*The Caravans— Gypsy Camp near Arles*) have depicted them. In the 1990s the films of Emir Kusturica, such as *Time of the Gypsies* and *Black Cat, White Cat*, exposed international audiences to Balkan accounts of Roma. Today, Roma are most conspicuously represented in reality shows such as *Gypsy Sisters*, *Big Fat Gypsy Wedding*, and *American Gypsies*. Nevertheless, Romani characters have also graced *Buffy the Vampire Slayer*, *MacGyver*, *X-Men*, *Law and Order: Special Victims Unit*, and *Criminal Minds*. In most renderings Gypsies are cast as a mix of thieves, fortunetellers, and exotic vagabonds. These various depictions are unified by a common theme: the stranger among us. Gypsies are familiar yet separate. They constitute a permanently marginal and potentially dangerous population who are inherently alien, unable to integrate into modern society, and capable of assailing national norms and values.[5]

This is particularly true in representations of, and responses to, Romani disparities. In many cases, segregation and disadvantage are portrayed as intractable expressions of an innate Romani desire to remain apart and preserve an itinerant lifestyle.[6] While ostensibly dedicated to aiding Roma, initiatives such as the Decade of Roma Inclusion stigmatize Roma, invoke poverty, and make a point of notionally separating them from the non-Romani population.[7] These attitudes are on vivid display in newspapers and magazines such as *The Economist*, where one headline declares that Roma are "Europe's biggest societal problem." To express the magnitude of Romani destitution, it opines that Romani settlements "rival Africa or India for their deprivation."[8] This article renders Roma as so fundamentally different that their communities have more in common with iconically impoverished countries than they do with Europe. In reality, many Roma are members of the middle class, own multistory homes, and work as salaried employees. However, the affluence of some Roma is ignored as identity and indigence are conflated. This discourse relies upon the fixity of stereotypes through which non-Roma construct and perpetuate Gypsy identity while Roma remain virtually powerless to shape dominant narratives about themselves.[9]

After a few weeks of hearing horses pass beneath my window and being told stories of dirty and dangerous *cigani*, I finally met a resident of a Romani settlement. One afternoon as I was disposing of my trash, a middle-aged man arrived on his *trokolica* and began sifting through the dumpster's contents. I approached him and explained that I was an American anthropologist who wanted to understand the histories and everyday lives of Roma living in the area.[10] Did he have a few minutes to talk to me? Yes, he replied. After telling me that his name was Endrit, he immediately asserted that he had not always lived in a shack. Born in Kosovo in 1968, Endrit spent his childhood in Germany where he attended school and excelled at gymnastics. He returned to what was then Yugoslavia as a teenager, eventually completing his mandatory military service, marrying, purchasing a home in Kosovo, and fathering six children. But Endrit's life changed forever in 1999 when war and ethnic cleansing enveloped the region. Fearing for his safety, he fled with his family to Belgrade.

Endrit's circumstances were the result of violent conflict and not a culture of poverty as so many Serbs assumed. Narratives underscoring *ciganski* foreignness fail to acknowledge the degree to which Roma have been embedded in European trajectories. Despite living in Europe for centuries, Roma were rendered as a people without history.[11] In reality, national and international crises, such as the geopolitical fragmentation of the Balkans, have fundamentally shaped their existence. As ethnic Serbs and ethnic Albanians sparred over control of Kosovo, Roma were not only displaced; their identity was splintered. Endrit, I would eventually learn, identified as neither a *cigan* nor a Rom. He was Ashkali. Endrit's ethnicity was the result of recent events in a centuries-long struggle over self-determination in Kosovo.

For most of its history, Kosovo has been home to a multiethnic population of Serbs, Albanians, and Roma. Today, Serbs view Kosovo as an indisputable part of their nation's territory, pointing to its role as a political and religious center of the thirteenth-century Kingdom of Serbia. However, the Ottoman Empire annexed Kosovo in the fifteenth century and Albanian-speaking people began to settle the area in greater numbers. When Yugoslavia was formed after World War I, Muslim Albanians had firmly replaced Orthodox Christian Serbs as Kosovo's majority population.[12] Ethnic tensions between the two groups had occasionally flared into violence, but Josef Tito's socialist government muscularly repressed any anti-Yugoslav sentiments. In an effort to build a unified nation, Roma were also integrated into the state apparatus alongside other ethnic groups. By the 1970s, Yugoslavia boasted antidiscrimination legislation, a prohibition on using the word *cigan*, and unprecedented access to education and employment for Roma.[13]

After Tito's death in 1980, ethnic ambitions were rekindled. By 1991 Yugoslavia was disintegrating as its constituent republics were declaring independence. With war erupting in Croatia and Bosnia, the Serbian government of Slobodan Milošević tightened control over Kosovo. In response, Kosovar Albanians increasingly called for self-determination and soon the Kosovo Liberation Army (KLA) was attacking Serbian security personnel. In 1999 urban warfare, shelling, and ethnic cleansing were occurring across the province as Serbs expelled Albanians. In an effort to end the conflict, NATO conducted a bombing campaign targeting strategic sites across Serbia. The offensive lasted seventy-eight days and resulted in the withdrawal of Serbian forces and a ceasefire. At the end of the war, 8,000–10,000 people had died with thousands more missing.[14] To forestall future violence and ensure the safety of returning Albanians, NATO stationed peacekeepers in Kosovo. Several years later, the Albanian-dominated government declared its independence from Serbia. The United States and most member states of the European Union (EU) recognized Kosovo's new status, but Serbia has steadfastly refused to abandon its claim to the region.

Although the war was fought between Serbs and Albanians, it deeply affected the lives of Kosovo's Roma. Prior to the conflict, Kosovo was home to an estimated 100,000–150,000 Roma, which some scholars have separated into two broad groups.[15] The first lived primarily in Serbian-dominated areas and was conversant in Romani and Serbian. In the 1970s and 1980s these individuals increasingly embraced a Romani identity that was in opposition to Albanian nationalism.[16] When the Milošević government forced Albanians out of public-sector jobs, these Roma, who generally backed the Serbian state, were hired if no Serbs were available.[17] The second Romani group resided in Albanian regions and spoke only Albanian, having lost proficiency in Romani approximately two generations earlier. Kosovar independence advocates urged these individuals to record their ethnicity as Albanian on the census to bolster the case for autonomy.[18] Eventually, Albanian-speakers would reject the label of Roma in favor of two alternate ethnicities: Egyptian and Ashkali.[19]

Beginning in the 1980s, evidence from Byzantine texts bolstered narratives of an Egyptian migration to Europe, while folktales described a Romani kingdom in North Africa.[20] Seizing on these stories, a movement to adopt an Egyptian identity was born, and in 1991 the Yugoslav government approved "Egyptian" as a census category.[21] Serbian nationalists were quick to support the Egyptian label for their own purposes, hoping it would simultaneously reduce the number of Albanians recorded in the census and prove to international governments that Kosovo was a multiethnic province, not an Albanian one. Firmly embedded within a specific geopolitical context, the creation and perpetuation of Romani and Egyptian identities was fueled by the disputes between Serbians and Albanians.

During the Kosovo War, *cigani* were targeted by both sides, their property was destroyed, and they were subjected to assault and murder.[22] Although the 1999 ceasefire was celebrated as the end of ethnic warfare, there was little relief for Roma and Egyptians. Albanians fighting for independence viewed Romani-speaking Roma and Egyptians, both of whom had relied on the state bureaucracy, as collaborating with the Milošević government.[23] In retaliation, Albanian refugees returning to Kosovo sought revenge for perceived past injustices. The KLA and other nationalist groups have been accused of rape, forced labor, and confiscating personal possessions.[24] Not expecting the Albanian victims to become victimizers, NATO peacekeepers did little to stop the violence. Even international efforts to shield Roma from retribution resulted in harm. The inhabitants of a United Nations refugee camp situated near a heavy metal mining complex were exposed to toxic levels of lead for over a decade.[25]

As brutality against *cigani* continued, a third identity, Ashkali, was popularized.[26] Ashkali attempted to mitigate the risk of reprisals by distancing themselves from Roma and Egyptians while stressing their affiliation with Kosovar Albanians, for instance by emphasizing their use of the Albanian language and ignorance of Romani.[27] With Ashkali ethnicity becoming increasingly common, international peacekeeping bodies such as NATO and the OSCE took notice. These organizations eventually accepted Ashkali as an independent group, arguing that self-determination was an integral component of an international human rights framework.[28] Relying on the support of these bodies, the Kosovar government, and its constitution, also acknowledged Ashkali as a category while Serbia added the classification to its 2002 census.[29] But even as their ethnicity gained recognition, Ashkali were still bound by enduring stereotypes of *cigani*.[30]

Despite stressing an allegiance to Albanian language and customs, brown skin marked Ashkali as aliens in an Albanian-dominated Kosovo. Like Roma and Egyptians, Ashkali were excluded from the postwar nationalist narrative and cast as hindering the development of an ethnically pure Albanian-dominated Kosovo. As a result Ashkali were forcefully expelled alongside Roma and Egyptians. Under the watch of NATO troops, 12,600 Romani, Ashkali, and Egyptian homes were partially or completely destroyed.[31] These and other acts of ethnic cleansing resulted in a mass exodus. Approximately a hundred thousand Roma, Ashkali, and Egyptians fled Kosovo, leaving as few as eleven thousand in the country.[32] Many families applied for asylum in Germany and other countries in the European Union, but most of these requests were eventually denied, resulting in forced repatriation to Kosovo. The largest percentage of those displaced, about half, sought safety in Serbia.[33] Endrit and his family were among this group.

In Belgrade, Ashkali were invisible refugees. Their history of eviction was publicly unnoticed and unacknowledged. To Serbs, who watched from a distance as Endrit rummaged through dumpsters, he was simply another *cigan.* They did not realize that his life in Belgrade was the result of being a bystander at the margins of the aspirations of others. Furthermore, nationalist ambitions resulted in the bureaucratic misrecognition of Endrit's status. Serbia's continuing claims to Kosovo officially rendered Ashkali internally displaced persons (IDPs), not refugees.[34] Because many Ashkali lacked identification or possessed invalid documents, they were unable to prove their citizenship, attend school, obtain routine public health care, get married, receive welfare, or purchase property. They interacted with the state only by suffering a medical emergency or by being arrested and imprisoned. Legal and economic exclusion facilitated spatial segregation. Having no place to settle, many Ashkali constructed their own housing in illegal settlements. Ashkali were so marginalized that they have been labeled the most vulnerable community in Serbia.[35]

Like numerous others, Endrit's family built a shack of discarded plywood, old doors, and tarps alongside other Ashkali in a field on the periphery of the city. The settlement, Zgrade, would eventually contain thirty-two structures sheltering approximately 150 people. Lacking secure tenure, sufficient living space, durable edifices, water, and sanitation, Zgrade was, according to UN-HABITAT's definition, a slum.[36] But the settlement was also a home. It was here that Endrit's daughter, Fatime, would meet and marry Bekim before moving into their own shack to start a family.[37] As months became years, Zgrade incubated Ashkali personhood. The everyday life of settlements generated belonging and solidarity, defining the place of Ashkali in Serbia and the world. Examining a Burundian refugee camp in Tanzania, Malkki notes that Hutu "located their identities within their very displacement, extracting meaning and power from the interstitial social location they inhabited. Instead of losing their collective identity, this is where they made it."[38] A similar process occurred in Zgrade. Although Ashkali identity was formed from the Kosovo War, living in Belgrade's settlements solidified it.

EXCLUDED PEOPLE AND DISCARDED COMMODITIES

Throughout Europe, Romani populations have been confined and controlled for centuries. The most horrific example occurred during the Nazi regime, when Roma were labeled an inferior race, sent to concentration camps, and exterminated.[39] Today, Roma are no longer overtly murdered by the state but they continue to be detained in sites across Europe. In Italy, for instance, state-sponsored "nomad camps" are often fenced, guarded, and surrounded by security cameras while residents must meet strict eligibility criteria.[40] In areas such as these, the normal rule of law is suspended and *ciganski* bodies are controlled.[41] While I am not equating nomad camps with concentration camps, there is a family resemblance between the two. In each case, *cigani* were confined, functionally stripped of citizenship, and rendered as nonpeople.

Foucault argues that modern states govern their populace through these conditions.[42] In the past, individuals deemed aberrant and a threat to social order were the subjects of explicit violence, but contemporary regimes rely less on openly taking lives. Instead, they subtly disallow existence through "indirect murder: the fact of exposing someone to death, increasing the risk of death for some people, or, quite simply, political death, expulsion, rejection, and so on."[43] Agamben builds upon Foucault's ideas, asserting that sites such as concentration camps, airport detention centers, and squatter settlements are "zones of indistinction," where noncitizens are defined, labeled expendable, and ultimately left to die.[44] These spaces are constituted through a state of exception, when governments portray certain events—such as migration, drug use, or an epidemic—as a national emergency. Then, citing security concerns, the state is able to justify abandoning legal norms and revoking the rights of those judged outside the national order. Citizenship is delineated by forging geographies for noncitizens.

In contrast to many other European countries where Romani camps were created, monitored, and controlled, those in Belgrade were characterized by the state's absence. While Zgrade was established after the Kosovo War, informal Romani settlements had been a feature of the urban landscape for decades. In the 1960s Roma established Deponija ("landfill" in Serbian) on top of a trash heap surrounded by industrial land. Over the next forty years it became synonymous with destitution, growing to over 153 shanties and 856 people.[45] But communities like Deponija were relatively rare until the 1990s. As Serbia was beset by war and economic collapse, settlements began appearing in parklands, under bridges, and on vacant commercial lots throughout the city. Eventually an estimated eight percent of Belgrade's area was occupied by squatter shacks.[46] Casting this as a national crisis, Serbs routinely attributed the proliferation of settlements to the influx of refugees and IDPs. In actuality it was the introduction of neoliberalism during the postsocialist era that played the most significant role.[47]

With the country's resources severely strained and prioritized for Serbs, authorities allowed *cigani* to construct makeshift homes on ostensibly unclaimed land.[48] Although the state did not publicly create and monitor settlements, it tacitly supported their existence through deliberate ignorance and lack of intervention. For instance, a municipal worker confessed to me that the city had no reliable record of the number of settlements around Belgrade or their location. Furthermore, no effort was being made to gather this data. But the state's inability to fund the infrastructure necessary to surveil and regulate *ciganski* bodies nonetheless resulted in an effective environment of domination. Settlements were clearly delineated from the rest of the nation because they existed in a vacuum. Withholding resources legitimized government portrayals of *cigani* as inherently Other. As sites like Deponija, Zgrade, and Polje became increasingly visible, they were branded as illegal, unhygienic, and substandard. Informal Romani settlements were icons of impoverishment and cast as a threat to public security, community health, and national safety. And their residents, *cigani*, were dangerous aliens, undeserving of rights or inclusion, let alone respect.

At a center of Agamben's work is *homo sacer*, a figure in Roman law who could be killed but not sacrificed. This illustrates the paradox at the root of Agamben's thought: politics is made possible by excluding those in whose name it is produced. This was exemplified in a tragic series of events that occurred in Polje. As segregated spaces outside the sovereign state, settlements had no right to electricity. To access the power grid, residents illegally siphoned electricity from neighboring streetlights. But municipal authorities routinely severed these connections and arrested offenders. When this occurred, families relied on candles to provide illumination. One evening, a family put their three children to sleep and went to visit a neighbor nearby. While they were away, a candle fell over and ignited their small shack. The fire spread so quickly that the children were unable to escape and burned alive. Although this incident was widely reported in the national media and thought to be heartbreaking, it not only failed to motivate a change in government policy but instead reinforced Serbian attitudes toward *cigani*. Newspapers decried the family as uncaring and reckless, while the police arrested the children's mother and charged her with neglect. These three children were the embodiment of *homo sacer*. They were viewed as vulnerable innocents who should have been protected, but it was the policies of the state—functionally ignoring settlements, their rickety wooden shacks, and lack of basic services—that allowed the children to be killed. In blaming the parents, Serbs exonerated the government and found another justification for consigning the Other to slums: *cigani* were an immoral people who permitted the death of their own children. At Auschwitz Roma were brutally slain, but in Polje they were abandoned to die.

Although *cigani* inhabited geographies of exception, the state's absence gave Ashkali and Roma an opening, albeit a limited one, to create their own sovereignty. Humphrey, in her examination of public transportation in Russia, asserts that while the state mechanics of exclusion shape everyday existence, so too do the ways of life of those who inhabit these spaces.[49] Individuals do not merely acquiesce to power. Through informal interactions and economies, they snub state strategies and generate their own localized forms of authority. Even within circumscribed environments, "everyday life 'throws in' its own exigencies and excitements. These burst beyond the confines of the notion of sovereignty and qualify it by responding to a different logic."[50] A similar set of relations also pervaded Romani settlements. While a denial of electricity rendered residents as *homo sacer*, it also refashioned social and political life through cooperative labor. Although the lampposts were monitored, an underfunded police force ensured that illicit connections could nevertheless be made and maintained. But wiring streetlights was a dangerous activity, which necessitated a series of rules and norms to govern residents. Through these actions, Ashkali and Roma established an order independent of the Serbian state. However, the primary avenue to micro-sovereignty was the trash.

Barred from the formal economy, Ashkali lived on its margins, searching dumpsters for resalable materials. Across Belgrade between 9,000 and 16,000 people derived a significant portion of their income from scavenging in dumpsters, landfills, and building sites.[51] For these individuals, who were predominantly Romani, Ashkali, or Egyptian, recycling was a profession. When Endrit left his settlement to search for trash, he spoke of going to work. Cardboard was taken to paper recyclers while metal products were offered to junkyards. If clothing or household items were found in good condition, they were hawked at local markets. While garbage provided cash, it was also a primary source of building materials, clothing, and food. Worn-out couches left on the roadside were stripped and their pressboard used as walls for shacks. Old clothes, ranging from Dolce and Gabbana sweaters to neon-orange construction vests, were salvaged and reworn. Rotten vegetables discarded by supermarkets were trimmed, washed, and cooked for dinner. If a particular item was needed— rugs for the floor of a shack, pots to cook dinner, or laces for shoes—it was sought in the trash.[52] Why pay for something, Endrit's wife, Drita, asked, when you could find it for free? Noting that almost everything he owned, wore, or ate came from dumpsters, one man proclaimed it was impossible to live without trash.

Garbage was a seemingly endless resource but it was also unpredictable. Some articles were impossible to locate immediately, forcing people to make do. When Bekim needed a new shirt, he had difficulty finding a suitable replacement and wore a woman's halter-top for two days. Scavenging was a constant struggle but it was nevertheless the most reliable method for improving one's living conditions. Refuting the comparison made in *The Economist*, one man told me, "This isn't Africa. You might not be able to buy a BMW from working in the dumpsters but you can do alright for your family." Ashkali repeatedly asserted that one could succeed, albeit only incrementally, if an individual scavenged consistently and had few expenses. Over the decade that Endrit lived in Belgrade, he was able to save enough to build a three-room brick house in Zgrade. A satellite dish was perched on the roof, a computer stood in the main room, and intricate blue Arabic designs adorned the white walls. Income from the trash allowed Endrit to build with sturdier materials and beautify his home, but he was still living illegally in a segregated settlement. Nevertheless, for those Ashkali who had left Kosovo with nothing, having a brick house was a crucial accomplishment.[53] Garbage made life bearable.

Endrit's relationship with trash was not only the product of war and displacement; technological innovations and burgeoning capitalism also played significant roles. Prior to the Industrial Revolution, scavenging was lauded as an efficient reuse of resources and an inherently moral enterprise.[54] In fact, trash contributed materials vital for the development of modern technology: a significant number of books that made the Scientific Revolution possible were printed on paper derived from rags.[55] The rise of mass production gradually altered ideas regarding trash-picking and the practice became synonymous with poverty and poor hygiene.[56] By the early twentieth century, capitalist narratives in North America and Western Europe framed disposing of the "obsolete" as essential to precipitate progress and economic advancement.[57]

This shift was delayed under state socialism, however, as nations were often beset by persistent shortages and citizens coped by intensively recycling.[58] In Hungary it was only after the introduction of a market economy and a focus on European integration that waste was associated with dirtiness.[59] Verdery contends that the postsocialist transition also played a significant part in structuring anti-Romani sentiment.[60] Their perceived roles as middlemen, market traders, and recyclers marked Roma as nonproducers, unlike the rest of the population who might be working multiple jobs to make ends meet. She writes that stereotypes of *cigani* as prone to laziness and thievery are "solidly rooted in the ideas of the socialist period: the productionist view that trade is bad and work is good (i.e., exchange is inferior to production), that it generates inequality, that it is illegal because it is 'like' the black market, that Gypsies aggravate shortage, and that for all these reasons they are criminals deserving punishment. As market reforms exaggerate all these problems of socialism, anger focuses on Gypsies, who have become their symbol."[61] Views of Roma were further augmented through their associations with trash, which was increasingly being cast as polluting and thus reinscribed the trope of dirty *cigani*.

Around the globe, waste is denotatively powerful. It has become a potent metaphor for social and economic marginality. The news media reifies garbage as an index of inequality, while anthropologists routinely employ the concept of trash as a metaphor to typify excluded groups.[62] In recent years, scholars have sought to critically assess the social, economic, and political lives of waste under the banner of "discard studies."[63] Research increasingly focuses on the institutions, policies, and technologies, which act to collect, manage, and transform garbage.[64] In an era characterized by globalization and neoliberalism, trash has become a lifeline for those whose previous economic niches were restructured or lost. Furthermore, governments and businesses depend upon scavengers, who play important roles in local and international recycling markets.[65] These interactions forge enduring bonds among individuals, corporations, and the state. Exploring the lives of informal recyclers on a Rio de Janeiro dump, Millar contests assumptions that waste work is evidence of economic exclusion. She writes, "To see the shift from Fordist wage labour to multiple forms of self-employment of the urban poor only in terms of a loss or disconnection prevents an understanding of how relationships of inequality are made and experienced in the world today."[66] Poverty, Millar argues, is created through new links to neoliberal capitalism, not isolation from it.

Examining Romani economies including recycling, Brazzabeni, Cunha, and Fotta come to a similar conclusion.[67] They assert that while scholars often describe Romani strategies as "niche," these practices are nevertheless firmly entrenched within commercial markets, albeit in unique ways. Highlighting the simultaneous internality and externality of Romani work within global capitalist networks, they note that it "is embedded in the modern economic system and created in relation to a milieu from which it cannot be dissociated, but which nevertheless cannot be fully characterised with reference to the modern economic system alone (such as being 'outside' it) without looking at the material processes that in each instance went into its fabrication."[68] Consequently, people like Endrit and Bekim not only exemplify a burgeoning trend whereby people rely on limited and unstable resources; their lives illustrate the complexities of being incorporated into an economic system only to be segregated within it.

These relationships were driven by the enduring materiality of discarded commodities. Contrary to popular wisdom, an item's worth is not extinguished when it is thrown away. A shirt in the dumpster is still a shirt and, once removed, can continue to fulfill its function as clothing. Ultimately, trash is an arbitrary state that need not be permanent. Commoditization is an ongoing process that lasts long after a thing is produced, sold, and abandoned. Appadurai notes that objects are not static but rather circulate in differing regimes of value.[69] As a result, a commodity's economic significance is tied to its social, political, and cultural framework. These differing registers allow a single item to have opposing values and meanings that are context dependent. In other words, one person's trash is another person's treasure. Appadurai observes that this disjuncture is particularly evident among extremely impoverished groups. For Ashkali, who had difficulty accessing commodities through ordinary channels, dumpsters provided an alternative. Consequently, an object's trajectory is not linear but circular, necessarily moving in and out of a trash state. As items shift between categories, they acquire biographies and histories.[70] Like people, commodities are socially constructed and possess social lives.

For Ashkali, trash was not just a source of material goods; it also provided symbolic capital. Recycling required fortitude, strength, and expertise. Furthermore, scavengers had to be able to identify valuable goods, know the market value of each item, and possess keen negotiating skills. They were connoisseurs, gaining their knowledge through an unconscious and measured familiarization with instruments of value.[71] Personal success depended upon one's mastery of the art of living, not institutionalized learning, wage labor, or government assistance. Parents saw their children's future in the dumpsters, not in the classroom. Youths were encouraged to go through the trash because it taught discipline and the value of labor. When a teenage boy refused, saying girls were watching, his father angrily responded that scavenging was not embarrassing; it was honest work. Taking pride in their abilities, individuals routinely showed off their best finds, such as a pair of barely worn designer sneakers, and bragged about the money they would generate. For Ashkali, garbage was not a sign of disadvantage and desperation; it demonstrated industriousness and integrity. But to Serbs, garbage marked Belgrade's scavengers as perpetually polluted outsiders. The very thing that seemed to promise success ensured that Ashkali remained marginal.

Given that trash fulfilled so many needs and represented potential wealth, it became a way of life. Men like Endrit and Bekim dedicated many hours each day to searching through dumpsters. Even outside these times, Ashkali routinely rummaged through every receptacle they passed. No opportunity was wasted because trash was fundamentally uncertain: you never knew what you might find. Serbs, on the other hand, passed dumpsters without reflection. To nonscavengers, trash was ready-to-hand. For Heidegger, ready-to-hand denotes everyday objects that are taken for granted and routinely overlooked.[72] They are unremarkable and uninteresting. For Ashkali, however, garbage was inherently conspicuous, expressive, and powerful. Much more than a simple source of cash, clothing, and food, it structured people's days, living conditions, relationships, and ethics. Millar notes that garbage can be a "form of living," which provides both an income and a worldview.[73] In Serbia, trash comprised the bedrock of an Ashkali economy, sociality, and morality and, as such, formed a complex nexus through which multiple meanings and relationships were negotiated.

Ultimately, the bibliographies of trash and the scavengers who collected it were strikingly similar. Consigned to settlements, Ashkali were stripped of humanity and abandoned by the state. Thrown into dumpsters, commodities were stripped of value and abandoned by their owners. Settlements and dumpsters were both excepted geographies that rendered people and things worthless. But these transformations were ultimately contextual and hence elastic. *Cigani,* in being discarded, were able to find worth in discarded objects. The Other world of Belgrade's settlements possessed its own regimes of value. It was through this process of resurrecting economic worth that scavengers were able to assert their own sovereignty by constructing unique social and economic spaces. Trash was not just a means of survival where none other existed; it was a byproduct of global capitalism that, through its vacillations between detritus and commodity, simultaneously challenged and consolidated Ashkali identity.

EVICTIONS AND ADVOCACY

Although Ashkali attempted to create a space of potential prosperity, they continually faced the threat of eviction. Serbian strategic documents labeled informal Romani settlements as urban blights that needed to be destroyed.[74] Authorities routinely prioritized Deponija's removal. Ashkali were well aware of these policies and frequently speculated about their own fate. As Endrit watched construction crews erecting new buildings adjacent to Zgrade, he was certain this heralded the impending demolition of his home. It would only be a matter of time, he remarked, until the settlement was leveled to clear land for apartments. Hoping to escape this precarious existence, Endrit considered returning to Kosovo. He had applied for a new home in a village near Pristina but nothing had materialized. Opening his wallet, Endrit produced business cards that he had collected from staff at UNDP, UNICEF, the Danish mission, and other organizations involved in the resettlement process. They made many promises, he said, but never kept them.

As Endrit predicted, the settlement was razed approximately six months after our conversation. He stood silently on the sidelines as his house with its delicate wall stencils was flattened by bulldozers. As occurred in other settlement removals, Zgrade's residents were dispersed across borders. Endrit joined a handful of others and returned to Kosovo. Participating in an international repatriation program, these families received new houses in a rural village. The Serbian state resettled many of those who wished to remain in the city, moving them into converted shipping containers situated in an industrial zone. A third group, including Bekim and five other families, relocated to a neighboring Romani settlement, Polje. Polje contained approximately forty households and was home to the horse carts and their Romani drivers that I had heard from my window. Its new Ashkali residents built shacks close to one another on the settlement's periphery. They hoped to retain their sense of community while avoiding entanglements with their Romani neighbors. But as soon as the Ashkali families settled in, they began worrying about Polje's removal.

The clearance of settlements like Zgrade attracted national and international media attention. One online article profiled Bekim, describing him as a Romani refugee, and recounted his search for a new home. This coverage reflected a growing awareness of Romani inequality, precipitated in part by the influence of nongovernmental organizations (NGOs). In Eastern Europe, NGOs have come to play an increasing role due to the neoliberal contraction of postsocialist states.[75] Of the many NGOs that operate in Serbia, several focus on Romani inclusion. Framing removals as human rights violations, activists have sought the support of European governments and organizations. Consequently, foreign dignitaries and donors would occasionally tour Belgrade and its settlements to assess the current state of Romani inequality. Designed to illuminate the hardships facing Roma, these excursions reinforced popular ideas of Roma as poor and needy. As a result, NGOs actually strengthened the boundaries around spaces of exception.

This was first illustrated to me when a bright van arrived at the front of Polje as Bekim, Fatime, Albin, Slobodan, and I chatted near Bekim's shack. A group of nine smartly dressed people emerged and began walking into the settlement. Albin informed us that it was a local NGO shepherding a delegation from the EU into Polje. As the visitors gingerly stepped over the detritus at Polje's entrance, one man loudly complained that his new shoes were getting dirty. Rolling his eyes, Bekim predicted nothing positive would come from this intrusion. "They never really help us," he said. The NGO staff led the group to Bekim's shack and, without introducing their EU companions, began their presentation. A member of the organization pointed to Albin, Bekim, and Fatime and explained in English that these individuals were Romani refugees from Kosovo. He then reviewed the legal status of displaced persons in Serbia and discussed how "these Roma" were the victims of systematic marginalization. NGO staff pointed at Albin, Bekim, and Fatime again, this time reporting that the family experienced difficulty obtaining identity documents and had been evicted from their previous settlement. The mission of the NGO, they continued, was to redress the marginalization of Roma by securing documents for individuals and legally fighting forced evictions. Switching to Serbian, they asked Albin to tell his story, which they translated into English. He solemnly explained that Polje's residents lacked running water, obtained electricity illegally, and did not permit their children to attend school. Gesturing to his surroundings, Albin said everything was substandard. To demonstrate the fragility of their homes, he shook the side of Bekim's shack.

By this stage, a number of Polje's Romani residents had joined our group. Unable to understand English and excluded from the proceedings, they began talking and joking with one another. This prompted one of the female visitors to loudly ask them to be quiet. She wanted to hear the

NGO's presentation, not a loud Romani conversation. At that point a member of the EU delegation spoke up, asking the Serbian staff to translate while he addressed the crowd. The man introduced himself as a Member of the European Parliament (MEP) and promised to work toward improving the lives of Roma by bringing Serbian laws in line with EU standards. When this occurred, he said, Romani rights would be expanded nationally and settlement demolition would cease. In response, Albin volunteered that Roma had experienced much greater freedom and security not long ago, under the Milošević regime. Characterizing Milošević as a strong leader, Albin praised him for keeping Kosovo safe. These statements elicited only silence from the visitors, who were aware that Milošević stood accused of committing war crimes and genocide.

The MEP changed the subject and asked Albin if any local churches provided food or assistance to Roma. Albin replied that some might help but he was unsure. Following up, the MEP queried the denomination of their church, to which Albin replied, Muslim. Again, an awkward pause followed as the MEP chose not to pursue the topic further. An NGO worker broke the silence, informing the group that they were late and had to leave immediately. The MEP congratulated the NGO staff on their work in the settlement and then promised to do what he could for its residents. Turning to leave, the MEP added that although he hoped for positive results, Polje's residents should not expect this to occur swiftly, if at all. As we watched them walk out of the settlement, Slobodan whispered that nothing would change; this was simply another effort to make money from the suffering of Roma.

The visit was one example of how the hardships endured by legally invisible refugees are packaged and sold to donors. The delegation was shown shacks standing amid a trash-strewn landscape and heard tales of impoverishment, but these interactions were all choreographed. Ashkali were to stand quietly as others discussed them in a language they did not understand. They were to speak only when prompted, and if residents behaved in a way considered disrespectful, they were immediately silenced. Polje's population became little more than generic representations of victimhood. The EU visitors ignored statements that fell outside this realm of discourse, such as Albin's praise of Milošević. Perhaps most importantly, Ashkali were consistently misrepresented as Roma. Members of the delegation remained completely unaware of the identity of those they were striving to aid. Consequently, the visit rendered Bekim, Fatime, and Albin visibly invisible.

Instead of gaining insight into the lives of Polje's residents, NGO staff and EU representatives were complicit in transforming Ashkali into *ciganski* stereotypes. This resulted, in part, from the perpetual need of NGOs to justify their mission and compete for funding.[76] To attract donors, NGOs in the Balkans co-opted popular images and narratives of Roma as a fundamentally needy yet deserving "problem population." The objective of the visit to Polje was not to understand Bekim's, Fatime's, or Albin's perspective. Ashkali were merely a tool to obtain EU support. Any awareness of the complexity of Ashkali and Romani identity would have endangered a simplistic and concise understanding of Romani impoverishment. It is through the distance of not knowing that activists are able to reduce suffering to a list of compelling bullet points that are deemed worthy of financing.[77] As a consequence the proliferation of Romani-centric strategies, directives, and initiatives has been criticized for profiting from disadvantage while reinforcing the very labels they sought to combat.[78] Historical portrayals are refashioned into a new, institutionalized Romani identity, which continues to be controlled by non-Romani politicians, scholars, and bureaucrats.[79]

NGOs and international agencies not only homogenized Roma but also pigeonholed national governments. Throughout the visit the EU was cast as a concerned and enlightened entity repudiating repressive Serbian policies. The MEP failed to mention that civil society organizations have criticized a number of EU states for committing rights violations: France illegally deported Roma, for example, while Slovakia built walls around Romani settlements. Spaces of exception also littered the EU. The most notable difference between these governments and the Serbian state was not exclusion but inaction. Serbia has historically exerted a much less forceful role in its management of informal Romani settlements. From 2009 to 2013 the government removed over twenty settlements in and around Belgrade but more than a hundred remained untouched.[80] Deponija has yet to be demolished. Despite policies pledging to reclaim land from squatters, these plans were seldom enacted. This inertia was an outcome of the state's inability to resettle displaced residents. Social housing vacancies were limited and attempts to construct new buildings for

Roma were often met with Serbian protests. Given the difficulties of securing alternate accommodation for Roma, the state was reluctant to raze settlements.

Consequently, it was private enterprise, not the Serbian government, that largely dictated when and where settlement demolition would occur. Similar to Roma and Ashkali, land developers were also ignoring state regulations. In contexts such as these, Ong notes that sovereignty becomes flexible "as governments adjust political space to the dictates of global capital, giving corporations an indirect power over the political conditions of citizens in zones that are differently articulated to global production and financial circuits."[81] Indeed, an underfunded Serbian planning authority had little choice but to accept an investor urbanism, where those with capital could effectively usurp public land.[82] This led to a graduated sovereignty, where private interests overlapped and destabilized state authority.[83] At Zgrade and elsewhere it was the unchecked capitalist endeavors of a burgeoning neoliberalism that largely propelled evictions. Interestingly, both settlement removal and the advocacy groups dedicated to ending this practice resulted from the state's retreat and the growth of private organizations. Investor urbanism and NGOs were trademarks of a neoliberal regime. The same processes produced the destruction of Endrit's home in Zgrade and the construction of his new one in Kosovo.

As NGOs, the EU, Romani rights activists, and the Serbian government wrangled with one another over the fate of settlements, Ashkali and Roma were expected to parrot the popular narratives of poverty and neediness. The EU delegation was not the only group wishing to experience Romani inequality firsthand. Each year a small number of journalists, researchers, politicians, and missionaries also wandered into Polje. When this occurred, Ashkali gave the same speech, tailoring their responses to fit the conventions of aid discourse: there is no work, we live in unhygienic conditions, and our children do not go to school. Narratives fit a formula that did not always reflect reality. Albin emotionally described how he inhabited a substandard shack in Polje, but his family actually resided in a container on the other side of the city. Crucially, neither Bekim nor Albin mentioned the utility of the trash or that it was possible for some settlement residents to earn enough money to build brick homes. And Ashkali never revealed that they were not Roma.

Year after year, advocates vowed to redress inequalities but tangible outcomes never materialized. Keenly aware that the EU visit was for the welfare of the NGO, Polje's residents became frustrated. Resigned, Bekim simply reiterated his earlier statement: "They never actually help us." Despite competing rhetoric between Serbian policies decrying the proliferation of unhygienic Romani settlements and NGO reports excoriating the removal of these communities, these debates rarely affected the lives of Ashkali. Both evictions and aid were rare.

Reminiscent of its physical position with the city on one side and fields on the other, Polje was in limbo between an unengaged Serbian government and ineffectual aid agencies. This uncertainty made informal Romani settlements sites of permanent displacement. They were simultaneously temporary and enduring. As a result, residents' lives were unceasingly precarious. Even those people who left Polje to settle elsewhere, like Albin and Endrit, could not find stability. They routinely returned to the settlement for the dumpsters that surrounded it. Whether they were relocated to containers, apartments, or Kosovo, these families never truly left Polje. Consequently, settlements impacted lives, economies, and socialities far beyond their borders. Rather than just temporary homes for refugees and migrants, informal Romani settlements became a discrete realm in which lasting insecurity and dislocation reconfigured experience.

SUFFERING AND BOREDOM

While artists, novelists, television producers, governments, and NGOs all perpetuate common narratives about Roma, so do researchers and anthropologists.[84] From the outset of this project I was concerned about how my own writing would be situated in regard to these narratives. What impact would it, and I, have upon the lives of Polje's residents? First, the topics that I sought to engage seemed prone to replicating long-standing assumptions. By studying the enduring displacement of people in excepted spaces, my work risked resembling the very stereotype that I most wished to challenge: that Roma choose to lead iterant lives on the margins of civilization. Second, I, a non-Romani white American male, would be telling a story about people whose lives were unlike my own in profoundly significant dimensions. Polje's residents and I were not only separated by differing ethnicities, nationalities, languages, and lived experiences but also by vast economic disparities. My own background, education, and embeddedness within a wage labor hierarchy would invariably structure any writing that I produced. And while I hoped for this book to be read by a "wide audience," I knew that group would not include the people it was about, many of whom were unable to decipher written Serbian, let alone English. In all likelihood, most readers of this text will share far more traits in common with me than with Polje's residents. Consequently, if Polje is an Other world, it is only because a world of assumed whiteness, housing, and paychecks is privileged, frequently taken for granted, and portrayed as normative.

Conscious of these issues and committed to a collaborative methodology, I determined the project's feasibility by first consulting with settlement residents and prepared to abandon the research if Ashkali and Roma did not want an anthropologist such as myself delving into their communities. It was at this point that I met Endrit. Not long into our first conversation, I explained that I hoped to spend months working with scavengers, taking part in their daily lives, and having them guide my project. But I also conceded that I was still learning Serbian, had never scavenged before, and was largely unaware of the social complexities and norms that suffused settlements. In thinking together about whether we might collaborate in this project, we discussed how his assisting me could be invasive and onerous. Having laid out my goals and concerns, I asked Endrit for his opinion: What did he think about my research and methodology? Was it appropriate and would anyone be interested in participating?

Rather than answering me directly, Endrit asked a question of his own: "What will you give me?" Would the project fund houses? Grant residents access to land? Guarantee that water and power was legally supplied to the settlement? Improve their lives? I replied that I could do none of those things. While I would assist in a personal capacity and provide whatever resources I could, my work would not lead to systemic improvements in his status, housing, education, or health. In fact, it might make things worse. Detailed information about his settlement, albeit disguised with pseudonyms, would be publicly available and could no doubt be used in ways we did not intend or foresee. Endrit thought for a moment before

THE OTHER WORLD 27

replying that I was the first person who had been honest with him. Journalists, NGOs, and government representatives all promised to change lives, he said, but no one did. Because I refrained from making similar pledges, Endrit declared that he would be honest with me: he was the leader of a nearby settlement and would be willing to speak more about my project. Two days later I visited his home, met other Ashkali, began the slow unfolding process of nurturing relationships, and was subsequently invited to conduct fieldwork with them in Zgrade.

Two years passed before I returned and began research.[85] By then, Zgrade had been razed and Endrit was living primarily in Kosovo. However, I located his daughter's family in Polje and I was invited to spend time with them. After speaking more about my project, they and their Ashkali neighbors agreed to participate. As we discussed, I would not conduct surveys, focus groups, and formal interviews. I also refrained from audio recording and public notetaking. I did not want people to feel as if they were being put under a microscope or subjected to unfamiliar practices. I would be present in the moment with people, what some anthropologists have called "deep hanging out."[86] Consequently, all quotes are from memory. To document events, I wrote copious field notes when I was alone or others were sleeping, usually late at night.

Although I attempted to be as unobtrusive as possible and integrate into the settlement, I was nevertheless a non-Rom and foreigner. Concerned about how an outsider like myself would be received, I employed a Romani research assistant to act as a facilitator, translator, and advisor. Slobodan was studying social work at the University of Belgrade and he assisted me approximately one day a week.[87] His conviviality, local knowledge, and Serbian language skills significantly eased the awkwardness of many early interactions and, as fieldwork progressed, his insights were invaluable. However, I quickly learned that my assumptions regarding insiders and outsiders were inaccurate. Aside from being Romani, Slobodan had little in common with Polje's residents. His family had lived in Belgrade for generations, owned a house, and were members of an educated working class. Upon meeting Slobodan, many of Polje's Roma actually failed to identify him as a Rom. Meanwhile, Ashkali residents routinely stressed their difference from, and at times superiority to, Roma such as Slobodan. He was thus never treated as an insider. Consequently,

Slobodan's Romani identity did not necessarily facilitate my entry into the settlement and, in some cases, complicated it.

My own positionality was also created and situated within the context of the settlement. First, Polje's residents steadfastly refrained from commenting on my ethnic or racial identity. I was never called a non-Rom nor was I labeled "white."[88] My difference was articulated through my nationality. When I was ignorant of local norms, asked about what trash to collect, mispronounced words, or confessed to being a vegetarian, I was called an American. Initially, my desire to live and work in Polje was attributed to this as well. As I returned from my first scavenging trip pedaling a *trokolica*—and Roma stared in confusion—Bekim loudly announced, "He is American!"

My nationality not only marked me as socially atypical but also was a signifier of wealth. In addition, Polje's residents were aware that I was employed as a professor and had been given a grant to conduct research in Serbia. However, conversations about my affluence were rare and, contrary to the stereotype of the begging Gypsy, only men in Bekim's and Endrit's households requested my financial assistance. Not only was it deemed rude to inquire about another's income; men took pride in being able to support their families. Accepting cash, especially from someone outside the domestic unit, was an admission that they had failed in this endeavor. Consequently, when Bekim or Endrit desperately needed money for food and other essentials, they quietly asked for "loans" that I did not expect to be repaid. My labor, on the other hand, could be and was publicly utilized. I carried water, prepared paper for recycling, watched children, and scavenged.[89]

But it was not my skin color, nationality, or wealth that most determined my place in Polje; it was my gender. I spent the vast majority of my time with men participating in their activities. In contrast, my interactions with women were much more circumscribed because significant relationships between men and women were largely restricted to familial settings. My eventual embeddedness in Bekim's household allowed me to speak with Fatime at length, but I could not replicate this with other female residents. Polje's women possessed their own sociality but it was one that I was unable to access. As a result, *Wastelands* focuses primarily on men, their viewpoints, and pursuits, even though women played crucial roles in the settlement. They maintained homes, prepared food, raised children, and exchanged knowledge. However, women were also among the most vulnerable residents of Polje. They were routinely the subject of sexual jokes and often expected to cede their agency, and bodies, to men. In exploring this context, my own gender limited my ability to engage women's experiences and perspectives. Thus I must acknowledge that my account of Polje is structured by my positionality within it.

While my first weeks in Belgrade were spent watching horse carts pass on the street below, I would become the one riding in a cart while Serbs stared at me from their windows. After a few months, I moved into Bekim's shack and ultimately became godfather to his two youngest children, who were born during my stay. As I grew familiar with Polje's residents, we spoke about how they wished to be represented. Endrit urged me to focus on the personalities and hard work of scavengers. They were individuals, he declared, each with his or her own history, aspirations, and agency. Rajim echoed this, instructing me to portray Ashkali as I knew them, as people.[90] Endrit, Rajim, and others wanted to be acknowledged as persons, not "poor *cigani.*" Consequently, this book seeks to counter monolithic depictions by providing an intimate account of the everyday. This is not a story of "the Roma" or "the Ashkali" but of Bekim, Endrit, Fatime, Harun, Jovana, Goran, Milica, and others. I aim to describe how people with diverse backgrounds are thrown together to endure life in an excepted geography. Hence, my focus is context, not culture.

Polje constitutes a very precise and circumscribed place. Informal Romani settlements are not the norm in Serbia or Europe. Likewise, Polje's inhabitants are not representative of the wider Romani community: the vast majority of Serbia's Roma live in houses, not shacks. When I asked a member of Slobodan's family what I should stress, he replied, "Be sure to tell everyone that not all Roma are the same." *Wastelands,* therefore, does not claim to represent Roma throughout Europe, Serbia, or even Belgrade; rather, it portrays a specific group in specific circumstances. Furthermore, I am not chronicling an eternal people or an eternal context; what follows is a series of bounded moments. The instability of Polje ensured that almost nothing remained the same. To depict it or the people who called it home as static is simply impossible. As a result, I have chosen to abandon the ethnographic present in favor of the past tense.

In situating Polje's residents in time and space, I also wish to resist attempts to homogenize their experiences of precarity and suffering. Anthropologists increasingly invoke precarity to make sense of how the twenty-first century's burgeoning economic insecurity has created fragile and vulnerable existences.[91] Allison comments that "where everyday efforts don't align with a teleology of progressive betterment, living can be often just that. Not leading particularly anywhere, lives get lived nonetheless."[92] Unsurprisingly, trash-pickers are frequently cast as the epitome of precarity.[93] Indeed, the contents of Belgrade's dumpsters were unpredictable and scavengers constantly struggled to provide for their families. But for Ashkali, much more was at stake. In addition to being economically marginalized, they were expelled from their homes in Kosovo, stigmatized as *cigani,* and segregated in slums. Facing chronic racism and inequality, they negotiated a continuum of structural, symbolic, and physical violence.[94] Kleinman, Das, and Lock argue that these traumas have societal origins and should therefore be conceptualized in terms of social suffering, which "results from what political, economic, and institutional power does to people and, reciprocally, from how these forms of power themselves influence responses to social problems."[95] However, while labels such as "precarious sufferers" draw attention to the severe effects of inequality, they do not always adequately reflect people's embodied realities.

Concepts such as experience, suffering, and precarity are, like all ideas, socially and historically constructed.[96] In contrast, individual responses to distress emerge from everyday life and can therefore be expressed in many different ways. Das aptly notes that any comprehensive understanding of precarity and suffering must ultimately decentralize theoretical discussions in favor of ethnography focusing on actual lives and encounters.[97] This is particularly true in excepted geographies where heartache is routine and remarkable. She writes, "suffering that is assimilated within the normal and yet not fully absorbed in it is much more difficult to decipher."[98] For Polje's Ashkali, shacks were simultaneously unstable structures and cherished homes, while scavenging was both evidence of marginalization and a source of wealth. Suffering was simply a daily reality and, as a result, it was not a cause for despair, regret, or anger. Instead, people like Bekim were bored.

Boredom is best conceptualized as an ordinary affect: public feelings that suffuse interactions, sensations, and ambitions.[99] When one examines impoverished populations, boredom is routinely linked to solitude and despair. For instance, Agamben notes, "the man who becomes bored finds himself in the 'closest proximity'—even if it is only apparent—to animal captivation."[100] Severed from humanity, bored individuals are encased in spaces that lack possibility. In his study of homeless Romanians, O'Neill adopts a similar approach. He defines boredom as a "persistent form of social suffering made possible by a crisis-generated shift in the global economy."[101] In Bucharest it signifies an estrangement from contemporary consumerism and downward socioeconomic mobility. Boredom is a feature of distress in the midst of existential crises, where individuals strikingly realize their alienation from the neoliberal order. Although I agree that boredom is a hallmark of social abandonment, Polje's residents, as Ashkali and Romani scavengers, were differently situated. Unlike homeless Romanians, Bekim never even contemplated the possibility of inclusion. He was always already the Other. Consequently, boredom was not an indicator of trauma but of normality. Poverty, marginalization, and violence were boring precisely because they were so ordinary. Suffering was, in Heideggerian terms, ready-to-hand. Reflecting upon this context, *Wastelands* seeks to reframe narratives and understandings of suffering by grounding them within the lives of Polje's residents and the trash that they collect.

Finally, I must clarify three choices I have made regarding terminology. First, debates continue to rage regarding the appropriateness and acceptability of the words Roma, Gypsy, and *cigan*.[102] For the purposes of this book I follow the preferences of Polje's residents and refer to them as Ashkali and Roma. However, because the epithet *cigan* is commonly employed in stigmatized and pejorative portrayals, I invoke it when communicating these narratives and perspectives. Second, informal Romani settlements have also been given a number of labels including slums, shantytowns, unhygienic settlements, substandard settlements, cardboard cities, and *mahalas*. Locally, communities such as Zgrade and Polje are simply called settlements (*naselja*) and I echo this convention. Third, I describe informal waste recycling as scavenging and those who do it as scavengers. In Polje, however, these terms were not in use. Searching through dumpsters was spoken of in euphemisms, namely as going to the trashcans (*po kante*) or to work (*rad*). In denoting these activities as scavenging, I aim to acknowledge the difficult, dirty, and desperate nature of this livelihood.

Each of the following chapters progresses chronologically and thematically. The first illustrates the diversity of Polje's residents and the economic and social bonds that tied them together. Governments, NGOs, journalists, and researchers routinely homogenized the inhabitants of informal settlements and dismissed them as impoverished *cigani*. However, Polje's population did not constitute a uniform group. From its founding almost three decades ago, the settlement was home to a varied collection of people. This chapter recounts the histories of a few of these individuals and in so doing explores the ethnic, religious, linguistic, and occupational differences that suffused Polje. Despite these contrasts, settlement residents shared one commonality: inhabiting an exclusionary space in which trash was the primary means of survival. Lacking social and economic affiliations elsewhere, Polje's denizens had no choice but to rely on one another. The ubiquity of barter, debt, and the sociality that accompanied them forged functional but volatile bonds. In an environment of displacement and privation, the never-ending struggle for commodities and cash created reciprocal relationships through an economy of trash.

Chapter 2 focuses on Ashkali attempts to establish homes in an excluded geography. Because the Serbian government considered informal settlements illegal, their inhabitants were denied basic amenities such as adequate housing, clean water, and electricity. Detailing people's struggles, this chapter explores how a domesticity of exception was wrought from scarcity and precarity. For instance, Ashkali collectively labored to transform shacks built from trash into respectable homes. Meanwhile, basic services had to be illicitly appropriated, which could result in arrest or electrocution. Although Polje's residents cooperated to survive, they also demarcated family from neighbor, contributor from competitor, through food and drink. The settlement's vulnerability was particularly evident after flooding that left the rest of the city largely unscathed. Losing what little they possessed and receiving almost no external aid, families worked to rebuild their shacks and recreate a marginalized area that was nevertheless their refuge.

Despite their physical segregation, Polje's residents participated in international networks by converting discarded value-laden commodities into cash. To make sense of this process, the third chapter examines the labor, embodied experience, and signification of scavenging. It follows Ashkali and Roma as they sort through dumpsters, recycle paper and metal products, sell salvaged goods at markets, beg, and engage in wage labor. Dumpsters were abject, but Ashkali earned their living and identity through these receptacles of disgust. Scavenging created a web of interactions and implicit understandings between Serbs and settlement residents. Destabilizing the boundary between private property and waste, trash-picking generated diverse but overlapping identities including the needy sufferer, the devious thief, and the entrepreneurial worker. Crucially, it transcended meaning and shaped Ashkali corporeality. Pedaling a fully loaded *trokolica*, stooping over dumpsters, and stacking tons of cardboard were physically debilitating. Consequently, trash work resulted in a life of pain. As Ashkali endured physical discomfort, social stigma, and economic marginalization, their afflictions were multidimensional and born out of garbage.

Chapter 4 charts entrepreneurial aspirations by following Bekim's efforts to achieve financial success. First, he attempted to increase his family's income by applying for welfare. Because the steps required to receive state aid employed technologies of governance to constitute biopolitical citizens, Bekim, as a *cigan*, was functionally excluded. As an alternative, he hoped to increase his scavenging revenue by emulating his Romani neighbors and collecting metal via horse cart. Bekim purchased a horse but was still unable to comprehensively support his family. If welfare was a function of state sovereignty, working with horses was the domain of a localized Romani sovereignty. Consequently, Bekim's desire to diversify his economic status was viewed as a betrayal of Ashkali values and he became increasingly estranged from these social networks. Bekim's identity and that of the trash he scavenged were intertwined. Just as he attempted to transform materials from commodities to garbage and back again, Bekim actively manipulated his own status both within the settlement and without.

Chapter 5 follows Ashkali as they negotiate the precarious transition out of informal settlements. Although formal accommodation boasted amenities like water and electricity, settlements provided access to important economic resources—trash—that could not be found elsewhere. For instance, state-sponsored apartments lacked storage space for recyclable paper, while container settlements and NGO-funded homes in Kosovo were situated in peri-urban and rural areas devoid of waste. On the other hand, those applying for asylum in the European Union temporarily received state benefits but were almost always repatriated to the Balkans. National and international resettlement programs, while ostensibly intended to improve housing, only succeeded in relegating Ashkali and Roma to other equally uncertain geographies. Prevailing economic, social, and political conditions ensured that spaces like Polje, although impermanent, were nevertheless enduring.

The conclusion lays bare the fragility of life in settlements by charting what appeared to be the impending eviction of Polje as trucks began dumping dirt, broken concrete, and other rubble near people's shacks. While Ashkali and Roma strained to cope, they were further burdened by the very people who purported to provide aid: a church group aiming to solicit donations from their American parishioners began recording emotional videos of scavengers. As Ashkali and Roma sought to scavenge resources from these interlopers, they also had to negotiate hunger, pain, violence, and death. Examining the events surrounding my final weeks in the settlement, I return to the concept of boredom. After years in Polje, I too had become bored, not with the people or the place, but with the enduring afflictions. As nights searching for food in dumpsters while attempting to avoid assault became common, I grew inured to the constant struggle. Rereading my field notes while preparing this manuscript, I was struck by the number of times I described being hungry, sore, and under threat. Yet, at the time, it all seemed routine and inconsequential. As a result, it is my desire to recount not only the trials that people faced but also the simple monotony of these extraordinary events.

1 The Sociality of Exception

Popular discourse routinely homogenizes Roma as a single ethnic and cultural group, but scholars frequently point out that few, if any, commonalities exist among the wide array of Romani peoples.[1] This diversity results, in part, from centuries of persecution and ghettoization by dominant European populations. Acton notes that Roma possess "a continuity, rather than a community."[2] In Serbia this was particularly true. Although many historic Romani neighborhoods and villages were composed of people claiming a unified identity, Belgrade's settlements became microcosms of heterogeneity as migrants and refugees from across the former Yugoslavia flooded into the city. Polje, for instance, was home to Ashkali, Bayash (alternatively Beyash or Boyash) Roma, and Yugoslav Roma.[3] These identities were reified through language: Ashkali primarily conversed in Albanian, while Bayash used Romanian, and Yugoslav Roma, Serbian. As a result, Ashkali were labeled Albanians while Bayash were dubbed Romanians. In addition to linguistics, distinctive religious, occupational, and economic practices further separated each group. Wanting to live among their own kind, residents created a ghettoized geography: Bayash in the center, Yugoslav Roma farther away, and Ashkali on the outer border.

While significant differences pervaded Polje's inhabitants, they were united by the shared experience of segregation. Romani geographies—whether formal communities or informal squatter camps—were isolated from non-Romani spaces as well as from each other.[4] Polje, for instance, was an island surrounded by risk. Residents venturing outside the settlement were targeted by police and surveilled by store clerks. Taking public transportation could result in the opprobrium of or confrontations by Serbs. Just walking down the street might end in physical assault. Because the settlement's population generally consisted of extended family groups, there was little impetus to brave these hazards and socialize beyond this residential network. As a result, people rarely left the settlement for reasons other than to search for trash, beg, or make purchases at neighboring convenience stores. Enclaves like Polje dotted Belgrade's landscape, each one forming a self-reliant community that was internally fragmented and separated from seemingly identical settlements nearby.

Lacking routine interactions with other Ashkali and Romani communities, residents were socially immobilized. Confined to Polje, sociality was unavoidable and unrelenting. With only one thoroughfare running through the settlement, residents were perpetually privy to the comings and goings of their neighbors. This was particularly true in the afternoons, when men returned from work and unloaded their carts. In good weather, residents were loath to remain inside their small shacks, so families sat outside. On these days, residents filled the margins of the lane, asking one another, "What's up, *cigan?*" and regaling passersby with tales of their day. Unable to draw from a common history or identity, people focused on their shared economic aspirations, discussing and appraising each other's finds. These conversations quickly evolved into financial exchanges as neighbors bought, sold, and traded items that they were unable to obtain any other way.

Because residents had limited opportunities for camaraderie or commerce outside of Polje, they created bonds, however tenuous, between one another. This was the sociality of exception. Examining a Palestinian refugee camp, Allan notes that in environments of privation, material and monetary exchanges transform disconnected individuals into cohesive communities.[5] She writes, "Economic exclusion and poverty represent more than an austere backdrop to camp life; they are, arguably, the conditions that now constitute it."[6] Distinctive relationships were precipitated by the common experiences of living in a segregated community, coping with economic marginalization, and being inherently vulnerable. In Polje intersecting affiliations were constructed from the discarded commodities of late capitalism. Garbage conventionally lacked worth, but as scavengers bought and sold these items, trash was imbued with value. These transactions not only fashioned a unique economic regime but also structured relationships. The bartering of trash and the establishment of social bonds were two aspects of the same process.[7] To illustrate the formative role that garbage played in Polje's sociality, this chapter explores the histories of each of the settlement's main groups—Ashkali, Yugoslav Roma, and Bayash Roma—and then describes how these categories were transcended through the shared afflictions, ambitions, and economies of trash.

POLJE'S NEWEST INHABITANTS

Arriving in Polje after the destruction of Zgrade in 2012, Ashkali built homes on the periphery of the settlement. Bekim's one-room shack was the first structure one passed upon entering Polje. But the simple edifice stood in stark contrast to his family's complex history. Born in Kosovo, Bekim was the youngest of five siblings. His mother was illiterate and unable to write her son's name. At his birth she asked a Serbian nurse to enter it for her on the official record. However, the nurse was unfamiliar with Muslim names and misspelled it. To this day Bekim must continue to misspell his name on all legal documents. Soon after his seventh birthday, Bekim's family fled to Serbia to escape the atrocities of the Kosovo War. Settling in a town not far from Belgrade, they moved into a three-room brick home with running water and electricity. Reminiscing, Bekim commented that he began learning Serbian while playing soccer with his friends, most of whom were either Romani or Serbian. At that age, he added, they did not know what it meant to be Serb, Bayash, or Ashkali. As an adult, though, he believed these ethnic differences were too much to overcome.

When Bekim was thirteen, his father relocated the family to Belgrade. They gave up their house and moved into a shack in Zgrade. Like other boys his age, Bekim began smoking and thinking about girls. Bekim's new friends mocked him for being single and introduced him to Endrit's daughter, Fatime. Bekim quickly became enamored and gave her a ring to signify his affection. However, it was not long before Endrit noticed the jewelry and asked Fatime where she had gotten it. Wishing to conceal the romance, she replied that she had found it in the trash. Endrit urged her to sell it but Fatime replied that she would rather keep the ring for herself. Not long afterward, Endrit saw his daughter walking with Bekim and their courtship was finally exposed. Fearing Endrit would attempt to separate them, Bekim proposed. Once Fatime agreed, Bekim spirited her away to his uncle's home, not far from where he had grown up. After consummating the marriage and confirming Fatime's virginity, Bekim quickly arranged a wedding celebration. Although Endrit was opposed to the match, there was little he could do. Several days later, he dropped his objections and asked for €1,200 ($1,500) bridewealth. Bekim negotiated with him and eventually paid €400 ($500). Bekim was sixteen and Fatime was fourteen.

The subsequent years were difficult for the young couple. Fatime quickly became pregnant but the child was stillborn, devastating both parents. Not long afterward Bekim's father died, leaving him without social and financial support. A few months later Fatime became pregnant once more. This time the child survived. But their third child, born the following year, did not live past infancy. Faced with death and poverty, Bekim hoped to build a better life for his family by relocating them to the EU. He paid human traffickers to smuggle them over the border into Hungary and they eventually settled in Austria, where Fatime's fourth child was born. However, Bekim began working illegally, was caught, and the family was deported to Kosovo. Soon, they were back in Zgrade.

Over the next four years Fatime gave birth annually, but only two of these infants survived past their first birthday. The couple rarely spoke of their deceased children as it elicited acute anguish. When Bekim quietly raised the topic one afternoon, he broke into tears. Weeping as he stared at the floor, he declared that all he wanted to do was look after his children. But try as he might, he was unable to provide them with a decent life. A shack, Bekim said, was no place for infants. He added that his babies should not suffer but they did. Sobbing, Bekim explained that despite all his efforts, nothing changed. With tears streaking his face, Bekim lamented that he was only twenty-four years old yet had already lost four of his children. "How can I live with that?" he asked. "For the rest of my life, how can I live with that?"

Each day Bekim struggled to make ends meet by sifting through the city's dumpsters looking for recyclable materials. Like most Ashkali, he concentrated on finding paper products. Discarded cardboard was relatively plentiful but collecting it on his *trokolica* was strenuous work. He earned only 4 dinars (4 cents) per kilogram and at this price a great deal of paper was needed to provide enough income to support Fatime and his four surviving children. With access to cash difficult, the trash also became the family's primary source of shoes, clothes, furniture, and food. Even when he was not on his *trokolica*, Bekim habitually searched every dumpster he passed. Fatime and the children did the same. At the age of nine, Bekim's youngest son was already bringing home items he found during trips to the local convenience store.

Not far from Bekim and Fatime, Gazmend and his second wife lived adjacent to one of the berms surrounding the settlement. Gazmend was distantly related to Endrit's father, while his wife was Drita's aunt. At sixty-four years old, Gazmend's face was an exercise in contrasts. His short, gray beard and wrinkles gave him a wizened look that was immediately contradicted by his boyish grin. Gazmend proudly boasted that his family had lived in Kosovo for three hundred years. However, during the violence of the war, he abandoned his home in Pristina and moved into Zgrade. Now living in Polje, Gazmend's shack was situated in a bucolic setting, free from the ubiquitous noise and trash that characterized the rest of the settlement. He reveled in the peaceful solitude of his surroundings. Not only did he avoid being a bystander to the comings and goings of Romani residents, Gazmend was able to elude police searching for illegal electric connections. The neighboring berms rendered his shack, and the light emanating from it, invisible to anyone on the main road.

Compared to many of the other shacks, Gazmend's was built of sturdy materials and kept free of debris. Remarkably, it sported a hinged window that could be opened. Because articulated windows were expensive and heavy, they were a rarity in the settlement. This feature marked Gazmend as both a master builder and a man of means. He had furnished the interior with spotless carpets, a couch draped with a fresh cover, and a wooden china cabinet containing neatly stacked dishes. A large rug depicting the

Kaaba hung on the central wall while prayer beads were placed on the table next to the couch. Like other Ashkali, Gazmend's Muslim identity was critical to his sense of self, but religious observance did not occupy a large part of his life. Although he avoided eating pork and celebrated the main Muslim holidays, Gazmend drank alcohol when it suited him. He also never fasted for Ramadan, claiming his advanced age and frequent illnesses made it too difficult.

Like so many of Polje's residents, Gazmend scavenged through the dumpsters. He worked longer and harder than most other men, despite being the oldest person in the settlement. Although he acknowledged that trash-picking was difficult, Gazmend believed that enterprising and disciplined people could realize financial success. He estimated that a pile of plastic in his front yard could be recycled for €20 ($25). It was nothing more than trash, he said, but it provided money. Gazmend remarked that he was able to live quite well off trash because, in Belgrade, everything could be sold. He even collected pieces of old bread, which he offered to farmers as pig feed. His income from bread, Gazmend bragged, funded his daily purchase of cigarettes. Without rent or electricity bills, Gazmend saved most of his earnings. He observed that even food could be found for free: discarded fruits and vegetables often filled the dumpsters in the back of the green market.

Given his achievements, Gazmend asserted that there was no excuse for being poor: if Ashkali and Roma were unable to get ahead, it was because they drank all night and then slept late the next day. Gazmend often noted that an individual "would find nothing if he stayed home." He complained that residents spent what cash they had on public displays of wealth such as large parties or weddings. Becoming visibly frustrated, Gazmend said that residents such as Bekim were responsible for their own poverty. But while Gazmend stressed the profitability of trash, the dumpsters were not his only source of income. Four of his six children lived in the EU and they regularly sent money to their father. On one occasion Gazmend demonstrated the significance of these remittances by removing €1,200 ($1,500) in cash from his wallet. He also produced a Western Union receipt, which he kept as proof that the money was not stolen should the police ever search him.

Unlike most Ashkali, Gazmend also had access to alternative accommodation outside of Polje. He continued to hold the title to his home near the center of Pristina, Kosovo's capital. But Gazmend preferred to reside in Polje. His painful memories of violence and discrimination dissuaded him from returning permanently. However, Kosovo was not his only option; Gazmend's daughters in Germany were frequently urging him to move into their apartments. But he steadfastly refused, saying he enjoyed his life in Belgrade. His current living conditions, Gazmend declared, were not so bad. Yes, he lived in a shack but he had everything he needed: a community, a home, electricity in the evenings, and steady work at the dumpsters. He acknowledged that it could all be destroyed, as Zgrade had been, but if this occurred another plot could be found. Gazmend was adamant that he would spend the rest of his life in a settlement. He planned to die in a shack.

In an adjacent plot dwelled Fadil, one of Gazmend's twenty-seven grandchildren. Fadil's young wife had recently given birth to their first child but their joy was tempered by the difficulties of raising a family in Belgrade's settlements. Fadil's father, Albin, also resided in Belgrade. He, along with Gazmend's youngest son, Fitim, lived in shipping containers approximately twenty kilometers from Polje. Regardless of the distance, the two men commuted to the settlement every day to search the dumpsters around the settlement. Remarking that neighboring junkyards offered the best prices in the city, Fitim believed he could make more money here than anywhere else in Belgrade. There were few other areas of the city with this concentration of residential buildings and, as a result, the abundance of discarded recyclable materials. In an effort to increase his earning potential, Fitim, with financial help from relatives in Germany, purchased a tractor to haul larger items.

The profusion of trash also drew other former residents of Zgrade to Polje, including Valon, Endrit, and Rajim. Soon after Zgrade's destruction, Valon's family received an apartment with running water and legal electricity but they lacked one important amenity: a place to store large amounts of paper for recycling. Consequently, Valon claimed a plot of land in Polje for his stockpile. While Endrit bragged about the running water and regular electricity that his home in Kosovo possessed, he could not find work. To earn an income, he came to Belgrade for several months each year accompanied by his wife, two daughters, son, daughter-in-law, and two grandchildren. They often stayed with Bekim and Fatime, making the shack home to as many as thirteen people. Like Endrit, Rajim's family also received a rural home in Kosovo but he sold his share to his brother and built a brick house on a small dirt track in the back of Polje. Given his proximity, Rajim could often be found in Bekim's shack chatting with Albin, Fitim, Valon, Gazmend, and Endrit.

Polje became an Ashkali social space because it was a critical site of resources: the dumpsters. Settlements provided access to an income that could not be found elsewhere precisely because they were on the margins. Excluded from mainstream regimes of value, scavengers made their own. The enduring materiality of garbage ensured that it remained useful even as Serbs abandoned it. Men like Bekim and Gazmend structured their days around the dumpsters and, as a result, the lives of Ashkali were intimately and inextricably tied to the trash they collected. Even those who no longer resided in a settlement, like Endrit, Albin, Valon, and Rajim, continued to rely on these spaces. Often considered a social blight or site of exclusion, settlements were essential to Ashkali survival in Belgrade.

YUGOSLAV ROMANI FAMILIES

Ashkali were a pervasive presence in Polje but they were in the minority. Most of the settlement's inhabitants were Romani, but several of these families, like Ashkali, were Muslims fleeing war. Sara, for instance, left Bosnia for Belgrade in 1991 to escape rising ethnic tensions. Having no home in the city, she and her children slept in public parks. The police repeatedly hassled the small family, forcing them to move from park to park. Once war erupted in Bosnia, Sara had no choice but to stay in Serbia. In search of greater permanence she built a shack in Polje. While Polje was new to her, settlements were not. Sara had lived in shacks her entire life. After settling into Polje, she fell in love with a Christian resident, converted, and became his wife. But the marriage was beset by difficulties and the couple divorced several years later. Now fifty-four years old, Sara had remarried for the third time and regarded Polje as her home. Yet despite living in Belgrade for decades, she and many of her children still lacked identity documents and official Serbian citizenship.

Out of necessity, Sara was one of the few women in the settlement who scavenged. Her husband seldom worked and could disappear for days at a time, leaving Sara as the main breadwinner for her two young grandchildren. The youngest, Bojan, was asthmatic and regularly had difficulty breathing at night. Making matters worse, he lacked an appetite and ate little more than bread, vegetable oil, and seasoning salt. On the rare occasions when Sara could afford meat, she was forced to buy bacon because it would keep longer without refrigeration. Given his poor health, Bojan caused Sara constant worry. She often prayed to Jesus, asking him to look after the boy. To earn money for food, she made three or four trips each day with her *trokolica* to search the dumpsters. By the evening Sara was exhausted and her muscles ached. She dreamed of taking analgesics to dull the pain but could never afford them. Reflecting on her experiences, Sara told me she had endured a hard life. If she died tomorrow, Sara said, she wouldn't mind. Shrugging, she added that she had little reason to live. Sara would be glad when her never-ending struggle ended and she could finally get relief.

Although all of Sara's children grew up in Polje, only her son Harun remained. Now thirty-two years old, he resided with his wife and six children in a shack ten meters away from his mother. Like Sara, Harun married a Christian and ceased to identify as Muslim. Whereas Ashkali gathered paper, he and many other Romani men collected metal to sell to junkyards. Dumpsters yielded only scraps of little value, so Harun shunned the urban routes favored by Ashkali and chose to scavenge in rural areas on Belgrade's outskirts. It was there that he could find larger items such as old boilers, bathtubs, sinks, stoves, and ovens. To cover the long distance and retrieve the heavy loads, Roma used carts pulled by horses. Horses were considerably more expensive than a *trokolica* and required much more care; however, unlike automobiles, carts could be legally driven by individuals without documents. Harun possessed a single gelding that he housed in a small shed next to his shack. He carefully tended the animal, resting him every other day. Although this was ostensibly for the benefit of the horse, Harun also needed the break. Like his son and nephew, Harun had asthma and was unable to labor for long periods without becoming winded.

Incapable of surviving solely through Harun's scavenging, the family was reliant on money from additional sources. While the children contributed by begging, the bulk of their income came from Harun's wife, Jovana. Born in Serbia and possessing identity documents that Harun lacked, she received welfare and child support payments. Jovana described their marriage as a good one, particularly compared to her first union. As a young woman, she wed while living in Sweden and then moved with her new husband to Germany. Realizing it was a bad marriage, Jovana left him a few years later and returned to her childhood home in Srem, a region to the west of Belgrade. The Kosovo War had recently concluded and Jovana remarked that as bad as things were in Belgrade, they were far worse in Srem. Hoping to improve her prospects, she moved to Polje, joining her brother, Miloš, and his wife, Milica. Soon after her arrival, Jovana married Harun. She often spoke wistfully of returning to the EU for its generous social benefits but because Harun lacked documents, Jovana resigned herself to a life in Serbia. Her marriage, however, had not prevented her from engaging in a series of sexual liaisons with other residents. For several months she conducted a very public affair with Rajim. Bekim believed that Harun was well aware of his wife's indiscretions but chose to ignore them. Harun was dependent on Jovana's child support payments, and if their marriage collapsed he would be destitute. Settlement residents commented that Harun was trapped.

Across the road from Harun and Jovana lived Aleksander. A rotund forty-three-year-old man with a bushy, gray-flecked beard, Aleksander spent his youth roving around the former Yugoslavia in a wagon. When traveling through Bosnia at the age of seventeen, he met and married his wife, Aisha. Although raised a Muslim, she became a Christian for Aleksander and now wears a cross around her neck. Aleksander recalled that while the nomadic life was difficult for the couple, he did not want to settle down. But once they began having children, he was persuaded that the growing family needed a permanent home. They eventually settled in Srem, where their youngest son was born. Unfortunately, the infant became ill and after numerous hospitalizations died at the age of three. The trauma of those years, Aleksander said, took a permanent toll on Aisha's health. She had two strokes in quick succession and suffered from seizures and asthma. Wanting to make a new start, Aleksander moved his family to Polje. Eleven years later, his four surviving sons had married and had children of their own. Aleksander's only daughter, still too young to find a husband, also lived with the family. With twenty-one people residing in his two-room shack, Aleksander was the head of the largest household in the settlement. He observed that guests often thought he was having a party because so many people were present. He had to explain that this was simply his family eating a meal together.

Similar to other residents, Aleksander came to the settlement to work. The men in his family collected metal while the women begged and received child support payments. Unlike Polje's other Roma, Aleksander owned a variety of livestock: three horses, fifteen sheep, and five goats. Twice a day he could be seen grazing his flock around the borders of the settlement. The sheep supplied meat for Aleksander's large brood while the goats' milk could be sold to Serbs. Customers often asked him to milk the goats in their presence to confirm the product was undiluted. While Aleksander remained at home with the animals, his sons increasingly abandoned scavenging in favor of wage labor at nearby junkyards. The hours were long and the work was grueling but it provided a guaranteed income. With this money two of his sons were able to purchase used cars. Although the vehicles were often in need of repair, they nevertheless marked the family as wealthy compared to their immediate neighbors. Their prosperity ultimately enabled Aleksander to secure accommodation outside the settlement. He bought four houses in Srem and needed one more to ensure that he and each of his sons had a legal home. Aleksander proudly boasted that two of these edifices were in the more affluent Serbian section of town. Like Gazmend, he credited his success to hard work and the inherent value of trash. Every one of Polje's inhabitants, he said, could own a home if they scavenged enough.

Aleksander's nephew, Imran, also resided in Polje but did so on a sporadic basis, ranging from a few days to a few weeks each month. The first time I met Imran's wife, she immediately displayed photos of their large two-story house on her cellphone. She did not want me to think that a shack was their permanent home or that they were dirty people. The couple stressed that they were unlike many of their neighbors. Imran had an international upbringing and spent most of his childhood in Germany, Italy, and Belgium. At the time of his marriage, Imran spoke German, Italian, Serbian, and Romani, but his wife, who was raised in Bosnia, only knew Romani. After moving from Bosnia to Belgrade, the couple began conversing solely in Serbian, which was the only language they taught to their children. Imran commented that he was rapidly forgetting Romani, wryly noting that he only used it when arguing with his wife.

Imran's family built a shack in Polje three years earlier, drawn to the economic potential of Belgrade. He believed that the only way to earn money was to follow jobs. Rather than going through dumpsters, he made a living buying goods from Chinese merchants and selling them to Serbian shopkeepers. He often complained about the poor quality of Chinese goods, saying he was careful to purchase only the best wares. If work was slow in Belgrade over the summer, Imran took his family to Montenegro and hawked binoculars to Russian tourists. Although he did not obtain his income from trash, Imran remained vigilant when passing dumpsters. He often peered inside but hardly ever found anything of worth. The economy, he declared, was simply too depressed for people to throw out valuable items. Imran was pessimistic about the future and did not believe his situation would improve. Smiling sardonically, he mused that at least desperation was nothing new. Serbia had been in crisis for twenty years and he was used to it.[8]

Polje's Romani inhabitants were conscious of the differences between themselves and their Ashkali neighbors. Noting that Ashkali rarely socialized with others, Roma remarked that they were cliquish. This arrogant attitude, Roma said, was outlandish considering that Ashkali were among the poorest people in Polje. In addition, Ashkali were viewed as unpredictable and violent. When I wanted to move into my own shack, Roma told me that the Ashkali section was too dangerous: men like Bekim would beat or rob me if given the opportunity. Stressing the disparity between the two groups, a Romani man remarked that instead of settling a disagreement with words, Ashkali relied on physical assault.[9]

For their part, Ashkali attempted to maintain cordial relations with their neighbors. When Gazmend and Bekim passed Roma in the settlement, they offered polite greetings. In private, however, Ashkali habitually portrayed Roma as dirty and immoral. On the rare occasions that Ashkali entered a Romani shack, they would silently assess its cleanliness, which was later discussed at length. Gazmend remarked that Romani homes were invariably filthy and possessed a fetid odor. After Bekim purchased a shack from Harun, Fatime spent several hours cleaning before allowing her family to move in. Ashkali also complained that Roma seldom bathed and routinely wore soiled clothes. Bekim disliked being around Aleksander for too long because, he said, the man often stank. Bekim's seven-year-old son echoed these statements, observing that his Romani playmates were all dirtier than he and his siblings. Not only were Roma filthy, they were thought to prioritize money over morality. Roma were cast as liars and thieves who begged, relied on welfare, and sold drugs instead of working. Consequently, many Ashkali would only befriend Roma "on the street," meaning they exchanged pleasantries but nothing more. If Roma invited Ashkali to share food, they were politely rebuffed. After being invited to Stanislav's home for dinner, Bekim declined by saying he was too busy. In private, Bekim revealed he was concerned that the food would be unsanitary. He wondered if Stanislav's family ever washed their hands.

BAYASH WEALTH

After passing Bekim's, Sara's, and Aleksander's shacks, an unofficial boundary was crossed. At the rear of the settlement, a cluster of approximately twelve homes surrounded a circular plaza. This was the oldest area of Polje and the domain of Bayash Roma, the most populous group in the settlement. Kept as slaves in Romania until the mid-nineteenth century, Bayash eventually migrated throughout the Balkans.[10] This persecution stripped Bayash of their ability to speak Romani and bequeathed a unique identity. In the late 1980s a group of Bayash from southern Serbia migrated to Belgrade seeking economic opportunities and settled on the vacant land that would become Polje. They chose a site on the edge of the city where they had easy access to the urban core, neighboring villages, and fields to graze their livestock. Looking back, Goran remembered those early years fondly, remarking that metal and other valuable goods were easily found. By the time that Zgrade was established in 1999, Yugoslav Roma were increasingly moving into Polje and competing with Bayash for resources. Goran reported that while these newcomers could be good neighbors, he was nevertheless wary of non-Bayash Romani groups. People like Harun and Aleksander, he said, belonged to a strange culture with distinctive customs. As a result, Goran did not approve of intermarriage between the two groups although it was occurring with increasing frequency. Like Ashkali, Bayash kept other residents at arm's length. Working and socializing almost exclusively with one another, Bayash were seldom seen in other sections of the settlement.

Bayash homes reflected the long tenure of their occupants. Whereas Yugoslav Roma and Ashkali assembled shacks simply and quickly, Bayash built them to last. Several were elevated on stilts to allow storage underneath, while others had gable roofs for better ventilation. In the rear, several stables were built to shelter horses. Given its long history of habitation, the Bayash area also contained a considerable amount of litter. Heaps of discarded wrappers, bottles, clothes, and building materials lined the road and conspicuously filled the spaces between homes. In addition, junked cars, steel drums, and scrap metal adorned the landscape. Much more than trash, the large piles of metal were tangible wealth and hives of activity. Men could often be seen disassembling cars, knocking concrete off pipes, or stripping wires. On some days, trucks, magnetic cranes, or robotic claws were brought in to lift and sort. As a result, the Bayash area had a palpable hustle and bustle that was absent elsewhere in the settlement.

Bayash scavenged metal like others in the settlement but used a far greater range of methods. A few traveled by horse cart to neighboring villages but they acknowledged that competition was fierce. Seeking a less contested market, some, like Jadran, purchased trucks and drove farther afield. He spent many hours on the road but was able to gather much more than those with horse carts. A few others diversified even more. Goran, for instance, purchased a boat to profit from the river traffic that passed through the city. He sold new steel drums to passing ships, took their discarded drums for scrap, and trawled the river for sunken metal objects. When Goran's boat arrived in port, Jadran was waiting with his truck to haul the payload back to the settlement. It was through cooperation that many Bayash residents were able to accumulate large quantities of metal. Working together, men within each household employed diverse yet complementary methods. The Bayash community also united to sell their metal. Each family contributed to a single collective cache, which was recycled only when it weighed over thirty tons. One individual, Goran's uncle-in-law, controlled the primary bank account for the group and managed the transaction, redistributing funds to each family based on their contribution. Selling in bulk yielded a significantly better price and allowed Bayash to maximize their scavenging returns.

These strategies, coupled with a long residency in Belgrade, allowed Bayash to earn considerably more than other inhabitants of Polje. In a normal month Jadran claimed he could gross €1,000 ($1,250). In comparison, the official average monthly salary in Serbia was 45,281 dinars ($475).[11] While a great deal could be made from recycling, Bayash families also had other sources of income. Men like Jadran and Goran, who worked in the informal economy, were considered unemployed by the Serbian government. Capitalizing on this classification, families applied for and received welfare and child support payments. Goran noted that if you had several children, these monies could significantly boost a family's monthly income. In addition, women occasionally begged, providing yet another source of revenue. Although Bayash appeared to be poor *cigani*, they were relatively affluent. When I asked Goran if the Serbs living around the settlement ever insulted him, he replied, "They can't look down on me. I have more money than they do."

Bayash may have lived in shacks in Polje but almost every family owned a well-equipped multistory house in their village. They sporadically returned to make repairs and maintain the buildings but no one intended to leave Belgrade.[12] Noting that there was simply no work in the rural regions of Serbia, Goran declared that the capital was now their permanent home. Bayash prosperity also allowed them to obtain medical care that was inaccessible to other residents. Although Goran possessed identity documents and could utilize government clinics, he refused, stating that Serbia's public health system was the worst in Europe. Instead, he and other Bayash consulted private physicians. These visits were expensive but they felt it was money well spent. Despite devoting significant resources to their health, Goran commented that his family had not prioritized education. The majority of Bayash children did not attend school and their parents saw little reason for them to do so. Goran felt it was ironic that his family was rich yet could not read or write.

Like Ashkali and Yugoslav Roma, Polje's Bayash population was not monolithic. Once the core families from southern Serbia established the settlement, others joined them. These individuals hailed from other parts of the country, lacked kinship ties with the core group, and were often impoverished. Bogdan, for instance, was considered the poorest Bayash in Polje. Although born a Yugoslav Rom, Bogdan had been married to a Bayash woman, Mirjana, for fifteen years. Originally from Srem, Bogdan and Mirjana began their courtship in Belgrade. At the time he was twenty-two years old and she was twelve. Moving to Polje a few years later, the family constantly struggled to make ends meet. When I spoke to him, Bogdan could not afford a *trokolica* and searched for metal by bicycle. Needing extra income, his wife and adolescent son begged. Bogdan possessed identity documents but Mirjana did not, which barred the family from receiving welfare payments. They were only able to survive, Bogdan said, through the assistance of other Bayash. His neighbors provided food, spare change, and materials for his shack, which was small and perpetually in need of repair. This charity was unique to Bayash. Ashkali and Yugoslav Roma occasionally aided each other but sustained financial support was nonexistent.

Reflecting on Bogdan's situation, Goran pointed to individual behavior. People lived in shacks, he said, because they did not work. Goran proudly stated that he searched for metal every day, except for holidays. With a grin, his brother called him a liar, adding Goran also worked on holidays. Although he complained about the increasing dearth of recyclable materials, Goran, like Gazmend, affirmed that it was possible to succeed in Belgrade. Both men easily admitted to having supplemental incomes— remittances and welfare—but these were never thought to mitigate their work ethic. Their attitudes expressed a strong moral sentiment: prosperous residents earned their wealth while those who struggled to make ends meet, like Bogdan or Bekim, were simply lazy. Of course, Bogdan and Bekim disagreed. Poorer individuals routinely blamed their situations on an environment of scarcity and attributed the financial success of others to unmerited advantages such as documents or moneyed family members. In each narrative, however, poverty was not attributed to discrimination, exclusion, or structural violence. The Serbian economy was difficult to negotiate but it was nevertheless considered a source of potential success, not a system of inevitable failure.

Although Bayash mirrored prevalent narratives in Polje, they were viewed by others as fundamentally aberrant. Bayash clearly possessed significant wealth yet their living conditions were regarded as the worst in the settlement. Pondering the disheveled appearance of the Bayash area, Bekim wondered how people with so much money could tolerate mounds of trash around their homes. Gazmend replied that they did not know how to live any other way. As further evidence of Bayash abnormality, he added that they begged despite getting a substantial income from other sources.

This, Gazmend said, clearly demonstrated their greediness. Ashkali also quipped that Bayash were insular and secretive, claiming the core Bayash families would never let outsiders enter their ranks. To keep and consolidate their wealth, Bayash men were purported to marry their first cousins, a practice that Ashkali regarded as incestuous.

NETWORKS OF RECYCLED CAPITAL

Most settlement residents were part of an extended family or cohesive ethnic group, but there were a few exceptions, like Dragomir. When I first met Dragomir, he was thirty-five years old and living on the outskirts of Polje. To reach his two-room shack, visitors skirted the main settlement and walked down a narrow path flanked by overgrown brush. Dragomir was accustomed to residing on the periphery both geographically and socially. He did not belong to any of the main groups in Polje and was at ease with his liminal status. Dragomir also resisted a definitive religious affiliation, saying he was raised Muslim but also felt comfortable with Orthodox Christianity. He relied on the trash to support his family but unlike other Roma, his wife, Snežana, did not beg nor did she receive welfare payments. While Dragomir conceded that his life was difficult, he declared that a shack in a settlement was all he needed to be happy. But he acknowledged that these conditions were much harder for his wife and children to bear. Nevertheless, he did not think that their lifestyle would ever change. If the government removed Polje, Dragomir said, he would simply build a new shack on the margins of another settlement.

Dragomir was born and raised in a city in southern Serbia, less than seventy kilometers from Goran's village. Abandoned at a young age, he spent most of his adolescence on the streets. It was not until his early twenties that Dragomir moved to Belgrade and began courting Snežana. The couple tried to keep their relationship secret, but when Dragomir gave her extra money to buy a large soft drink from the store, Snežana's parents realized what was occurring. Angry, they beat her. Snežana's elder brother, however, supported the match and the couple quickly married. While Dragomir was in love with his wife, he was concerned that Snežana, who was thirteen years old, was too young. He became acutely aware of Snežana's age when he returned from work to find her playing with dolls. After asking an older relative if he should "give her back," Dragomir was told that marrying an adolescent bride was ideal because the couple would grow up together. This is exactly what happened, he said. But Snežana's youth did present a challenge when their first child was born. Because she was fifteen at the time, the hospital would not release her or the baby into Dragomir's custody. While the couple considered themselves to be man and wife, the Serbian state regarded their relationship as statutory rape. Consequently, Snežana was only allowed to leave the hospital with her parents. Over the next decade she had four more children, all girls. Dragomir wanted a son but he remarked that he would always love his children, regardless of their gender.

Unlike the other men in the settlement, Dragomir did not collect metal or paper to recycle. Instead, he searched the dumpsters for discarded clothing, shoes, housewares, perfumes, and books that could be resold. Because these small items did not require a *trokolica* or horse cart, Dragomir rode a bicycle that sported an improvised milk crate basket. He regularly vended at local markets but also sold his wares within Polje. Residents bought whatever pieces of scrap metal he found, promptly recycling them to junkyards. In addition, Dragomir was able to supply a range of goods that no one else in the settlement could. If Bekim's antenna broke, he went to Dragomir to find a replacement. If Harun needed a car battery to provide electricity during the day, he asked Dragomir. Even Serbs living in the neighboring buildings would visit Dragomir's shack to purchase articles they could not locate elsewhere. In addition, Dragomir was a skilled carpenter and electrician. Residents who were unfamiliar with building a shack or wiring it routinely requested his assistance. Dragomir's utility, rather than ethnic affiliation, made him a central figure in Polje.

While selling items was Dragomir's primary business, every male in the settlement traded goods with one another.[13] Polje's residents were excluded from the mainstream Serbian economy, so neighbors were a vital source of commodities.[14] Each afternoon as men returned from scavenging, neighbors inspected each other's *trokolice* and bid on the most desirable merchandise. These transactions not only allowed buyers to gain articles they could not locate themselves but also provided an immediate though unreliable income for sellers. Making deals was an essential feature of settlement life and occupied a significant portion of everyday interactions. Even the shortest conversations were often laced with offers and counteroffers. Bargaining played such a central role because these commodities, many of which were found in the trash, lacked a clearly demarcated value. Unlike items in a store that were unambiguously priced, in part based on fixed production costs, those from the dumpsters were free of these constraints. Worth could be constantly negotiated and renegotiated. This inherent instability ensured that residents spent extended periods interacting with one another in an effort to establish value. Repeated conversations, in turn, built bonds across ethnic, economic, linguistic, and religious divides. As merchandise and capital flowed around Polje, people were unavoidably and inextricably tied together.

The most frequently traded items were either difficult or impossible to obtain from scavenging. For instance, cellphones comprised the bulk of transactions and were vital to everyone's lives. Most residents could only afford older models that were no longer available in stores. Thus, neighbors had little choice but to rely on one another. The cellphone trade was brisk with buying and selling occurring at all hours. A single phone could move from person to person to person, circulating throughout the settlement for several weeks. In the course of an hour, one phone was purchased, swapped, and sold again, as it passed between four owners. Given the ubiquity of phones, sellers could be confident of finding a replacement within minutes. As a result, individuals had no hesitation about relinquishing their cellphone if the right price was agreed upon.

Cellphones were ostensibly kept for their utility but they also served as an effective method of storing wealth. Residents lacked bank accounts and were reluctant to keep extra cash in their shack, where it was vulnerable to theft. However, surplus money could be used to purchase a smartphone, which would be carried at all times. When the family needed the cash, the phone was easily sold. These phones were also tangible demonstrations of success. For many people in the settlement, a cellphone was the most expensive item they would ever possess. Consequently, narratives about wealth were frequently narratives about cellphones. Residents compared phones and engaged in long debates about who possessed the better and more prestigious model. The few people who could afford smartphones displayed them whenever possible by publicly playing games or browsing the internet.

Cellphones were the most popular items to circulate in this fashion, but other costly commodities were transacted in a similar pattern. Shacks were regularly on the market as people moved in and out of the settlement or existing residents relocated a better plot or larger home. Over the course of a year, a single shack could have three or four different owners. Alongside cellphones and homes, horses and *trokolice* were also frequently bought and sold. For example, in a four-year period, Harun resided in over ten shacks and owned eight horses. The lives of these commodities, in fact of all objects in Polje, mirrored those of their owners. They were fundamentally unstable. Just as settlement residents endured permanent displacement, so too did their belongings.

While trading was an integral part of settlement life that bound people together for mutual benefit, it was also an adversarial contest in which each party sought to benefit at the expense of the other. The best deals were achieved by exploiting the inexperience of one's neighbors. Because many goods were found in the trash, their value was opaque. Maximizing profit was dependent on knowledge of an object's resale potential. A stranger to junkyards, Dragomir was often unaware of how much certain metal items would realistically fetch. As a result, it was possible for a clever individual to buy scrap from Dragomir and resell it for twice the price. This was not deemed immoral because it was the consumer's responsibility to identify and avoid fraud. After purchasing a computer from a Bayash family, Bekim asked for a refund, saying it did not work and he had thrown it away. Showing me the phone he received as compensation, Bekim boasted that he had merely hidden the computer and would eventually sell it. If Bayash were dumb enough to believe him, Bekim said, they deserved to lose their money. Similarly, Endrit's nineteen-year-old son, Agim, declared that there were many "stupid *cigani*" in the settlement and he was more than happy to deceive them.

Despite persistently bidding for items, few people had cash on hand to pay for them. Consequently, debt was a staple of life in Polje, as it was in many settlements.[15] Purchasers routinely attempted to negotiate payment plans, which could last from a few days to a few months. Generally, the seller turned over any item, whether a cellphone, *trokolica*, horse, or shack, to the buyer while awaiting reimbursement. However, a few residents, such as Dragomir, always demanded cash. For people like Bekim, this often necessitated arranging loans from a third party. While individuals living outside the settlement would act as lenders, they invariably charged interest, sometimes as much as fifty percent. This could be avoided by borrowing from your neighbors. Smaller amounts, typically less than 3,000 dinars ($32), were obtained from anyone willing to front the money and were often repaid in a matter of days. However, almost everyone was in a similarly precarious economic position and finding lenders in Polje could be difficult. It might take several hours to organize a loan and often required a significant amount of cajoling if not dissembling. Bekim's quest for 4,000 dinars ($43) to pay for a new *trokolica* illustrates this process.

He began by listing those in the settlement who would be most willing to help: Marko, Harun, Miloš, Gazmend, and Endrit. But Marko was already in debt, Harun was trying to secure a loan himself, Miloš was not speaking to Bekim because of an earlier argument, Gazmend was still waiting for Bekim to pay off an existing debt, and Endrit was away in Kosovo. Searching for another option, Bekim decided to reach out to a Romani neighbor. Phoning Đorđe, Bekim pleaded with him, saying his family was suffering and needed to buy food. Đorđe replied that he was trying to purchase a house and consequently did not possess any extra cash. Continuing to plead, Bekim lowered his request to 2,000 dinars ($21). But Đorđe refused once more and suggested Bekim look elsewhere. To demonstrate his desperation, Bekim listed his potential sources, stressing their inability to assist him. Before Đorđe could respond, Bekim guaranteed he would return the money within four days, five at the absolute most. When Đorđe hesitated, Bekim added that there was a good chance he could even do it in two days. Bekim repeatedly vowed that the loan would be repaid quickly. Ten minutes after the conversation began, Đorđe finally agreed. Grateful, Bekim made small talk for a couple of minutes before hanging up. Turning to me, Bekim said bluntly, "I lied." There was no way he would be able to meet the deadline. But given his lack of other options, "What else can I do?" he asked.

Episodes such as this were commonplace. Borrowers regularly suggested unrealistic timetables, aware that lenders were also in financial need and wanted to be repaid as quickly as possible. Once debts came due, many attempted to stall by claiming they were robbed, harassed by police, or dealing with an emergency. Others simply disappeared from the settlement for several days if not longer. Delaying tactics were met with anger and occasionally violence. If a payment was missed, the creditor immediately threatened to repossess the item or assault the borrower. When Bekim was unable to compensate Harun for his shack, he begged for more time, saying the money was needed to feed his children. Harun unflinchingly replied that Bekim must either pay up or move out. Panicked, Bekim quickly secured another loan and reimbursed Harun. Afterwards, Bekim bitterly complained that settlement residents were mercenary and unwilling to assist one another. Bekim demonstrated his point a few weeks later when Marko was unable to repay him. In a rage, Bekim declared he would burn down Marko's shack with his family inside if the debt was not settled. Reflecting on residents' behavior surrounding economic transactions, Sara simply commented, "They treat each other like shit."

Almost everyone in Polje relied on credit and struggled to meet multiple commitments. Because most loans were to others in the settlement, a web of debt bound residents together. Money received in repayment was often passed to another individual to settle an additional obligation. As a result, tardiness had wide-ranging consequences. On one occasion Veljko purchased Bekim's *trokolica*, promising to pay at the end of the month. When the day arrived, Veljko defaulted because Stanislav was late in settling his debt. Although Bekim angrily warned that he would repossess the *trokolica*, this did not occur. The *trokolica* was of little use to Bekim, who needed the cash to repay Gazmend. Bekim decided to wait until Veljko had the money but this necessitated arranging another loan to tide him over. Seeing Stanislav begging and therefore knowing he would have cash, Bekim asked to borrow 2,000 dinars ($21). Bekim promised to reimburse Stanislav once Veljko fulfilled his commitment. In the end, Stanislav would repay Veljko, who would pass it on to Bekim, who in turn would return it to Stanislav. Circular obligations such as this occurred regularly.

For the largest loans, residents relied almost exclusively on the wealthier members of their ethnic group. Ashkali approached Gazmend when they were in need of over €50 ($63) and he often acquiesced to their requests. Bekim could borrow up to €400 ($500) at a time and take several months to repay it. Gazmend estimated that Ashkali across Belgrade collectively owed him over €3,000 ($3,750). But loans between extended families were not exempt from the machinations and conflicts that pervaded indebtedness in the settlement. In fact, family relationships were often monetized. When Sara left Polje, she sold her shack to Harun rather than giving it to him. At the time, Bekim remarked that only a Romani mother would charge her child for a home. But Bekim's relationship with his family was similar. The following week his elder brother, Ezgon, refused to give Bekim a child's bicycle on credit, instructing him to get a loan from a Bayash family. Bekim was livid that his own brother would demand cash but he soon adopted an identical policy. After Ezgon failed to hand over a cellphone charger despite being paid, Bekim insisted that his brother settle all transactions immediately.

When negotiation, threats, and cajoling did not result in a mutually agreed upon deal, residents occasionally accessed their neighbors' resources without consent. Petty theft was ubiquitous in Polje. If people were not around to watch their belongings, others had no difficulty purloining them. Cash, cellphones, car batteries, metal, and tools were routinely targeted but any item of use or value could be taken. While poverty motivated burglary, Polje's living conditions facilitated it. Shacks lacked locking doors, allowing thieves to easily enter a vacant home, rummage through belongings, and remove sought after items. In an effort to thwart burglars, Ashkali hid extra cash and electronics in the ceiling. Sometimes, the items were so well concealed that their owners had difficulty finding them again, setting off frantic searches. As with trade and loans, robbery was structured by the material and economic constraints of life in Polje. Thievery was so prevalent that when Fadil's dog went missing, he immediately assumed it had been stolen. Fadil angrily declared that nothing was safe in Polje, not even pets. The next day the dog returned, having simply run away. Fadil was embarrassed at his mistake, but his neighbors assured him that theft was a perfectly reasonable theory given the realities of settlement existence.

VOLATILE RELATIONSHIPS

As men negotiated prices, requested loans, and sought to obtain new cellphones, they also swapped pleasantries, made small talk, and shared settlement gossip. However, their differing backgrounds restricted conversations to a few common topics. To create rapport, residents joked with one another. This drew in all of Polje's inhabitants no matter their age, gender, language, or ethnicity. But like trading, jesting was ubiquitous, unrelenting, and dominated by men. Dragomir commented that there were only three things to do in life: eat, fuck, and joke. In fact, the final two items were inextricably intertwined: sex was the primary subject of settlement humor. Breast size, penis size, pubic shaving, and male homosexuality were all fair game but the most popular topic was infidelity.

Although actual adultery was a serious offense, it was perfectly acceptable, even encouraged, to joke about having affairs with other men's wives. Harun often remarked that Fatime had nice breasts, adding he would "fuck her like crazy." When faced with these statements, Bekim and Fatime both laughed. Bekim regularly told Dragomir that Snežana had a hot body and it was only a matter of time until he had sex with her. I was also incorporated into these discussions. Only a few weeks after I began visiting Polje, Bekim looked at his eldest son, Besart, and pointing at me said, "You know, he is going to fuck your mother." Without missing a beat, the nine-year-old responded, "No, he is going to fuck your mother." Pretending to consider the matter, Bekim retorted, "My mother lives in another settlement but yours lives right here. He is definitely going to fuck your mother."[16]

While female residents occasionally made fun of a man's sexual prowess or suggested that a neighbor coveted them, male voices controlled these conversations. Women were publicly invoked as the object of male desire and, as a result, denied agency. Sexual jokes produced a shared discourse but one that built relationships among diverse men by placing women in identically subservient positions. According to male narratives, female roles—whether among Ashkali, Roma, or Bayash—were largely confined to passively providing for the sexual needs of men. Although Fatime laughed at jokes about herself, she nevertheless found ways to strategically resist them. When men attempted to implicate me in explicit narratives about her, Fatime informed everyone present that I could not discuss her sexuality because I was godfather for their family and must be respectful. This allowed her a temporary and selective reprieve from men's attention.

Over time, trading and joking led to the establishment of formal bonds between individuals from different ethnic groups. While intermarriage was considered inappropriate, godfather or *kum* relationships were fostered. An important figure throughout the Balkans, a *kum* customarily provided spiritual guidance for a couple's children as well as serving as the best man at the wedding. The godmother, *kuma*, was traditionally the *kum*'s wife, but now Serbian couples are increasingly appointing each independently. Present for marriage and baptism, a *kum* and *kuma* play a central role in a family's life, offering emotional support and advice. The institution of *kum* in Polje resembled this Serbian practice in some regards but was also unique. While Serbs nominated a single *kum* for their nuclear family, Ashkali and Roma chose a different individual for each of their children. Because families grew quickly, often with a newborn arriving each year, residents generated an expanding network of affiliation. For example, Fatime's sister's husband was *kum* for her first child while Endrit asked Rajim to be *kum* for his son. As more children were born, a *kum* from outside the parents' ethnic or economic group was preferred and neighbors were frequently asked. The *kum* for Bekim's second child was a Romani man who lived a few shacks away while Harun's son had a Bayash *kum*. But these relationships, unlike Serbian traditions, were wholly focused on men: talk of godmothers was nonexistent. Consequently, *kum* affiliations crosscut settlement divisions and formally tied disparate families together but it did so, like trading and joking, through men.

As different groups invited one another to be *kum*, identity became a socially acceptable topic of conversation. Normally, it was impolite to question a resident about his ethnicity or religious beliefs, but a potential *kum* expected these inquiries. When Sara's ex-son-in-law, Marko, moved into the settlement, Bekim initially suspected he was a Serb. Marko's light skin, freckles, and red hair were not traits normally associated with Roma. It was only after he suggested that Bekim be *kum* for his next child that Bekim began asking about his ethnicity and religion. Marko then disclosed that he was half-Serbian but identified as Romani. Reciprocally, Marko inquired about Bekim's Muslim beliefs and practices. These conversations tended to discount differences in favor of similarities. Bekim, for instance, explained that he considered the Christian God and Muslim God to be the same being. The only real difference, Bekim added, was that Christians crossed themselves, went to church, and celebrated saints' days. Marko nodded in agreement, saying, "God is God." Through a *kum*, settlement residents actively constructed relatedness.

Despite narratives stressing mutual understanding and confluence, some Ashkali emphasized the utilitarian nature of *kum* relationships. In private, they noted that being *kum* was simply about getting along with one's Romani neighbors. Rajim declared that the role of *kum* originated within an Orthodox Christian tradition and was incompatible with Islam. If Ashkali were truly concerned about their religion, he said, they should not participate in the practice. Rajim conceded that this was difficult to do: he was *kum* for Agim. Being *kum* was an inescapable aspect of life in Belgrade's settlements. It was simply what people did. Ashkali needed allies and this was the most reliable way to forge essential bonds.

But these relationships were inherently fragile. If one party felt the other was being disrespectful or not fulfilling their required duties, public friction quickly developed. Harun's Bayash *kum* complained when Harun attempted to charge him for a pile of scrap metal. A *kum*, he said, should be given such items for free. The man vowed to sever their bond if Harun continued treating him in this fashion. Although a *kum* was appointed for life, these ties could nevertheless be broken. This occurred when Bekim suspected that his son's Romani *kum* was taking drugs. From then on, the two men passed each other in the settlement every day but refused to acknowledge the other's presence. Bekim also disowned his daughter's *kum* after the man abused and abandoned Bekim's sister-in-law. Consequently, only half of his children had a godfather. In some cases, relationships were strained even before the child was born. A few weeks after Marko asked Bekim to be *kum*, clashes over loans created hostility between the two men. At that point, all talk of godfathers ceased and Marko left Polje soon afterward.

Disagreements were a constant feature of settlement life. While most were money related, there were other causes as well: a joke deemed too severe or insulting, accusations of theft, or evidence of sexual indiscretions. Many conflicts arose over domestic matters. For instance, parents responded aggressively if neighbors attempted to discipline their children. When Harun yelled at Bekim's son for blocking the lane, Bekim became incensed. Declaring that Harun did not own the road, Bekim made it clear that any other attempt to police his son's behavior would result in violence. While quarrels routinely led to threats, these were often nothing more than posturing. In the rare instances that physical confrontations ensued, they were brief and usually consisted of only a few well-placed punches. Rather than assault, the most common method of dealing with disagreements was to ignore the other party: Bekim simply stopped speaking to Harun. Nevertheless, given the relatively small size of the settlement and the constant social interaction, total avoidance was impossible.

Feuds frequently materialized but they ended just as swiftly. Generally, no one held a grudge for more than a couple of weeks. It took Bekim only six days before he reconciled with Harun. Even serious arguments could be forgotten. Less than two months after two men came to blows, they were drinking beer together and joking. Rajim noted that no matter how adversarial a relationship became, sooner rather than later the tension would dissipate. As neighbors traded, formed bonds, and then broke them, interactions careened between indifference, friendship, and conflict. These vicissitudes resulted from the confined segregation that all residents endured. Lacking other ties in Belgrade and reliant on the settlement for work, its inhabitants had no alternative but to get along. It was almost impossible for an aggrieved party to leave Polje. Long-term disputes were especially untenable because economic marginalization forced individuals to maintain links with each other. No one could afford to lose a potential source of commodities and loans.

Differences suffused Polje but everyone was motivated to transcend them. The only way to survive the shared experience of privation was through cooperation, dependency, and support. As a result, residents were more concerned with their neighbor's scavenging skills and ability to loan money than with their history and background. Bekim knew Marko's work habits and income long before he was aware of his ethnicity. Economic utility rather than a shared heritage or tradition became the basis of relationships. These transactions shifted support from kin and ethnic groups to heterogeneous strategic networks, making tactical associations the norm. Neighbors bargained for cellphones, mothers sold shacks to sons, and brothers demanded payment in advance. While customary relationships were becoming transactional, transactional relationships were becoming customary.

Ultimately, settlement relatedness was not the result of Ashkali or Romani cultural patterns but rather a political economy of trash. It was an artifact of life in a state of exception where value was constantly being negotiated. Items from the dumpsters and other secondhand goods were assigned worth through arbitration. Unlike at stores where commodities had a clear provenance and price, Polje's merchandise was recycled and hence severed from formal trade networks. It was primarily through interactions that previously discarded items were invested with value. But this process was unstable. An object's price was agreed upon in the moment and could easily change if resold. Consequently, value was derived from the exchange itself, not the actual commodity, which in many cases was nothing more than trash. Similarly, sociality was a series of bargained transactions that were equally volatile. *Kum* bonds, like cellphones and loans, circulated around the community. Relationships, like material goods, were recyclable; they were used, discarded, and resurrected as needed. Polje's transactions, and hence its social cohesion, stemmed from the inherent disposability of commodities.

Garbage and segregation fundamentally altered people's material and social lives. Marginality made sociality. Examining precarious spaces such as Romani settlements, Agier notes, "Those who inhabit these places are 'stuck' on the margins of the neo-liberal world order. However, their 'stuckness' is also productive of new formations of place, culture and politics."[17] As Ashkali spent more and more time living in settlements, these new values and behaviors were normalized. What had been exceptional became increasingly ordinary. But these transformations were not confined only to settlements. Rajim, Fitim, and Valon, despite possessing accommodation elsewhere, returned to Polje each day and thus continued to participate in a shared social life. Moving out of the settlements did not end one's precarity or neoteric ways of being in the world. Polje and other communities like it were not just places for impoverished *cigani;* these spaces created a new and increasingly dominant form of affiliation. Consequently, the proliferation of settlements in Belgrade has precipitated a radical restructuring of people's collective worlds.

2 Precarious Domesticity

Bekim was exhausted. Out of breath, shirtless, and sweating, he sat hunched over on an old couch. Bekim was moving homes in the midst of a heat wave. Domestic tasks such as this were intimately interwoven with work, sociality, and the threat of violence. After purchasing Miloš's old shack for €50 ($62.50), Bekim and Fatime spent the morning cleaning their family's new abode. It was a laborious task. Cigarette butts, uneaten food, muddy clothes, and plastic bottles littered the inside, while rubble surrounded the exterior. Bekim and Fatime devoted several hours to sweeping out the dirt, disposing of the debris, and making minor repairs to the walls and roof. Although Miloš and Milica left their old carpets, Fatime was adamant that they were too filthy to use. Folding and carrying three large, heavy carpets from his old shack, Bekim placed them over the existing rugs. With Harun's help, he then brought in the family's three pieces of furniture: two couches that doubled as beds and an old dresser that served as a television stand and cupboard. Meanwhile, Fatime strived to make their new shack look as homey as possible. On the wall she hung a decorative rug and a large frame containing several family photos.

While the couple completed the final touches, Rajim and Aleksander were outside chatting amicably and drinking beer. Rajim had just finished his last bottle and sent his twelve-year-old son, Altin, to purchase more. As Altin sped out of the settlement on his bicycle, he passed Branko, a retired Serb. Branko owned a garden in the neighboring fields and, unlike the other Serbs who traversed the settlement, he routinely greeted residents. He saw Bekim and me sitting in the shade and commented that the heat was nothing compared to what he had experienced in Iraq, where he had worked as a contractor. Unconvinced, Bekim simply waved as Branko continued on his way. Soon Harun, then Marko, loaded their horses with metal and drove to the neighboring junkyards. Watching them leave, Bekim complained that the price of metal had dropped by fifteen percent over the past few months. Life, he lamented, was only becoming more difficult.

Standing up, Bekim began preparations to go to work. But before leaving Polje, he wanted to visit Dragomir's sister, who, he had been told, was selling a large cache of scavenged items. We walked to her shack, where Bekim inspected three bags of goods pulled from the dumpsters. The bags contained clothes, shoes, toys, purses, and bedsheets. After a brief negotiation, Bekim paid 800 dinars ($8.40) and we carted the bags back to his shack. He planned to sell the merchandise at the market the following day. He was particularly pleased with the shoes and estimated that he could recoup his investment with them alone. As we passed the men drinking, Rajim stood up and followed us, eager to inspect Bekim's purchases. Rajim agreed that the shoes were nice but he thought the rest was junk. Bekim quickly dismissed him, saying he needed to leave for work. Because he had spent all morning moving, Bekim was unable to go scavenging earlier. Furthermore, the down payment on the shack had consumed what little cash he possessed and he had no money to purchase his family's dinner. Bekim knew the only way they would have a full meal was if he managed to find scrap metal, which could be sold before the end of the day.

Before Bekim could depart, he needed to repair a flat tire on his *trokolica*.[1] He began extracting the inner tube as Dragomir walked by on his way to the rear of the settlement. Calling to Dragomir, Bekim asked if he could connect his new shack to the power grid. Dragomir readily agreed and glanced at Bekim's handiwork. He pointed to the pliers Bekim was using and declared they were his. Bekim immediately returned them and then provided Dragomir with the necessary implements to wire the shack. While Bekim resumed fixing his tire, Dragomir and I attended to the electricity. When we were finished, Dragomir demanded a bottle of soda as payment for our efforts. Gesturing to his bare chest, Bekim replied that he lost his shirt during the move and did not have a spare. Without a shirt, he would not be admitted to the convenience store. In response, Dragomir removed his own and handed it to Bekim, who quickly left for the shop.

Bekim spent the remainder of the day pedaling up and down the alleys sifting through dumpsters. Luckily, he returned home with a few hundred dinars in his pocket. He used this cash to purchase his family's dinner: a bottle of soda, three loaves of bread, and a pound of sliced bologna. This was their main meal of the day. After eating, Bekim, Fatime, their children, and I settled on the couches and watched television. It was then that a passing neighbor informed us that a group of skinheads was loitering outside of Polje. Bekim was concerned that they might try to attack the settlement. As long as the Serbian men remained in the vicinity, no one would leave Polje for fear of assault. Despite the threat, the children soon fell sound asleep and even the adults grew weary. Ready to doze off, Bekim pulled out cushions from the couches, turning them into beds. He then maneuvered the door into the frame and secured it with a chain. Fatime and I lay down on opposite sides of the room with the children between us. Finally, Bekim unscrewed the single exposed lightbulb and took his place next to Fatime. As usual, the television stayed on all night at full volume, blaring newscasts, Serbian folk music programs, Spanish telenovelas, and American action movies. The sound and light was thought to deter rats, the bane of settlement life. Indeed, I could hear rats scurrying over the roof and hoped they would not enter the shack. Just as I was about to drift into unconsciousness, Bekim whispered that he was pleased that he had found a suitable place for his family to live.

Bekim's day typifies life in the settlement. Residents were continually shifting from one event to the next, juggling household demands with the difficult realities of poverty and exclusion. But they were not just striving to make due and get by; they were attempting to build an enduring home. Polje's community was born out of its precarity. To Serbs, however, this would seem absurd. Whether in casual conversations, media portrayals, or government directives, settlements were routinely conceptualized as fundamentally impermanent. Residents were labeled squatters while their shacks were slated for removal. However, for Bekim and his neighbors,

Polje was the greatest constant in their lives. Ashkali and Roma had lost or abandoned their houses elsewhere and now the settlement was their only haven. If it was not home, where else was?

Examining the daily struggles of Bekim and others, this chapter explores the ways in which Polje's residents produced domesticity in a segregated zone built on trash. Almost all of the trappings of home—a domicile, food, and electricity—were sourced, in one way or another, from the dumpsters. Consequently, households were made and maintained through garbage. Objects that Serbs deemed worthless, Ashkali and Roma routinely refashioned into life's necessities. Once more, the biographies of scavengers and waste paralleled one another. Through processes such as collecting items to build and beautify a shack or sitting down to share a meal of salvaged vegetables, material and social spaces were generated. In this context, trash was not simply circulating in an alternate regime of value; it also created families.

But even as residents worked to construct lasting homes, these efforts were inevitably disrupted. Less than a week after Bekim's family moved into their new shack, heavy rains pummeled the settlement. They woke to discover the floor soaked with water. The rugs and even the children's clothes were sodden. Realizing that the location was prone to flooding, Bekim purchased another shack and moved yet again. This would be his sixth relocation in two years. Within the confines of Polje, there was no security; displacement was the norm.

BUILDING A SHACK, MAKING A HOME

From a distance the shacks gracing Belgrade's settlements appeared to be a uniform testimony to poverty. They were small squat structures, composed of irregular wood scraps and covered in fraying tarps. Windows were broken, walls were riddled with holes, and roofs leaked. However, closer inspection revealed a host of variations and no two shacks were the same. Each edifice was the cumulative result of individual expertise, cooperative labor, and the city's detritus. Because the trash supplied the items necessary to build and maintain the abodes, each shack was a testament to resourcefulness. To provide insulation against the cold winter wind, Sara lined the walls of her home with large cardboard advertisements. The billboards, which also functioned as decoration, depicted a pouting blond woman in an evening dress holding a translucent bottle of perfume. These images of wealth and beauty stood in stark contrast to the potato peels and dirty clothes scattered over the floor. Yet the billboards, like the clothes, had come from the dumpsters. Everyone's home was built from garbage. As a result, shacks were much more than domiciles; they occupied the intersection of sociality, materiality, and economy. I discovered this firsthand when I attempted to assemble my own shack.

Wanting to live full-time in the settlement, I first sought the permission of Endrit and Bekim, who readily agreed and volunteered to assist me. However, my attempt to make a home in Polje was beset by a number of challenges. The first was finding a location. Existing residents had already claimed all of the suitable plots within the center of settlement. The margins possessed plenty of available space but this would result in greater interactions with Serbs. Although Branko was amicable, others were not. Gazmend recalled surveying one potential site on the edge of Polje, when a passing Serb, Igor, informed him it was forbidden to build there. Contemplating the exchange, Gazmend noted that no matter where Roma and Ashkali went, no one liked them. Gazmend, however, would not be discouraged. A few days later he arrived with several men and began erecting his shack. As it took shape, Igor walked by again but this time said nothing. Even after Gazmend moved in, Igor refused to acknowledge his presence. Tired of the silence, Gazmend stopped him one day and asked why he never said hello. They were neighbors, Gazmend reminded him. Igor replied that he had not seen Gazmend. This, Gazmend told me, was bullshit. They now greet each other but say nothing else. While Gazmend and Igor reached a détente, minor conflicts could escalate. After several months of exchanging insults with Dragomir, a Serb living in a nearby apartment building threatened him with assault and arrest. Dragomir was concerned for his family's safety and quickly relocated his shack from Polje's periphery to its center. Residents were acutely aware of their vulnerability and chose to live in the settlement's core to minimize their risk. Segregation was a strategy for protection. Consequently, Bekim suggested that my shack be placed at the back of his plot. The space was cramped but it would ensure my security. I agreed and began gathering the materials I would need.

At its most basic, a shack consisted of a simple frame with makeshift walls, a ceiling, door, window, and roof tarp. As with many items, these supplies could be scavenged or purchased. Conscious of the potential cost involved, Bekim, Endrit, and other Ashkali urged me to do the former. When Drita returned to the settlement with two large sheets of plastic for my roof, she proudly declared that there was no reason to buy anything. However, this approach necessitated ingenuity and patience. A number of items could be used as construction materials and a savvy builder needed to be flexible. Discarded door jams, 4x4s, or posts made excellent frames while plywood, doors, or the backs of couches could function as walls. But as the days passed, I learned that suitable pieces of wood were seldom discarded. Acquiring sufficient supplies would take weeks. Dragomir had been stockpiling wood for over a month and still did not have enough to add another room.

Realizing the difficulties of building a shack out of found components, I decided to purchase materials instead. This would cost between €30 ($37.50) to €70 ($87.50) depending on the number of items I required. To mitigate the expense, Endrit advised me to scavenge the beams and window while paying for the rest. However, others gave me the opposite advice. Regardless of the approach I chose, buying supplies was not straightforward. I would not be patronizing a store or acquiring new merchandise. Everything would come from fellow scavengers. But given the relative rarity of these components, it was doubtful that a single person would possess all of them. I might need to source each one from a different individual. Whether I collected the materials myself or someone else did it for me, it was impossible to escape the indeterminacy and insecurity of relying on trash.

Once all of the constituent parts were amassed, building a shack was relatively simple. It never took longer than a day and was often finished in three to five hours. Ethnic and family groups cooperated, usually with three to six men working together. Less experienced men relied on others to oversee construction. When Bekim needed to erect a stable for his horse, Gazmend took control, complaining that the younger generations built too quickly and with little skill. Although it might take him more time, Gazmend asserted that his structures would last longer than those made by others. The men labored as a team, with Gazmend barking orders while Bekim, Valon, Agim, Endrit, and Fitim lifted boards and nailed posts. Similarly, Aleksander's sons worked under his guidance when their family needed a new domicile. Those who lacked knowledgeable relatives hired architects such as Dragomir. But no matter who was supervising, the building process was invariably the same.

The first step required digging holes, approximately ten centimeters deep, to house the vertical support beams. Minimally, one beam was put in each of the four corners. Larger shacks would ideally have additional pillars located at the midpoint of each wall. However, few could scavenge or afford this many beams, leaving most shacks either small or unstable. Once the timbers were in place, the holes were packed with rubble. With the beams secured, walls were created using flat boards. In most cases, old doors were repurposed for this task. Front doors, bathroom doors, and closet doors—in a variety of sizes, colors, and materials—could all serve as walls. Any featuring decorative glass or mirrors were strategically positioned at the top to function as makeshift windows or vanities. But fashioning doors into walls limited the height of the structure. Consequently, builders often affixed scraps of plywood or pressboard to the tops of the walls. Old couches, once torn apart, yielded several panels that were ideal for this task. Additional scraps were employed to fill any gaps between the main planks, the door, and the window. These elements were all affixed with nails bought from a local hardware store. In an attempt to save money, builders purchased smaller nails and used them sparingly. Sometimes an entire wall was attached with as few as twelve nails.

The final step was constructing the ceiling and roof. Two rafters, positioned in an X, were placed on top of the structure. A volunteer then scaled the walls and, carefully balancing on top of them, nailed ceiling planks to each rafter. Having seen how few nails were used and the flimsiness of many of the materials, I was concerned that the shack would collapse each time anyone climbed on top of it. However, this never occurred. With the building completed, the roof was covered with a tarp or plastic, which was weighted down with bricks, tires, or other debris. Compared to gathering the components, shack construction was quick and straightforward. All anyone needed for a fully functional home was a few hours and a supply of doors, doorframes, couches, nails, and a tarp.

But before I could buy any of these items, another opportunity presented itself: the vacant shack next to Bekim's was put up for sale. Its owner had relocated to another settlement several weeks earlier but kept his shack in case he needed to return.[2] Now that the owner was satisfied with his new home, he was offering to sell his old shack for €80 ($100). The price was about average for a one-room structure. Smaller shacks could be bought for as little as €50 ($62.50), while larger ones in good condition could fetch over €100 ($125). However, this shack was in need of repair. The roof had sprung several leaks, the rugs were wet and mildewed, the walls were riddled with holes, and the door was off its hinges. Gazmend joked it was so poorly built that a strong wind would blow it over. Bekim agreed that the shack was falling apart but, he added, this was true of most structures in Polje. He believed it could be transformed into a livable home with a minimal amount of effort. Given the delays and difficulties I had experienced, I decided this was the best option and bought the shack.

A couple of days later, Bekim, Agim, Slobodan, and I began renovations. The first step was to remove the carpets. Pulling them up, we discovered that the floors underneath were covered with cigarette butts. Soon the air was filled with ash so thick that we were forced to shield our noses and mouths with our shirts. Hoping to sweep up the debris, Agim fashioned a rake by nailing a square wood block to a makeshift handle of plywood. Although the two pieces detached every few minutes, Agim swiftly reconnected them and continued with his work. Once the dirt floor was exposed, it was necessary to level it. We walked to Polje's outskirts where a layer of loose white sand covered a buried gas line. Scooping the sand into buckets, we carried it back to the shack, dumped it onto the floor, and leveled it with Agim's improvised rake. Because the area around the gas line served as a communal toilet, we had to watch our step to avoid trodding in feces. After six trips, a three-centimeter layer of sand lined the floor, which Bekim then covered with a layer of cardboard.

With the floors finished, we turned to the holes in the walls. Strips of carpet and scraps of wood were nailed over the largest gaps, while foam from old couches was stuffed in smaller ones. The last item to fix was the leaky roof. Agim quickly scaled the structure, and while it shook ominously, the shack supported his weight. Next, Bekim, Slobodan, and I handed him large pieces of rubble, which he used to better secure the weathered plastic. Surveying our work, Bekim conceded that the shack was now markedly improved. Nevertheless, many of the beams were rotted and it was extremely unstable. But, Bekim said, these were issues that plagued most shacks. His was no different. When you lived in a settlement, this was what functioned as a home.

Like me, most residents also purchased and renovated preexisting shacks rather than building their own. Finding an available home was relatively easy given the fluid nature of the settlement population. Residents were constantly looking for structures that were in better repair, in a better location, or larger. Having inside knowledge of who was planning to depart, local inhabitants were usually the first to make an offer. Consequently, individuals seeking to move into Polje were often limited to homes that residents held in low regard. But this did not deter newcomers, who knew that they could later exchange their initial domicile for another. As a result, a single structure could change hands repeatedly. When I first arrived in Polje, Bekim was living in a small shack at the mouth of the settlement, but a year later he sold it to a fellow Ashkali. When the man was sent to prison, a Romani woman from southern Serbia bought it. Several months later, she returned home and gave the shack to Dragomir. He sold it to a family from Srem but they only stayed for a couple of months. Finally, less than two years after Bekim moved out, Dragomir's brother-in-law bought it.

In many cases, these movements were the outcome of persistent and overlapping misfortune. For instance, as flooding forced Bekim's family to look for a new shack, Marko's family sought to sell theirs after an unexpected run in with the authorities. Marko's wife had been stopped by the police a few days earlier and asked to produce identification. Unable to do so, she was taken into custody. Subsequent background checks revealed that their children were not attending school as required by law. If this continued, the family would no longer receive child support payments. Marko relied on this money and could not afford to lose it. Consequently, he decided to move his family back to Srem, where his children were enrolled in school. Hearing about Marko's difficulties, Bekim immediately offered to purchase his shack for €50 ($62.50). After making a small down payment, Bekim secured the rest of the cash from a loan shark and moved in. However, over the next three weeks, Bekim was unable to earn enough money to settle his debt. In lieu of cash, the loan shark demanded the shack as compensation and evicted Bekim's family. Once again, Bekim had to search for a new home. Events such as these were commonplace. Every family in Polje routinely experienced difficulties maintaining a stable household as chronic adversity drove relocations.

In the midst of this turmoil, perhaps because of it, people strove to turn their shacks into homes. Constructing and renovating shacks might take more effort but beautifying them was just as crucial. Each time Bekim and Fatime moved, their new domicile was immediately adorned with family photos. But, as with building materials, embellishments came from the trash. The frame containing the photos originally held an English-language motivational poster urging travel agency employees to work together. A few months later, when Bekim found an almost empty can of blue paint in the dumpsters, he used old clothes to smear it over the outside of his shack. Fatime then added a floral sticker with a homily written in incorrect English: "Love is what make you smile when you're tired." Fatime also decorated the interior, hanging rugs and fabric appliques on the walls. For a few weeks, a small plant was placed next to the television. Each of the settlement's residents personalized their living area in a similar fashion. Drapes, velveteen, garlands, religious images, and cardboard were often used.

A shack was much more than a collection of old doors and wooden beams. It represented a series of transformative relationships that revolved around trash. First, it embodied a globalized capitalism that produced a plethora of durable commodities that, once discarded, could be resurrected and repurposed. Second, a shack's materials, which were often sourced from a variety of individuals, reflected the networks through which scavengers traded these goods and imbued them with value. Third, the knowledge and skill necessary to erect an edifice demonstrated people's unique ability to convert seemingly worthless scraps of wood into a functional dwelling. Finally, by adding décor, families attempted to create a semblance of domesticity and stability amid the chaos of exception.[3] Working within an environment of overwhelming constraints, camp residents actively forged a space of normalcy that contested the hegemony of sovereign power.[4] Consequently, homes were constructed materially, socially, and politically.

I discovered the significance of shacks as homes when my own was at last completed. No sooner was it deemed fit for occupation than Bekim and Fatime expressed concerns. How would I, a single man, cook for myself? What if the electricity went out? What if someone tried to rob me while I was sleeping? What if a rat bit me? Their objections revolved around a single issue: a shack with one occupant was not a social unit. I needed to be part of a family who could look after me. They suggested that I abandon my shack and move in with them. Even though Endrit and his family were also residing with Bekim and Fatime, I was told that one more person would not make a difference. I gratefully accepted their invitation and joined the eleven other people who called their shack a home.[5]

FOOD INSECURITY

Shacks were a space to make a home, but it was food that sustained the community, nourished both physical and social bodies, and facilitated relationships between neighbors and within families. Significantly, this context was structured by the commoditization of food. Polje's residents were accustomed to spending their limited cash on staples acquired from convenience stores (*prodavnice*). Surpassed only by dumpsters, *prodavnice* were the second most visited destination outside of the settlement. This was the result of two factors. First, because the absence of refrigeration rendered storage impractical, Polje's residents purchased food for immediate consumption. Second, a chronic lack of cash ensured that families could only afford to buy a few items at a time. This necessitated making several trips to the *prodavnica* throughout the course of the day. When adults tired of the journey, they sent their children.

Prodavnice were a ubiquitous feature of Belgrade's landscape and several lay in close proximity to the settlement. But residents preferred one shop in particular, which was situated just across the street from Polje's entrance. Too small to accommodate aisles, its walls were lined with shelves containing cookies, potato chips, canned foods, and cleaning supplies. In the rear, refrigerated cabinets and a freezer held cold drinks, milk, ice cream, and frozen meats. A small deli counter provided cold cuts and cheeses while cigarettes and instant coffee were stocked by the cash register. Outside, a small selection of seasonal fruits and vegetables was available. Although the *prodavnica* sold a limited choice of goods, this did not trouble Ashkali, whose needs seldom ranged beyond a few key items including soda, coffee, bread, seasoning, processed meat, potatoes, tomatoes, onions, and peppers.

While the *prodavnica* saw a constant flow of Ashkali and Roma, Serbian customers frequented it as well. Convenience stores were one of the few sites at which Polje's inhabitants regularly intermingled with their Serbian neighbors. Shoppers of different ethnicities tended to ignore one other but interactions at the register were unavoidable. Ashkali engaged in small talk with the cashiers, who, in turn, sometimes remembered the customer's preferred brand of cigarettes. But when Ashkali were out of earshot, clerks spoke of *cigani* as potential thieves and complained about their numerous visits. Consequently, Polje's residents did not linger in the *prodavnica* lest they become the target of suspicion or aggression. When leaving the shop, they were reminded what happened to those outside the Serbian nationalist project: on the *prodavnica*'s exterior, a mural depicted Ratko Mladić. A hero to many Serbs, he was convicted of genocide and crimes against humanity for his role in the Bosnian War. Passing the *prodavnica* several times a day, Ashkali and Roma were confronted with his image and the implied consequences of Otherness.

While the *prodavnica* was a site of routinized anxiety between Serbs and Ashkali, its commodities lubricated relationships among Polje's diverse residents. A carbonated drink or a cup of coffee was an essential feature of most interactions. In some cases, clear rules governed the purchasing and distribution of these beverages. For example, a host was always required to provide refreshments for guests. Likewise, individuals who assisted in communal tasks, such as building or wiring a shack, expected to receive a bottle of soda as thanks. However, when chatting alongside Polje's thoroughfare, the responsibility for supplying drinks was ambiguous and had to be negotiated. Extended discussions regarding beverages were particularly meaningful because drinks were the only items that residents bought and shared with one another. The signification of coffee and soda came from their status as commodities. Unlike almost everything else in Polje, they could not be found in the trash. To serve beverages required cash. As a result, purchasing refreshments accorded formal value to reciprocal and neighborly relationships. But like the cost of soda, this value, while important, was minimal. A bottle of soda would foster brief comity but these bonds were fundamentally impermanent.

In contrast to soda and coffee, which were purchased at the *prodavnica*, water was obtained illegally, usually from a fire hydrant just outside of the settlement. Water was used only for cooking or washing and never as a beverage. However, the onerous steps required to access hydrants generated its own sociality. Most families went for water each day, typically in the afternoon when men had returned from work. Empty plastic bottles scavenged from the trash were loaded onto horse carts or *trokolice* and transported to the hydrant. Once there, residents faced a challenge: every hydrant was sealed with a heavy metal cap intended to prevent unauthorized access. To open the spigot, a sturdy metal rod was inserted into the cover and twisted. This process required strength and agility. First, an individual had to negotiate the modest pool of water—a hallmark of use— that ringed the hydrant. Attempting to keep their feet dry, residents gingerly stepped onto small shaky rocks placed in the pool. The rod, functioning as a makeshift lever, was then placed in the spigot and twisted. It took a great deal of force to move the valve and men could make several attempts before they were successful. But as soon as the spigot was opened, water gushed everywhere. This forced the individual to move immediately or become drenched. On several occasions, people miscalculated and ended up stepping completely into the pool, flooding their shoes. Once the hydrant was flowing, one bottle at a time was placed under the spigot. Given the small aperture of the containers and the torrential flow, most of the water fell on the ground, enlarging the hydrant's pool.

Like many other tasks in the settlement, fetching water encouraged interaction and cooperation. In the late afternoon, a line could form by the hydrant with people amicably chatting. They exchanged settlement gossip, recounted scavenging stories, and negotiated trades. While waiting one day, Bekim entertainingly described finding a dildo in a dumpster. Everyone broke into laughter and a few jokingly speculated the price it would have fetched at the market. When it was Bekim's turn, he utilized a shared lever that was left at the hydrant's base. But because the implement was communal and frequently reused, it was prone to warping, breakage, and loss. If this occurred, individuals asked other members of the settlement for help. Bekim regularly went to Aleksander or Dragomir to borrow tools when he was unable to open the hydrant. At times, however, residents discovered that no amount of ingenuity or improvised levers could loosen the cap. City authorities occasionally locked the hydrant, rendering it inaccessible for days or weeks. During these periods, Polje's inhabitants swapped information about other sources of water such as hidden spigots behind high-rise buildings or junkyards with unguarded hoses. The constant hardship of accessing water created connections as the community shared, and attempted to overcome, mutual struggles. Unlike soda and coffee, the sociality of water came from its procurement, not from its consumption.

Whereas illicitly accessing water inspired conversation, scavenging food did not. Polje's population, routinely lacking the cash to purchase their meals, were accustomed to acquiring a significant portion of their nourishment from the trash.[6] However, residents rarely discussed this in public. Food insecurity, although ubiquitous, was shameful. This was illustrated one afternoon when I passed Jelena, a Bayash woman, sitting outside her shack preparing wild snails for dinner. Without prompting, she immediately explained that her family had enough money to purchase staples. Jelena declared that she merely liked the taste of snails, pointedly noting that she was not poor. Food, more than any other aspect of domestic life, was viewed as a bellwether of poverty. Residents felt no embarrassment scavenging through trash or living in a shack, but going hungry signaled a fundamental failure. Furthermore, a family's sustenance needed to come from a store and not a dumpster. As with drinks, the moral value of food lay in its commoditization. It was not enough that a family had prepared a meal; that meal must have been bought. Anyone unable to do so was viewed as irresponsible, lazy, and destitute.

Given this connotation, few families admitted to foraging for food in the garbage. Nevertheless, economic necessity drove all of Polje's inhabitants to find at least a part of their meal in the dumpsters. Similar to fashioning a shack from old doors, Ashkali and Roma appropriated discarded provisions and recycled them. What Serbs deemed to be rotten or inedible, scavengers could view as a windfall. But they only procured a select range of items. Meat and cooked food were always rejected for fear that they were spoiled. Meanwhile, packaged foods such as candy and potato chips were only retrieved if they were unopened. In contrast, Polje's residents readily salvaged raw vegetables. They particularly favored tomatoes, peppers, onions, and potatoes. To find these foods, Ashkali and Roma routinely searched dumpsters at the rear of supermarkets. Large stores consistently discarded significant amounts of produce as these items began to wilt and mold. This was made possible by an increasingly global food regime that valued freshness and equated it with blemish-free foods devoid of decay. To meet customers' expectations, supermarkets became accustomed to throwing away items that were still edible. Consequently, it was the tastes and commodity cycles of transnational capitalism that provided scavengers with sustenance.

The timing of supermarket disposals varied, however. This made locating a vegetable-filled dumpster a matter of luck, but doing so could feed a family for a couple of days. For instance, in a single dumpster, Bekim and I unearthed two large bags of potatoes, two plastic baskets of strawberries, two bags of spinach, two bags of lettuce, two bunches of radishes, seven bell peppers, eight chilies, a bag of oranges, and a bag of bananas. When we returned home, Fatime carefully examined each item to determine its edibility. She immediately discarded the lettuce and spinach, both of which were wilted. The bananas and strawberries were bruised and several had molded but with careful trimming, Fatime was able to salvage a quarter of them. While a few of the oranges were also moldy, most were in good condition and saved. In contrast to the greens and fruit, the vegetables were nearly pristine. Fatime cooked the bell peppers and chilies for lunch while she placed the potatoes and radishes in the cupboard for later. In the end, she served about half of the food we retrieved, transforming trash into sustenance.

Like all women in Polje, Fatime managed and prepared meals.[7] For this purpose she kept a small selection of pots, mixing bowls, and utensils in a cupboard under the television. An adjacent cast-iron stove was used for cooking and baking.[8] Although each day's menu varied, Fatime fixed three dishes on a regular basis. The first was *čorba*, a soup made by combining boiled beans with a roux of flour and oil. She frequently prepared *čorba* when scavenging had been unsuccessful and cash was scarce. Soup required only a few inexpensive items and yielded a substantial amount. Another popular dish consisted of sliced potatoes baked with oil and salt. Whenever possible, a salad of tomatoes and onions dressed with vegetable oil and seasoning salt was also served. In addition to these three staple dishes, other options included sliced bell peppers baked in oil and salt, omelets, pasta with ketchup, fried battered zucchini, and baked mushrooms. The family's diet was predominantly vegetarian because most of their food came from dumpsters. About once or twice a week, Bekim tried to find enough cash to buy a few slices of bologna. On rare occasions he could afford to purchase chicken legs, which Fatime baked with rice. Regardless of the entrees, bread accompanied every meal. It was filling, cheap, and never scavenged.

Throughout Polje, meals were served and consumed in a similar fashion. Because shacks were small and lacked a dedicated dining area, one had to be created. At lunch and dinner, Fatime began by laying several sheets of newspaper on the floor. She placed the hot food in the center and arranged individual plates around the periphery. Finally, half a loaf of bread was set beside each plate. Summoned to eat, diners sat cross-legged in a circle on the newspaper and served themselves. Each individual was careful to take only a small portion, as there was seldom enough to go around. Ashkali eschewed knives and forks, preferring instead to scoop up their food, whether potatoes or salad, with bread. Bekim and other scavengers often came to eat with their hands stained black from dumpster residue. Given the difficulty of getting water, hand washing was seen as a needless waste of resources. Consequently, the loaves of bread became dotted with dark fingerprints as a meal progressed. Ashkali ate quickly but always left a small amount of food on their plate because to do otherwise implied that the diner was still hungry and Fatime had not provided enough. As soon as an individual was finished eating, he or she stood up and left the circle, often sitting on one of the couches against the wall. No one waited for others before retreating to the sidelines. When the dining area was clear of people, Fatime picked up the plates, stored any remaining food in the cupboard, threw the newspaper out the front door, and swept the floor. With all evidence of the meal removed, the shack was transformed into a living space once again.

The act of eating not only created a bounded physical space but also underscored familial relatedness. Whereas soda and coffee were shared with guests and friends, food was not. Anyone visiting an Ashkali or Romani household at mealtimes either politely left or watched from a distance as the family ate. This was an accepted part of life in Polje and residents never resented being excluded. This custom also applied to all family members who lived in another domicile. Once Endrit moved into his own small shack in Bekim's backyard, he no longer ate meals prepared by his daughter, Fatime. As a newcomer to the settlement, I was never offered food and quickly became accustomed to sitting on the sidelines.

However, one day this unexpectedly changed. After spending my first full morning scavenging with Bekim, we returned to the shack to find lunch prepared. I took my usual seat on the couch but Fatime immediately told me to eat with everyone else. When I hesitated, both Bekim and Fatime became insistent, saying that I had worked hard and must now replenish my strength. On the days that I labored with Bekim, he demanded that I share their food, but on the days that I did not, I remained a spectator. By the time I moved into their shack, my daily scavenging activities had secured a permanent place for me at mealtimes.

I discovered that families were not only linked through kinship; they were also constituted through production. In Polje, families were laboring units whose members contributed to its collective well-being. Consequently, only those who assisted in maintaining and perpetuating the household shared in its food. When Endrit relocated, he no longer contributed to Bekim's family and was excluded from meals. I believe that this pragmatic approach resulted from the lived experience of settlements. Polje's residents were strangers surrounded by chronic scarcity. Competing for meager resources, every family was on its own. The extended support systems that suffused villages were absent in Polje. Yet to survive, it was necessary to rely on one's neighbors. These practical bonds were lubricated with the exchange of inexpensive purchased commodities: coffee and soda. In contrast, trash was for family. Not only did families scavenge in the dumpsters together, they consumed its bounty at mealtimes. This was not simply about producing a meal but also about how it was eaten. Spouses, parents, and children sat together on the ground in a uniquely demarcated social space. Through scavenged foods and commoditized beverages, Polje's residents delineated family from neighbors, insiders from outsiders. Kinship was created through garbage.

WIRED

Perhaps the greatest domestic struggle was for electricity. Lights, cellphones, and televisions required power but Polje was not connected to the Serbian grid. To circumvent this barrier, residents attached wires to municipal lampposts and siphoned their electricity. These furtive connections were free but also inconvenient, illegal, and dangerous. Power was only available after the streetlights were switched on and this varied with the sunrise and sunset. In winter the lampposts illuminated as early as four o'clock in the afternoon, but in summer this did not occur until eight o'clock at night. Residents' lives were regulated by these shifting times, waiting each evening for their lights and televisions to turn on. But even when the electricity was flowing, a family's use was limited. The current was notoriously weak in large part because six to eight shacks drew from a single cable. Turning on the television invariably caused the lights to dim. Even if residents could afford larger appliances such as refrigerators, there was never enough power to operate them. Consequently, each household was generally restricted to a television, a DVD player, a lightbulb, and one or two cellphone chargers.

While the current from streetlights was anemic, it was nevertheless dangerous. Residents working on active wires hardly ever escaped unscathed. Bekim used only a pair of rubber-handled pliers, resulting in a flurry of sparks and mild shocks. In addition, exposed cables crisscrossed the settlement and presented a considerable hazard. Individuals taking shortcuts between shacks or looking for a secluded place to urinate ran the risk of accidentally treading on a live wire. Casual electrocution was so common that people joked about it: stepping on a dead cable during the day, Agim began to jerk erratically while smiling. Given the danger, experienced men such as Dragomir, Endrit, and Rajim performed most electrical tasks. Consequently, when Bekim needed to connect his new shack to the grid, he asked Dragomir for assistance.

Like building a shack, electrical work did not take long and could be accomplished with very few materials. To wire his new home, Bekim supplied Dragomir with nothing more than a half-meter-long pipe and a power strip. Similar to everything else in Polje, electrical connections were made possible by recycling garbage. All the supplies Dragomir required could be found in the trash heap at the rear of Bekim's shack. When Dragomir was ready, he began searching the detritus until he located a brick. Using it as a makeshift hammer, he drove the pipe into the soil beside the shack. This would act as a ground. The power strip would be suspended from the ceiling and function as an outlet. The plug had already been removed and two wires, one red and one blue, dangled from the cord. The red wire would be connected to the ground while the blue would be wrapped around the main cable. However, the cord was too short to reach either the pipe or the cable.

Unperturbed, Dragomir returned to the pile of trash. He quickly located three severed cords that still possessed plugs. Threading the cords through his fingers and gripping them tightly, Dragomir forcefully tore off the plugs. He then put the cords in his mouth and used his teeth to puncture and remove the plastic covering. With the interior red and blue wires now liberated, Dragomir employed the same technique to strip a few centimeters of the casing from each of their ends. Twisting the exposed tips of each of the blue wires together, he formed a strand approximately four meters long. Dragomir repeated the process with the red wires before rummaging through the debris field yet again. This time he picked up a plastic shopping bag and tore it into pieces. With these, he fashioned covers, which were tied around each join. Inspecting the two extended wires, Dragomir boasted that he was able to accomplish the entire task without tools.

Ready at last, Dragomir took the power strip inside and passed its cord through a gap between the shack's wall and roof. He joined the lengthened red wire to its counterpart on the power strip, covered the connection with plastic, and wound the other end around the grounding pipe. Dragomir then covered the pipe with a small piece of concrete to prevent anyone from accidentally stepping on it. Picking up the blue wire, he also attached it to the power strip. However, the cord was still too short to reach the cable, which lay two meters away. Once more, Dragomir searched the debris. This time he was able to find an abandoned section of cable, which he fastened to the blue wire before placing it on the ground. Rather than cover the join with plastic, Dragomir simply laid a small piece of concrete on top of it. He added additional weights at intervals along the cable to ensure that it remained stationary. Finally, he twisted this subsidiary line around the end of the main cable. Both were quite thick and it required some effort to get them to bend around each other. Setting the cable down, Dragomir put concrete slabs above and below the connection. He was finished at last. The entire project took about forty minutes. Surveying his work, Dragomir commented that the cable quality was poor and could result in fires. Bekim's shack could easily burn to the ground. But, he added, this cable was all they had so it would have to do. The trash used to wire a shack might have been freely available but it was also dangerous.

Connecting a shack to the main cable was only the first link in a chain that ran approximately three hundred meters from the settlement to the lamppost. The cable was not a single span; it consisted of shorter inter-linked sections, much like the wires Dragomir constructed. If bought from neighboring stores, it would cost 30,000 dinars ($315) to cover the required distance. This was an expense that men like Bekim and Dragomir could not afford. Instead, inhabitants purchased low-quality, worn, and discarded stock from Roma at a much lower price. Once enough segments were amassed, the cable was surreptitiously laid toward a lamppost. Several streetlights adorned the area immediately adjacent to Polje's entrance but they were never utilized. These lampposts were clearly visible from the main road and any illicit wires would be highly conspicuous and removed immediately. Instead, residents snaked the cable in the opposite direction through bushes and pastures. Given how well the cable was camouflaged by the vegetation, some residents worried that unsuspecting Serbs would accidentally step on one of the joins in the darkness and become electrocuted. Fortunately, this never occurred.

The most vulnerable section of the route was the final few meters. The cable emerged from the high grass and crossed an unpaved road, where it was particularly susceptible to detection. In an effort to conceal the cable, Polje's inhabitants buried it under the road. This project, unlike wiring a shack, could not be accomplished alone. A group of several men was needed to complete the work quickly and avoid discovery by passersby or the police. Polje's work teams were uniquely composed of a mix of Ashkali and Romani men. Because members of both ethnicities drew electricity from a single cable, they were collectively responsible for maintaining it. This was the only task in Polje that elicited cooperation from its diverse residents. Consequently, cable work created a distinctive comraderie among neighbors. In fact, it was through participation in these groups that I was introduced to, and formed friendships with, Romani residents such as Dragomir and Miloš.

Burying the cable was simultaneously an exercise in vulnerability and levity. When residents caught sight of men leaving the settlement bound for the streetlight, they often joked about calling the police and having the group arrested. While everyone laughed, this joke underscored the danger of cable work. Residents were well aware that the authorities monitored the neighboring lampposts and detained anyone caught tampering with them. Compounding this issue, there was simply no way for cable workers to conceal their presence. The lamppost was exposed and visible from all directions. In addition, all cable work was done during the day when the power was off. Polje's residents had a choice of risking arrest or electrocution and they chose the former.

Once the men arrived at the lamppost, the work began. The most arduous task was digging a shallow trench directly across the road. As with any project, the tools available were limited. They used a solitary digging implement, often a pickaxe borrowed from Aleksander. One man dug furiously until he became exhausted, at which point another took over. As others in the group kept watch for the police and waited for their turn, they occupied the time with teasing and joking. Cable work might have been risky but it was also humorous. In one instance, the digger was so intent on his task that he failed to realize that his pants were drooping. Before long, the top of his hirsute buttocks was noticeably exposed. Amidst muffled snickers, Dragomir gave Bekim his phone. Casually walking behind the man, Bekim took several photos, eliciting howls from those present. Sexual banter was also commonplace. Men bragged about the size of their penises and their sexual prowess. These conversations were more explicit and incorporated taboo subjects that were rarely broached within the confines of Polje. For instance, men routinely accused one another of being faggots (*pederi*). Eventually, one would grab another from behind and pretend to have intercourse with him as everyone erupted in laughter. Given the constant discussions of homosexuality, they joked that repeatedly burying the cable would make me gay. Because cable work was restricted to younger and middle-aged men, it allowed these individuals to perform a particular type of masculinity, one that was deemed inappropriate in the presence of women and children.

Even as the members of the work crew laughed and teased one another, they remained vigilant. Bekim often glanced up at the neighboring apartments wondering if police or police informants were watching. On some occasions, these suspicions seemed to be justified. When a man appeared on a balcony with what looked to be a camera, Fitim immediately speculated that the Serb was taking photos for the police. Rather than hiding his face in fear, Fadil became defiant and began making obscene gestures. Agim registered his anger by pulled down his trousers and mooning the building. However, not all exchanges with Serbs were confrontational. A few minutes after the potential photographer retreated inside his apartment, an older Serbian woman came walking down the street. She warmly greeted Rajim and asked if he had built his chicken coop yet. Rajim replied that the tips she had given him were quite helpful. Pleased, she promised to visit him later and see the coop for herself. Acting as if our illegal activities were simply another job, Rajim said he would return home after his work on the road was finished. She casually bid us farewell and continued on her way.

As soon as the men completed digging the trench, they laid the cable inside and buried it. Now remained one final task: connecting the cable to the lamppost. This was by far the most stressful part of the entire procedure. Anyone found tampering with municipal lighting faced a day in jail and a costly fine of 120,000 dinars ($1,260). Given the penalty, only two individuals worked on the lamppost. Rajim typically acted as the electrician, while Fadil or Dragomir assisted him. All others kept a safe distance, prepared to scatter into the fields at the first sign of the police. Everyone was on edge. I learned very quickly that this was serious business.[9] Fortunately, wiring the streetlight was simple and took just a few minutes. First, Rajim unscrewed a single nut at the lamppost's base and removed a small cover. Inside, three thick wires were bolted to a horizontal plate. Rajim loosened one of the bolts, slid the settlement's cable underneath it, secured the contact, and replaced the cover. Their mission complete, the men cut through the fields to their shacks hoping that no one would notice the black cable emanating from the lamppost. But they would have to wait until sunset to know if their efforts were successful.

Even if their shacks illuminated as planned, the men could not celebrate. Residents knew that it was only a matter of time until the electrical connection was severed. Every sunset was a waiting game. If the settlement remained dark, conversations ceased and chores were abandoned as residents enlisted each other's help in searching for the cause. For instance, when Gazmend's lights failed to activate one evening, he immediately yelled across his yard for Dragomir. The men shared a subsidiary cable and Gazmend wanted to know the state of Dragomir's electricity. Dragomir reported that his home was also dark and began checking the wiring in the rear of their shacks. After finding nothing amiss, Dragomir summoned

Bekim, Marko, and me, as we had been chatting nearby. Dragomir explained the situation, adding that he was unable to examine the rest of the cable because he did not want to leave his wife and children unprotected. Could we do it? Having little choice, Bekim agreed and we set off through the dark fields. As was often the case, none of us possessed a light. We awkwardly stumbled through the brush, following the cable as best we could, looking for abnormalities, and hoping to avoid accidental electrocution.

Expeditions like ours occurred on a regular basis, sometimes as frequently as every other night. We hoped that a falling branch, grazing sheep, or careless child had accidentally detached one of the cable's tenuous joins. In these situations, repairs were quick and easy. We would simply need to twist the ends together to reestablish contact. However, there was a chance that the damage could be more serious. On some evenings, repair parties discovered that the cable had been severed or removed. Polje's residents alternately blamed police, farmers, or skinheads but were never able to identify the perpetrators with any certainty. Suspecting that every Serb was a potential saboteur, inhabitants refrained from discussing electricity when farmers were walking through the settlement. This caution stemmed from the difficulty of mending a cut or stolen cable. In these instances one or more sections would have to be inserted to span the gap and obtaining additional cabling would incur a significant cost and could take days. As difficult as this was, it paled in comparison to police crackdowns. Several times a year, police intensified their enforcement efforts, patrolling the lampposts, removing any cabling, and forestalling all wiring attempts. When this occurred, Polje could be without power for weeks. But sooner or later the police would relent and the cable would be attached yet again.

Cable maintenance took a great deal of effort and was a constant source of anxiety. As Bekim, Marko, and I lurched through the fields, we quietly complained about spending so much time struggling with the electricity. Bekim criticized men like Gazmend and Endrit, who expected to have power without taking any of the risks. Although burying the cable inspired comraderie among participants, the daily management of electrical connections could easily create tensions between neighbors. Bekim, Marko, and I were halfway to the lamppost when we heard Dragomir yell that we should return immediately. Unsure of what was occurring, we sped back to the settlement. We burst through the last set of bushes only to see the warm glow of light emanating from every shack. Dragomir and Gazmend greeted us with sheepish looks on their faces. There was nothing wrong with the cable; the streetlights had merely been switched on later. While everyone laughed at the mistake, Marko asserted that it was perfectly justified. Resigned, he noted that almost every day the cable malfunctioned. Why should tonight be any different? Indeed, difficulties with the electricity were so common that they had become a part of life. Residents expected the cable to fail as a matter of course. Dysfunction was the norm.

While power outages at sunset frustrated residents, those later at night terrified them. Under the cover of darkness, skinheads raided settlements and assaulted their denizens. These episodes were rare but they began with the assailants cutting the electricity. Consequently, Polje's residents assumed that a blackout was the precursor to an attack. Whenever Bekim's shack was plunged into darkness, he and Fatime panicked. Bekim ran to the window, pulled aside the curtains, and nervously peered out. Meanwhile, Fatime woke the children and held them crouching under the window to avoid being seen. If Bekim was unable to assess the situation, he darted into the street wielding a makeshift weapon while I remained in the shack to protect Fatime and the children. Fortunately, each time the settlement experienced a power outage during my tenure, it was the result of an accidental disconnection. But these incidents reinforced the vulnerability and danger of life in Polje. A power failure could just as easily herald a fallen branch as a home invasion.

Efforts to maintain the cable encapsulated the struggles of Polje's residents. Bekim, Dragomir, and Rajim spent an inordinate amount of their lives working to access an amenity that Serbs simply took for granted. Electricity exemplified Ashkali and Romani exclusion from the Serbian state and its apparatus. When the power failed, the settlement's inhabitants were reminded of their segregation. In her analysis of a Palestinian refugee camp in Lebanon, Allan notes that in a discriminatory environment, siphoning electricity becomes an assertion of basic rights.[10] The ordinary practices of accessing this resource, such as wiring connections, are meaningful acts but ones that often lack an explicit organized resistance. She writes, "Configured around a more dispersed logic of everyday consumption and immediate need rather than ideology or factional politics, these practices are charged with political meaning, if not always polit-ical intent."[11] In Polje, cable work was similarly motivated by necessity as well as a realization of one's marginal relationship with the state.

Although residents blamed the government and the police for many of the challenges associated with obtaining electricity, the authorities were seldom faulted. One man commented that he understood why the police removed their electrical connections: the cable was illegal and enforcing the law was their job. What really upset him was the conduct of ordinary Serbs. He wondered aloud why his Serbian neighbors refused to allow Polje's residents to live in peace. Everyone in the settlement, he said, was just trying to survive through honest work in the trash. Why were Serbs purposely making difficult lives even harder by cutting or stealing the cable? He concluded that sabotaging the cable was an attempt to force residents to abandon the settlement. This, he assured me, would never occur. He and others were angry because Serbs treated them like vagrants rather than neighbors. Whether telling Gazmend where he could build or surveilling cable workers, Serbs thought of Polje's inhabitants as illegiti-mate occupants. But Gazmend, Fitim, and others saw the settlement as their home. They might live in shacks but they deserved to be regarded with respect and courtesy. Unfortunately, they were not. More than any other domestic issue, electricity reminded Ashkali and Roma that no mat-ter how hard they labored to create a home in Polje, they would never succeed. This motivated some people to look elsewhere for security. When Fadil confided that he was considering applying for asylum in Germany, he stated that anywhere was better than Serbia. As proof, he reminded me of all the times the cable was stolen.

DESTRUCTION AND RECONSTRUCTION

Despite residents' constant efforts to build a stable community, they could easily lose everything and regularly did. In May 2014 a stationary low-pressure system released days of record-breaking rain, causing the Sava River and its tributaries to swell. Widespread flooding occurred across the country, affecting 1.6 million people and causing over €1.5 billion ($1.9 billion) in damage.[12] Fortunately, Belgrade appeared to have avoided much of the destruction that occurred elsewhere. Although water inundated several homes, the majority of damage was confined to uninhabited parkland along the Sava's banks. Government officials and media outlets quickly declared that the city and its inhabitants had been spared. However, these reports failed to mention that settlements across Belgrade were devastated.

These communities were particularly susceptible to flooding because they were built on undesirable land. Polje lay on a sunken plain and became inundated even as the neighboring apartments remained dry. Residents watched in shock as water suddenly began pouring into their shacks. Those at home stacked belongings on sofas and beds, thinking they would be safe. But the water continued to rise, reaching well over a meter in some areas. Carpets, clothes, beds, and couches were all ruined within a couple of hours. While the destruction was swift, reconstruction was not. The murky foul-smelling water took over a week to recede. When the ground finally emerged and residents could sort through what remained, they realized that virtually nothing could be salvaged. Most families had to completely rebuild.

Gazmend's home was particularly hard-hit. When viewed from the surrounding berm, his shack looked like a submerged island in a small lake. Fortunately, Gazmend and Fadil had taken their families to Albin's container as soon as the water entered their shacks. But Gazmend did not want to inconvenience his son and returned to Polje after only three days. They settled in the small shack built by Endrit, one of the few in Polje that remained dry. To provision his rickety new abode, Gazmend waded knee-deep into his old dwelling and recovered everything he could. From dumpsters he scavenged odd pieces of wood, intent on reconstructing his former home. Gazmend then used money from his children in Germany to buy the remaining components. Within two weeks, he was working on his old plot, resolutely pushing a wheelbarrow laden with beams, planks, and windows. Gazmend finished only days later and proudly gave me a tour. He had cleaned his entire plot of land, carefully removing the detritus deposited by the flood. In the center his rebuilt shack was outfitted with new wall hangings, rugs, and furniture, erasing all signs of damage. Gazmend boasted that he had completely restored his home. His hard work, however, was for naught. Within a year, the shack was underwater once more. Realizing the futility of rebuilding, Gazmend abandoned his bucolic location and reluctantly moved inside Polje. Despite these set-backs he had no intention of leaving. The settlement, Gazmend reiterated, was all he needed.

Sara's shack was similarly swamped with water but, unlike Gazmend, she had no other place to go. Her family found a dry area nearby and slept outside on carpets donated by other residents. She was grateful for the support but noted that it took a crisis for her neighbors to provide assist-ance. Lacking the money to purchase materials, Sara had to wait until she could scavenge the items needed to construct a new shack. Only after sev-eral weeks was she finally able to build another home. She chose a site at the opposite end of the settlement but, like most of the land in Polje, it remained in the floodplain. After every heavy downpour, the floor was drenched in water. It then took days for the carpets to dry and the increased humidity aggravated her grandson's asthma. To allow him to rest easier, Sara made impromptu beds out of cushions and slept with Bojan outside. She repeatedly vowed that she would rebuild her shack on higher ground but never found the resources to do so. After a year Sara left Polje and moved with her husband to Srem.

Aleksander's family was also among those who lost their homes, but their relative wealth allowed them to escape many of the hardships that Sara endured. As soon as the water began to rise in their shack, Aleksander loaded his extended family into three cars and drove to higher ground. They spent the first night sleeping in their vehicles, with each car housing seven people. Realizing it would be at least a week before their land was habitable, the family moved to one of several shelters set up by the Serbian state. But Imran remarked that this accommodation was too noisy and crowded so they returned to Polje three days later. With their shack still underwater, the family found a new site and began living out of their vehi-cles. Aleksander chose an elevated plot located down a service road in the back of the settlement. The parcel remained unclaimed by other residents because it was uneven and covered with bushes. Erecting shacks in this terrain would be difficult if not impossible. Aleksander, however, used his financial resources to hire a small bulldozer to clear and level the area. Now with considerably more land at their disposal, the family no longer had to remain cramped in a single dwelling. In a little over a week, they built five shacks and two stables. Imran was pleased that each nuclear family had its own home but he was concerned about the sturdiness of the new buildings. They salvaged a significant amount of wood from the old shack and these materials were damaged, rotten, and fetid. Indeed, Imran's concerns were justified. After only a few days, the roof of one home collapsed completely. Luckily, it was uninhabited at the time.

While the flood destroyed their shacks in Belgrade, Aleksander's homes in Srem were not damaged. The vulnerable structures in his town were surrounded with sandbags provided by the government and volunteers. Across the country a number of programs were in place to protect home-owners. Consequently, Aleksander had no fears about leaving his houses unattended. But Polje's other residents saw none of this aid. A valid title was the first condition for resettlement or reconstruction support, which excluded many Ashkali and Roma.[13] The government not only discounted those living in settlements, the flood was used as an opportunity to repur-pose this land through international aid. When the United Arab Emirates donated new housing for displaced persons, the units were built on the site of a former settlement, where Bekim had spent his childhood playing with friends.

Although the Serbian state failed to acknowledge Polje's residents, one NGO attempted to provide assistance. Much like the crises themselves, aid tended to appear without warning. One afternoon Bekim and I saw two Serbian women walking from shack to shack checking off names on a clipboard. They were preparing to distribute household items to those affected by the flood. Hoping to receive a parcel, Aleksander, Harun, and Fatime walked to the entrance of the settlement, where they found a parked van. Government and NGO staff almost never drove their vehicles into Polje. Harun reasoned that this was because aid workers, while seek-ing to help Roma, were ultimately scared of them. We approached the van and found a man pulling out bags filled with diapers, clothes, and food. His shirt was decorated with multihued churches and emblazed with the words "The United Colors of Orthodoxy." After unloading approximately twenty parcels, he boarded the van and drove away. The Serbian women then emerged from the settlement with Milena, a Romani resident, and began distributing the bundles to specific families. The NGO had sur-veyed the settlement a few days earlier and recorded the names of each household. However, several had been absent and therefore were not on the list. These families, including Bekim's, Gazmend's, Aleksander's, and Harun's, would receive nothing.

Those excluded quickly became irate. Fatime loudly announced that she had been at the doctor when the survey was conducted and demanded that the woman give her a parcel. Aleksander complained that people with undamaged homes were being handed food while he received nothing. Instead of assailing the NGO workers directly, residents focused most of their grievances at Milena. As a member of the settlement, she was expected to lobby on her neighbors' behalf. Instead, Milena suggested that the families on the list share their items with those who were omitted. But this did not occur. Residents with packages snubbed the entreaties of their neighbors. Incensed, Fatime began screaming at Milena, calling her a whore and lesbian. Milena sought to avoid Fatime's wrath by walking back into the settlement. Unrelenting, Fatime picked up several rocks and hurled them at Milena's back. When it became clear that Milena would not engage, Fatime turned her anger on a neighbor clutching an aid parcel. Fatime demanded to know why she had not told the NGO about her household. As before, Fatime was ignored. In the chaos the NGO workers departed. Having no other recourse, Fatime and the others returned to their shacks, complaining that NGOs were not concerned with equity. They loudly remarked that wealthy families had received goods, all of which they could afford to purchase, while poor residents had been given nothing. A few days later, Imran alleged that Milena had sold the contents of her package to other residents. He added that the whole exercise was nothing more than an opportunity for her to make money. To my knowledge, this was the only aid the settlement received.

While Belgrade was able to withstand heavy rains and a rising river, Polje was not. Shacks, furniture, and clothing were swiftly ruined but those with resources and cash, like Gazmend and Aleksander, were able to emerge from these crises quicker than others, like Sara. While misfortune could promote a certain amount of generosity among residents, ultimately this was limited. Residents were willing to give Sara their old rugs but no one would share their NGO relief packages. These parcels supplied some families with essential items but they also highlighted the unpredictability and inadequacy of aid. Furthermore, NGO staff had no knowledge of the settlement and even appeared to be fearful of its inhabitants. Assistance was arbitrary and impersonal, reinforcing the divisions between responsible Serbs and needy *cigani*. Most importantly, the NGO visit exacerbated differences within Polje. Rather than easing a crisis, this intervention strained relationships between neighbors. A natural disaster destroyed people's homes but aid destroyed people's friendships. Consequently, the flood fundamentally shattered every aspect of the lives residents had worked so hard to create in Polje. Worst of all, everyone knew it would happen again. Polje's residents remained vulnerable to the next catastrophe. Gazmend and Sara might have rebuilt, but it was only a matter of time until their shacks were flooded once more.

In Polje, an excepted geography built upon trash, domesticity was constantly under threat. Because the settlement was a space apart and situated on land deemed unsuitable for habitation, it was fundamentally exposed. Rain, heat, snow, and wind that seldom impacted the rest of the city could wreak havoc in Polje. This was compounded by the lack of basic services such as water and electricity, which were accessed illegally and, in doing so, could result in arrest or death. To purchase food, residents patronized a shop bearing the portrait of a Serbian war criminal. The alternative, however, was to collect rotten vegetables from the dumpsters.

While trash provided a lifeline for Polje's residents, it also consigned them to an uncertain and risky existence. No one could predict when and where food or building materials would be found. Because shacks were constructed with nothing more than wood scraps, they were rickety, dangerous, and easily destroyed. Substandard wires could malfunction and burn down homes. Despite these challenges, residents worked diligently to create a patina of normality by transforming garbage into décor, shacks into homes, and strangers into neighbors. But constancy was impossible. The inherent precarity of trash ensured that Polje was both materially and socially unstable. Shacks and support networks could easily collapse, forcing Polje's residents to continually make and remake their homes and domestic lives. This was an arduous process but it had become habitual. Safety and security were illusory.

The flood had a lasting effect on the settlement. Seeking higher ground, families like Aleksander's abandoned the center for the periphery. While the core of Polje was hollowed out, the Bayash area was deserted entirely.

After saving money for years, Bayash families decided to finally purchase several hectares of land not far from Polje. They erected brick houses and eventually received municipal power and water. Other families departed Serbia altogether. Fadil, for instance, never returned from Albin's container. Hoping for a better life in the EU, he hired a human trafficker to smuggle his family across the Hungarian border. These and other exoduses significantly reduced the settlement's population. Half of Polje was now uninhabited. In the midst of this reorganization, Romani and Ashkali homes became intermingled. Once more, the settlement was transformed.

3 Abject Economies

Ashkali and Romani trash-pickers were a ubiquitous sight in Belgrade, pedaling *trokolice* along busy streets and searching through the contents of dumpsters. Scavenging was a powerful nexus of identity, economy, and corporeality. First and foremost, Polje's residents conceptualized these routine and repetitive activities as a job. Several times a day, scavengers left Polje to make a carefully planned circuit, visiting as many as eighty dumpsters. Each trip covered a distance of about two kilometers and took approximately two hours to complete. To ensure nothing of value was missed, scavengers delved to the bottom of each receptacle and tore open every trash bag found inside. Ashkali primarily sought paper products, while Roma concentrated on metal, plastic, or clothing. Because no one claimed an exclusive territory, scavengers roamed wherever they could pedal. As Polje's residents moved from dumpster to dumpster, they routinely saw their neighbors but never stopped to have a conversation. Friendly banter was reserved for the settlement. They were on the streets to earn a living, not socialize.

To Serbs, though, scavenging was not real work. Searching dumpsters, they said, was nothing more than a sporadic activity that required little effort and no skill. While these views were accepted as common knowledge among Serbs, they were rooted in historical transformations and contemporary identities. Prior to the Industrial Revolution, reusing garbage was considered efficient and responsible. However, as workers moved from farms to factories, productive action was increasingly equated with paid employment.[1] Capitalist manufacturing espoused wage labor as a hegemonic ideal, making it a powerful technique of governance.[2] With alternative forms of labor cast as illegitimate or detached from the "real" economy, responsible citizens were delineated from indigent outsiders. Despite these stereotypes, trash-picking was nevertheless intimately connected to global capitalism. Ashkali and Roma transferred discarded materials to transnational recycling corporations and thereby comprised a critical link in the waste-industrial complex. Polje's residents did not reject the formal economy nor were they excluded from it. Scavengers were biopolitical projects who were relegated to the margins.

But dumpster work was not only an exercise in retrieving commodities and creating identities; it was fundamentally corporeal. Sorting through trash and breaking down boxes wrecked one's body. As I scavenged day after day, I quickly realized that what appeared to be a simple task was extremely arduous. To reach anything inside a dumpster, I had to strain and stretch, pushing the metal rim painfully against my ribs and contorting my back uncomfortably. Getting at objects in the lower third of the receptacle was particularly grueling. This required hoisting my body onto the rim, supporting my weight with my arms, and cantilevering into the dumpster. Bobbling unsteadily, I quickly grabbed the item I needed before I lost balance completely. The entire maneuver took strength and concentration. However, this was only the first step.

Boxes had to be pummeled, kicked, and torn until they lay flat. Then they were stacked onto a *trokolica* and pedaled to the next dumpster. As more paper products were added, a *trokolica*'s weight increased considerably. A full load could surpass two hundred kilograms. By the end of each circuit I was exhausted. I often returned to the settlement hot, drenched in sweat, and out of breath. My back, arms, and legs were perpetually sore and my hands were peppered with cuts and lacerations. This was typical. Bekim and Agim, both in their early twenties, routinely complained of chronic pain. By the time Ashkali were in their forties, the strain of scavenging impaired people's ability to function. Drita could barely pedal a *trokolica,* while Gazmend was unable to lift heavy items. Dumpster work took an unmistakable and permanent toll on bodies.

While pain permeated daily labor, so did revulsion. Scavenging was a dirty, malodorous enterprise. A potent stench greeted anyone leaning over and peering inside a dumpster. Sifting through debris and ripping open trash bags released a miasma of smells and textures. Throughout this process it was impossible to avoid the gunk that festooned every dumpster. My hands became black with the remnants of discarded meals, dirty diapers, and wet coffee grounds. My clothes grew stained and putrid. Due to a lack of running water, these garments were worn for days at a time. Everyone stank. In the heat of summer, when the odor was even more overpowering, I would become nauseous. This was compounded by near-constant hunger, a result of persistent food scarcity. On the final circuit of the day, I occasionally skipped a row of dumpsters, unable to face the stench. Ashkali fared no better. When we returned home, Bekim often refused food, saying his appetite was ruined.

Trash was a material and financial resource but it was also abject. Abjection denotes that which is expelled or cast off, but Kristeva most closely associates it with food, waste, and signs of sexual difference.[3] Existing in and around bodily boundaries, the abject is fundamentally transgressive. Kristeva writes: "It is . . . what disturbs identity, system, order. What does not respect borders, positions, rules. The in-between, the ambiguous, the composite."[4] Abjection simultaneously creates a system of meaning and belonging—of me and not-me—and subverts it. Importantly, the abject triggers visceral responses: horror, vomiting, crying, shame. For Ashkali, the abject was inescapable. Scavenging not only produced deeply physical reactions through the body and its senses; it also was inherently disturbing.

Examining dumpster divers in Seattle, Giles argues that a dumpster's abjection makes it revolting, in both senses of the word.[5] Trash evokes physical disgust while concurrently destabilizing and even inverting normative economic ideals. Just as the abject delineates the me from the not-me, it separates commodities from countercommodities. Abandoning objects in dumpsters transforms them into materials that contravene order itself. Belgrade's dumpsters certainly confused boundaries: between worthless trash and valuable commodity, between spoiled vegetables and a good meal, between unemployment and work. As a result, dumpsters, like settlements, were socially excised from Belgrade's landscape. Trash existed in a space of exception. Once again, the biographies of Ashkali and the biographies of trash were intimately intertwined. This chapter explores the abject economies that dominate life outside of the settlement: recycling paper and metal, selling goods at the markets, begging, and wage labor. During each of these activities, Ashkali not only negotiated revulsion but did so by navigating the transnational flows of commodities, countercommodities, and capital.

DUMPSTER IDENTITIES

Because garbage was generated through an individual's actions, not an object's inherent qualities, scavenging was socially constituted through visibility. Personal possessions only became collective waste through the process of disposal: taking an item out of the home and placing it into a dumpster on the street. Public abandonment socially signaled that a commodity's value was extinguished, transforming it into trash. But while the notional line between a commodity and trash was clearly demarcated, being placed in a dumpster did not strip an item of its materiality or utility. A discarded shirt could be reworn, repurposed as a rag, or burned as fuel for a stove. Because trash was an unstable category that was perpetuated through communal behaviors, scavenging became a radical act. Removing items from dumpsters subverted the irreversible progression from valuable commodity to valueless garbage. Furthermore, Ashkali were not only reviving wealth, they were doing this by publicly appropriating the former property of Serbs. Consequently, gathering refuse required traversing a shared interactive space where liminal objects moved from Serbs to Ashkali. This material flow created a complex knot of social meanings that were continually negotiated and renegotiated.

One example of these exchanges, and the signification that they produced, occurred on the margins of dumpsters. In most cases Serbs simply threw their trash away, but occasionally they hung bags on a dumpster's exterior. These parcels were left to help struggling *cigani* and contained items meant for reuse, including old clothes, worn shoes, and broken electronics. They were simultaneously garbage and gifts. As Mauss notes, gifts bond givers and receivers in a web of meaning and, in so doing, engender a social hierarchy.[6] In Belgrade, dumpsters adorned with bags reinforced the notion of charitable Serbs and destitute *cigani*. In leaving these donations, Serbs expressed a desire to help those who had nothing. This act ostensibly condemned the collective social and economic conditions that consigned *cigani* to settlements while lauding their individual efforts to redress inequality. By separating their trash, Serbs visibly declared their morality. However, this gesture of giving required no social or physical interaction. Serbs simply left their parcels, confident that the contents would aid an underprivileged family. The actual lives and experiences of their Ashkali and Romani neighbors were never interrogated. Nor were the structural factors that relegated these individuals to segregated settlements.

For Ashkali, these gifts held a different meaning. If a scavenger saw a plastic bag outside a dumpster, he immediately became optimistic. Perhaps it held a good pair of shoes, a nice jacket, or a radio. Unfortunately, a bag's contents seldom lived up to expectations. Although Serbs assumed that *cigani* were eager for anything they had to give, this was not the case. Ashkali were only interested in items that they could wear or sell. If a shirt or pair of shoes was old, damaged, the incorrect size, or unflattering, it was immediately rejected. Household electronics contained far more plastic than metal and therefore were only valuable if they functioned, which few did. Generally, most gifts were, as far as Ashkali were concerned, nothing more than junk. In these cases, the parcel was returned to the side of the dumpster, often with Ashkali complaining that Serbs must think that they lacked standards and pride. One man, upon opening a bag only to find a pair of shoes riddled with holes, told me that no one was so poor that they would take them. Instead of replacing the shoes for another scavenger to find, he threw them into the dumpster. The gift was firmly refused. In doing so, Ashkali recast an act that Serbs viewed as charitable into one of derision.

Although Serbs were unaware of the genuine needs or perspectives of scavengers, Ashkali were mindful not to dispute the dominant Serbian narrative of *cigani*. On the infrequent occasions that Serbs offered books, paper, clothes, or knickknacks directly to Ashkali, these interactions were brief but cordial. Ashkali were careful to be docile, polite, and always thank the individual. While ostensibly motivated by compassion, giving items to scavengers was also about convenience. Carting heavy refuse to the dumpsters was onerous and dirty. Simply handing everything to *cigani* saved time and effort. As with care packages, these donations were not always welcomed. Bekim complained that Serbs hardly ever parted with anything of value. Nevertheless, he took any goods he was offered. Not to do so, I was told, would be rude and could result in missing valuable merchandise. Ashkali were materially dependent upon Serbs and, as a result, needed their goodwill. Bekim had little choice but to be gracious and accept whatever he was given, regardless of its value. But as soon as he was out of sight, Bekim often threw the majority of the donation in the nearest dumpster. Yet again, gift-giving created an illusion of charity while allowing Serbs to discount Ashkali labor. An exclusionary social hierarchy was imposed through goodwill.

Unfortunately, the material that Ashkali sought the most, metal, was almost never given away. Serbs were aware that junkyards paid for scrap and would only part with old piping, broken boilers, and dilapidated refrigerators for a price. However, this had not always been the case. It was only after the breakup of Yugoslavia and the subsequent economic downturn that Serbs sought to profit from recycling. Charity had limits. When Bekim spotted workers remodeling an apartment, he asked if he could take their debris. In response, the supervisor offered to sell an old water heater, a metal bathtub, several pots, and two bags of clothes for 1,200 dinars ($12.60). After some negotiation, Bekim agreed to pay 1,000 dinars ($10.50). However, because he only had 400 dinars ($4.20), Bekim was forced to cycle back to Polje and arrange a loan. He made the trip as quickly as possible, worried that the laborers would sell the materials to someone else. But when he returned, the metal was still waiting for him. The workers were pleased to earn some extra cash while avoiding the hassle and expense of transporting the bulky items to the city dump. Once the transaction was concluded, Bekim loaded everything into his *trokolica* and pedaled to the junkyard. Serbs charged for metal but they possessed scant knowledge regarding its value. As a result, Ashkali were regularly able to make two to three times their initial outlay. Bekim disliked paying for metal but it benefited him much more than gifts from Serbs.

Because locating metal was difficult and unpredictable, Bekim spent the majority of his time searching for paper products. Magazines, newspapers, and cardboard boxes could be found in abundance. Hoping to maximize their yield, Ashkali strategically targeted dumpsters behind convenience stores and supermarkets. It was here that empty shipping boxes were thrown away en masse, potentially enough to fill an entire *trokolica*. If a scavenger spotted any empty boxes lying outside a *prodavnica*, he often asked permission to take them. Brief interactions with store staff occurred regularly, but in these instances Ashkali were not met with sympathy. In most cases, staff allowed us to remove the boxes but watched us intently, worried that *cigani* would steal any unguarded merchandise.[7] We encountered the same response when visiting large supermarkets. Although garbage was discarded via a bare loading dock, we were still treated with suspicion and disdain. Employees rarely handed cardboard items directly to us. In some instances, the boxes were tossed in the trash for us to immediately remove. In others, staff kicked them off the loading dock, forcing us to pick them up from the ground while dodging incoming boxes flying toward our heads.

In these instances Ashkali were no longer viewed as impoverished and worthy of charity; they were now impoverished and prone to theft. Serbs, including several who worked in retail establishments, routinely told me that if store employees were not vigilant, *cigani* would use scavenging as a cover to shoplift. This shift in identity from struggling people in need to devious thieves occurred, in part, because the line separating the public from the private was particularly thin at retail spaces. Stores were openly accessible as was their merchandise. Furthermore, scavengers were the antithesis of customers because they took items without making payment. Although boxes were deemed trash, their removal destabilized the order of capitalist enterprise. Consequently, Ashkali were transformed into thieves. This led to discernable surveillance and hostility. As potential criminals, *cigani* deserved to have boxes thrown at them. Ashkali were well aware of their status and bristled at being cast as deceitful. Scavenging, Bekim repeatedly said, was an honest job to earn honest money. However, if an opportunity presented itself, he did not hesitate to exploit it.

Searching the dumpsters one morning before sunrise, Bekim and I saw a supermarket delivery truck unloading. As usual, we approached the staff and asked if they were discarding any cardboard. A stock clerk grudgingly agreed to give us their empty boxes, which he punted off the loading dock. Soon our *trokolica* was full and we returned to Polje. When we were safely within the confines of the settlement, Bekim rummaged under the layers of cardboard and proudly produced four large cases of Twix candy bars. Apparently, the stock clerk had become confused and given us boxes filled with merchandise. As soon as Bekim realized this, he concealed the Twix cartons and acted as if nothing was amiss. In his view, this was simply Serbian incompetence working to his advantage. Once inside his shack, Bekim exultantly told the story to his family. They were pleased at the unexpected windfall and speculated how much money the candy would fetch. In the meantime, there was no food in the cupboard so one box was consumed for breakfast and lunch. By the end of the day, Bekim had sold the three remaining cartons for 3,000 dinars ($31.50), less than a quarter of their retail value. This income did not last long—it was gone within two days. Opportunism such as this was rare but significant. It provided unexpected capital and a rejoinder to exclusion but simultaneously induced insecurity.[8] Unfortunately, the incident significantly affected Bekim's recycling work.

The stock clerk eventually realized what had occurred and, seeing Bekim scavenging, confronted him. The man called Bekim a thief and demanded the candy be returned. Bekim defiantly refused, saying it had been legitimately discarded and the employee was at fault. If the supermarket manager wanted proof, Bekim added, he could check the security tapes. The store determined that their employee was responsible for the loss and deducted the full amount from the man's paycheck, leaving him fuming. In retaliation he threatened to have Bekim beaten if he ever again took cardboard from the supermarket's dumpsters. Suddenly, Bekim was unable to access his largest and most reliable source of paper products. To compensate for the loss, Bekim spent longer scavenging each day. It took over a year before he quietly began returning to the supermarket's dumpsters. Still fearful, Bekim scavenged quickly and was always prepared to flee in case any angry staff emerged to assault him. In the end, Bekim earned relatively little from the candy and it came at the expense of his livelihood and safety. Even though the employee was found to be at fault, Bekim was punished. Bekim's inherent vulnerability ensured that Serbs could easily take reprisals for any transgressions, whether real or imagined.

While store employees closely monitored *cigani*, so did the police. This occurred primarily through identity checks. Under Serbian law, every individual was required to carry government-issued identification. Serbs were rarely asked to produce their documents but *cigani* were regularly stopped. Anyone lacking the necessary credentials was subject to a fine, possible detention, or worse. The slightest police scrutiny could quickly dredge up a host of past infractions. As discussed in the previous chapter, what began as a simple police check ended with Marko's family leaving Belgrade. Ashkali were particularly vulnerable, as they seldom possessed sufficient identification. Two days before Marko's wife was taken into custody, Bekim and I were also stopped. While we were strolling down the road, a black SUV pulled up beside us. Bekim was accustomed to these inspections and he halted immediately. The officers rolled down a window and asked for our documents. I showed my passport but Bekim was unable to produce any credentials. He politely explained that his IDP papers were at home. To substantiate his claim, Bekim added that only a few days earlier he had shown his identification at the station, as requested by the officers who had stopped him the previous week. The police admonished Bekim but released us and drove off. Visibly relieved, Bekim confided that he lied; he had no proof of his IDP status and had never been to the station. Because he lacked the proper records, Bekim said, duplicity was his only option. Over the next several weeks Bekim made a point of avoiding the police, walking blocks out of his way to evade any patrol cars he spotted. When he saw a Romani family being questioned, he immediately turned around and fled down an alley.

Scavengers were surveilled during the day but at night they were assaulted. Searching dumpsters in the evenings and early mornings could be extremely dangerous. Bekim, Agim, and Fitim all told stories of being chased or beaten. Endrit had survived a stabbing, which left three scars on his back. Despite the risk, Ashkali and Roma kept visiting the dumpsters after dark because of the opportunities it afforded. Some stores disposed of produce and cardboard only after closing. Around midnight, the dumpsters could yield a bounty not found during daylight hours. Consequently, Endrit continued making scavenging circuits into the early morning, each time passing through the alley where the assault occurred. Not knowing what he would encounter, Endrit was in a constant state of fear. To minimize their vulnerability, Polje's residents avoided groups of Serbian men, but keeping a distance was no guarantee of safety. Whenever I went scavenging with Ashkali at night, a moment invariably arrived when I was told to flee because an attack seemed imminent. We always escaped physical confrontations but the threat of violence never disappeared.

As they rummaged through the stench of dumpsters, Ashkali had to negotiate a space physically and discursively dominated by Serbs. In it, *cigani* were assigned multiple identities. They were a pitiable people who deserved aid. They were criminals who should be beaten. They were noncitizens who must be surveilled. Within a few blocks, Ashkali could be given gifts, sold metal, interrogated by the police, mistreated by store employees, and chased by skinheads. These various encounters occurred because scavenging was fundamentally disruptive. It resurrected abject commodities, complicated notions of public and private property, and blurred the line between worth and worthlessness. But as Ashkali moved from one dumpster to the next, they had little control over their immediate environment. Scavengers could only throw useless gifts in the trash, be polite to the authorities, and avoid confrontation. This was an inescapable, and therefore mundane, feature of dumpster work. Like other aspects of scavenging, it was boring.

CARDBOARD, COOPERATION, AND CORPORATIZATION

Returning to the settlement with a *trokolica* brimming with paper was only the first part of the recycling process. Ashkali then needed to navigate relationships with each other, cooperating to prepare their paper for recycling. Once this step was completed, they finally turned to multinational corporations. These businesses controlled the recycling trade and had a pervasive presence in Polje: a large metal "basket" (*korpa*) for storing cardboard stood beside almost every shack. These receptacles were 1.5 meters high and occupied a sizeable footprint on residents' plots. Baskets had a permanence that residents did not. As the shack beside it was bought and sold, the *korpa* remained in place. This was because baskets were the property of Belgrade's recycling consolidators and each was emblazoned with a company's logo. Residents were completely dependent upon these corporations to transport, weigh, and purchase their paper. Consequently, capitalist enterprise was visibly, materially, and economically integrated into settlements.

As the most recent arrivals, Ashkali lived in a newly settled area of Polje that lacked recycling baskets. Bekim, Gazmend, and Endrit stored their paper on the ground, usually in an area to the rear of their shacks. To the untrained eye, these low expanses of cardboard appeared to be nothing more than worthless trash. But they were, in fact, tangible wealth. The densely packed mounds could measure as much as thirty-five square meters and be as deep as twenty centimeters. Given the space, Ashkali were able to accumulate large caches before recycling. Bekim typically waited until he possessed around a ton of paper but Endrit preferred to have at least two tons. They then phoned a consolidator to schedule a pickup within forty-eight hours. A day before the truck's arrival, Ashkali saturated the mound with water. This would make the paper heavier and, in theory, fetch a higher price. But the recycling companies were well aware of this tactic and attempted to counter it by paying less per kilogram for damp paper. Nevertheless, Ashkali still felt the practice was advantageous and so it continued.

I became familiar with the procedure soon after my arrival. It was the middle of winter and Endrit had been amassing paper for just over two months. With the truck slated to appear the next day, he visited Gazmend and retrieved a large plastic bin that measured a meter on each side and was open at the top. Endrit in turn gave the bin to Bekim, who asked Fitim to transport it on his small tractor to a water source. The police had locked the fire hydrant so the men drove to a creek at the rear of the settlement. Fitim positioned the tractor close to the stream as Agim and Fadil arrived with the buckets used to haul sand for the floor of my shack. The men quickly formed a relay chain, with Agim scooping out the algae- and trash-filled water, passing the bucket first to Fadil and then onto Fitim, who emptied it into the large bin. Agim commented that this was the recycling task he disliked the most. Transporting water was messy, heavy, cumbersome, and always strained his back. As each man became winded, he alternated position or rested on the sidelines while others filled the gap.

When the bin was three quarters full, Fitim draped an old blanket over the top to prevent water from splashing out and drove to Endrit's pile. Now the chain was reversed: one person filled the bucket from the reservoir, handed it to an intermediary, and then onto a third individual, who threw the water on the paper. Once the bin was emptied, the process was repeated. Passing a bucket full of water back and forth was strenuous work but that did not stop everyone from joking. In addition to the usual ribald accusations of having affairs with other men's wives, Agim grabbed Fadil from behind and pretended to sodomize him. Laughing, Bekim said that I now knew Agim was gay. Finally, after the third trip, Endrit was satisfied that his paper was suitably wet. The men went home tired but realized that the following day would require even more exertion.

At seven o'clock the next morning, Fitim and Valon arrived at Bekim's shack. Inside, Bekim, Endrit, Agim, and I were waking up. Fatime and Drita had risen earlier to stoke the stove and prepare coffee. We chatted amicably until the thunderous sound of a diesel engine disturbed our conversation. The truck had arrived. Braving the cold weather, we emerged from the shack and greeted Miško, a Serb in his mid-thirties. He had been driving his recycling truck for twelve years and Polje's residents knew him well. Miško briefly exchanged pleasantries with Endrit before standing back and letting us get to work. We would have to load the cardboard onto the flatbed manually.

One by one, Endrit, Agim, Bekim, and I stooped over, gathered bundles of paper, and threw them onto truck. The only effective way to separate the overlapping layers was to grip two or three pieces of cardboard and roll them into a large cylinder. Although appearing simple, this method took practice to master. If too much paper was used to create the roll, it grew heavy and unwieldy. But without enough material, it would not hold together. Dry and rigid cardboard would not bend into a roll but if too wet, the bundle dripped, sagged, and fell apart. Even for the adept, this was a messy business. Everyone's hands and clothes quickly became soaked and stained. As we burrowed further down into the pile, the grime increased. Rancid pizza grease and decayed vegetable matter had composted into brown goo that was riddled with earthworms. Since children also used the mound as a toilet, lifting up a layer of paper could reveal a pile of feces.

While we labored on the ground, Fitim stood on the truck bed packing the paper as tightly as possible. He intermittently added a layer of dry cardboard in an attempt to disguise the cargo's true wetness. Eventually, he wandered off to complete other tasks and Valon took his place on the truck bed. Valon quickly grew bored and, to break the monotony, began flailing riotously. As his antics elicited laughs, Agim continued the fun, lifting

Bekim into the air, spinning him around, and throwing him onto the card-board. As usual, work and horseplay occurred simultaneously. Sex jokes also abounded, despite Endrit's attempts to shield the women and children from such lewd language. The constant merriment provided a welcome distraction from our grueling task. Repeatedly bending over, wrestling with the soggy cardboard, and hefting the heavy rolls to the truck was backbreaking. I was exhausted after little more than an hour. My back hurt, my arms were sore, and my legs ached. I was not alone; everyone felt the strain. When Drita emerged from Bekim's shack with cups of instant cappuccino, we were all grateful for the break. Like most labor, loading the truck was simultaneously entertaining, debilitating, and abject.

It took two hours to completely fill the truck with paper. However, we had only cleared a portion of Endrit's stockpile. Multiple trips to the recy-cling depot would be necessary. Miško had stood silently on the sidelines as we loaded the truck but once the process was finished, he sprang into action. He covered the paper with netting and ushered Endrit into the cab. A few moments later, they headed off to the recycling center. When I rode along on later trips, I discovered that Miško became much more talkative during the drive. He was extremely gregarious and alternated between sober conversations about the Serbian economy and joking about sex. Miško recounted the difficulties he faced earning a living wage and claimed to survive only by working long hours. During one journey he confided that the flood had damaged his small apartment but he was una-ble to afford the repair costs of €1,200 ($1,500). Although the Serbian government provided a portion of the funds, Miško complained that the state was not doing enough to help its people, especially working-class individuals. Ashkali did not mention that, in comparison, they received nothing after their shacks were completely destroyed. As Miško bemoaned his life, his passengers carefully censored their responses, sympathizing with his struggles while never discussing their own. Ashkali had similarly measured reactions to Miško's ribald humor. When he bluntly stated whose wife he would like to fuck, Ashkali did not find it amusing. During one drive with Bekim, Miško declared that having sex with a *ciganski* woman would bring seven years of good luck. He lightheartedly suggested that the ideal candidate was Fatime and proceeded to mimic her moans of pleasure. Miško chortled at his impersonation as Bekim silently fumed.

After a twenty-minute drive, Miško pulled the truck into the depot with Endrit. A string of warehouses lined one side while a parking lot filled with collection and delivery vehicles was on the other. In the middle stood a large scale operated via an adjacent control booth. Miško immediately drove onto the scale and the truck was weighed. Next, he proceeded to the rear of the compound, dumped his cargo, and returned to have the vehicle weighed once more. Then, an attendant calculated the total number of kilograms and paid Endrit. The advertised rate was five dinars (five cents) per kilogram but this amount was adjusted for two factors: the wetness of the paper and the disbursement method. Given that Endrit's paper was clearly damp, the attendant accepted only two thirds of the total weight. That sum would be reduced further, one dinar per kilogram, if Endrit was paid in cash rather than by bank transfer. Few Ashkali possessed documents, let alone bank accounts. Consequently, they had little choice but to take the cash price. The payment process was quick and Ashkali seldom spent more than fifteen or twenty minutes at the depot. Once the sale was concluded, Miško took his passenger to the closest bus stop.

These transactions placed Ashkali firmly within the global waste economy. Scavengers were one link in a long supply chain that moved materials from Serbia to the European Union. Companies such as Miško's collected paper from vendors, packed it in bales, and shipped them to a handful of processing plants. Paper recycling was still a nascent industry in Serbia and lacked the extensive state support found in the EU. Consequently, the largest processor in the nation had less capacity that its EU counterparts but was still able to exceed national demand and export over seventy percent of its production.[9] Given the EU's substantial investment in recycling, it was increasingly cost-effective to send Serbian raw materials abroad. In 2009 a German company built a large plant in Hungary designed to process paper from neighboring countries such as Serbia.

While transnational recycling plants were proliferating, Ashkali were exhausting their bodies. To load Endrit's paper, we spent all day lifting wet, fetid cardboard. When he returned from his third and final trip to the depot, Endrit proudly reported the total weight: ten tons. But because the paper was damp, he was only paid for seven tons, netting 28,000 dinars ($294). This represented two months of sifting through dumpsters, breaking down boxes, contending with store clerks, and avoiding assault.

This, Endrit said, was success. When we were at last finished, I collapsed in Bekim's shack. Feeling the strain in every muscle of my body, I tried to move as little as possible. Bekim and Agim did not fare much better. However, they commented that such pain was the norm. It was simply the life of a scavenger.

Like Endrit, most Ashkali could amass between a ton and a ton and a half of paper a week, netting 4,000 dinars ($42) to 6,000 dinars ($63). The only way to survive on such a meager income was by living in a space of exception. Paper scavengers could not afford an electricity bill, let alone a house. Segregated settlements were made possible by segregated economies. Ashkali were not excluded; rather, they were relegated to the lowest ranks of the recycling industry. Paper consolidators relied on cheap labor just as scavengers relied on trash. This not only consigned Ashkali to a world of poverty; it created an existence where pain and abjection were the norm.

SCRAP METAL

While paper accounted for the bulk of their recycling, Ashkali preferred to collect metal. It was worth more by weight, could be independently transported to a range of recycling facilities, and the onerous tasks of wetting paper and loading Miško's truck were avoided. Furthermore, Ashkali could recycle small amounts of metal on a daily basis rather than waiting for weeks or months to accumulate a stockpile. Most importantly, all payments for scrap were in cash and no one was penalized for lacking a bank account. But Ashkali could never abandon paper for metal. Scavengers using a *trokolica* were limited to local dumpsters, which contained only small items such as aerosol cans, tins, curtain rods, automobile headlights, shower hoses, and old pans. On occasion, Ashkali bought scrap from other residents but these were gathered from the same area and comprised similar articles. Consequently, metal could never supply the bulk of Bekim's revenue but it did provide supplementary income. For instance, he once went to the junkyard with nothing more than three olive cans, the metallic portions of a suitcase, a large pot, and a few sections of pipe. He received only 500 dinars ($5.25) but used this money to purchase bread and soda for lunch. Metal served as an immediate source of cash to tide a family over until their paper was sold. If Ashkali were able to obtain larger items, it represented an important but infrequent windfall.

Trips to recycle metal took Ashkali outside population centers and provided an escape from the constant public scrutiny inherent to dumpster work. The junkyards lay approximately two kilometers from Polje and straddled a secondary road between rural and industrial areas. These businesses were primarily consolidators, which received objects from building sites, demolition contractors, and automotive wreckers. Junkyards set prices independently and offered different rates for various categories of metal such as aluminum, sheet metal, iron, and copper. Metal was the most developed recycling sector in Serbia and, as a result, Ashkali could choose to patronize any one of several businesses ranging from large enterprises to more limited family-run establishments. While transactions with Ashkali and Roma accounted for a minority of their overall commerce, junkyards were nevertheless accustomed to dealing with scavengers.

After Bekim, as mentioned earlier, procured the water heater, bathtub, and pots from construction workers, he piled the items into his *trokolica* and pedaled to a compact rural house surrounded by fields and large piles of scrap. To entice customers, smaller junkyards such as this tended to give better rates. However, these businesses lacked the resources of their larger neighbors and were chronically short of cash. Ashkali could be turned away or given an IOU, which would be honored a few days later. Consequently, the first question that Bekim asked the attendant was if he had cash. The answer was yes. The attendant offered a price of thirteen dinars (fourteen cents) per kilogram for everything in the *trokolica*. Although Bekim believed he could get a dinar more per kilogram elsewhere, he was hesitant to leave, worried that other junkyards might be unable to pay him. Deciding not to take a chance, Bekim agreed.

Before weighing the metal, Bekim informed the proprietor that he wanted additional money for the water heater because it contained copper. Copper commanded a considerably higher rate than other metals and, as a result, Polje's residents were adept at locating and removing copper wires, conductors, and other parts with few if any tools. But because Bekim had not done this, the proprietor refused to pay extra. Not wanting to lose valuable income, Bekim decided to keep the water heater but placed the rest of his items on the scales. They weighed 100 kilograms and

Bekim received 1,300 dinars ($13.65). Tucking the money in his pocket, he suggested that we try another junkyard. This time he chose one of the largest in the area, knowing that they were less restrictive.

After cycling a few blocks, we passed through an open gate in a tall metal fence and found ourselves in a spacious compound. At the rear stood an administrative building flanked by three scales of increasing size. Mountains of iron and aluminum, including wrecked car bodies and oil drums, littered the perimeter. Not only did this junkyard possess significantly more metal than the previous one, multiple workers were sorting and processing its stock. It would certainly have cash on hand. Bekim pedaled his *trokolica* into the center of the courtyard and we waited for an attendant to appear. It was a hot day so I proposed moving to a shaded area closer to the wall. Bekim replied that we could not. Pointing out several cameras, he said we needed to remain in the open. After numerous thefts, the junkyard monitored visitors closely and he did want to be accused of robbery. Although patronizing junkyards altered the positionality of scavengers—they were now autonomous customers, who sold materials instead of taking them—*cigani* were still surveilled and distrusted.

We stood in the sun for fifteen minutes before a worker appeared. Pointing to the water heater, Bekim assured him that it contained copper. The man was skeptical but summoned two of his colleagues to open it. As Bekim predicted, several auburn components were revealed. Seemingly impressed, the attendant estimated that they totaled two kilograms of copper and offered Bekim 680 dinars ($7.15). Although some junkyards paid as much as 400 dinars ($4.20) per kilogram, Bekim did not want to go through the hassle of removing the copper. He agreed and the attendant added an extra 40 dinars (42 cents) for the rest of the water heater. When combined to what he had received previously, Bekim was able to sell the metal for 2,020 dinars ($21.20), giving him a profit of 1,020 dinars ($10.70). As we headed back to the settlement, he commented that this was a good return for a couple of hours' work. In most instances, however, it required much more effort to earn this amount of money, as the following events illustrate.

In need of cash one afternoon, Bekim looked to metal. He had collected a few pieces of scrap over the past couple of days and hoped to supplement it with a small pile that Dragomir was selling. However, he could not afford the price. Harun was facing a similar situation, so the men decided to jointly purchase Dragomir's metal and combine what little they had scavenged earlier. Still, this was not enough to yield a sufficient return. Desperate, they elected to harvest the springs in their outdoor couches. The furniture was in poor condition but it provided a comfortable place to sit and chat with neighbors on warm days. At that very moment Aleksander was perched on Harun's couch talking to Jovana. Bekim brusquely ordered him to get up and called for Harun's twenty-six-year-old brother, Ahmed. He and Bekim lifted the couch and placed it in Harun's *trokolica*. Crossing the road to Bekim's shack, they piled his couch on top. Ahmed steadied the payload as Bekim and I pushed the *trokolica* to the rear of the settlement. We stopped in a cleared area and dumped the couches on the ground. Ripping off a section of fabric, Ahmed removed a handful of foam, set it alight, and stuffed it back inside the cavity. Soon, both couches were ablaze.

While the fabric, foam, and wood burned, Ahmed and Bekim left to complete other errands. Bekim's family needed water but his *trokolica* had a flat tire. Stray rocks, broken glass, precipitous curbs, and overzealous children all contributed to regular punctures. It was not unheard of to have two flats in a single day and it was rare to go a week without needing to fix a tire. Much more than a ubiquitous source of frustration, flat tires jeopardized a man's ability to scavenge. Without a functioning *trokolica*, Bekim could not haul paper and metal back to the settlement. On this occasion he borrowed Harun's, loaded it with empty bottles, and pedaled to the hydrant. Bekim arrived only to find the impromptu lever had broken. He returned to the Polje and scrounged a wrench from Aleksander. After filling his bottles, Bekim went to check on the couches. The fire was almost extinguished, leaving only a pile of black ash, springs, and hinges. Bekim used a long stick to fish out each piece of metal and placed them in the *trokolica*. He then rode to Harun's shack and loaded the rest of their supply: two more sets of couch springs, several metal tins, and a few pieces of aluminum siding. Ready to depart, Bekim called Ahmed and we headed to the junkyards.

Bekim pedaled the *trokolica* while Ahmed and I perched over each of the wheels, clinging to the basket. As Bekim navigated through the small lanes, he asked Ahmed about his past. Slowly, Ahmed recounted his story. Like Harun, he had grown up in Polje. He eventually got married and had two children but his wife grew unhappy. After a few years, she left him and took their children back to her hometown. Three months later he was arrested for theft and spent two years in prison. Ahmed had been released only a few days earlier and was trying to rebuild his life. He was unable to afford a *trokolica* or shack so he was temporarily living with Harun. When Bekim asked about his time in prison, Ahmed shrugged. It was not so bad, he said. And it did come with one advantage: all prisoners were given identity documents. His status as an undocumented Bosnian refugee had finally ended. Ahmed commented that at least now he did not worry about random identification checks by the police. Bekim, who still lacked his own documents, agreed that there were some benefits to incarceration. But before the conversation could continue, the right tire blew out. Bekim stopped the *trokolica* as Ahmed and I dismounted. To avoid further damage to the tire, Ahmed pulled the tire and inner tube completely off the wheel. As we began walking down the road, the exposed metal rim scraped piercingly against the asphalt.

After a few blocks Bekim turned the *trokolica* over to Ahmed and sat down on the curb. He could not go to the junkyard because he owed the proprietor money. Bekim agreed to pay it back with his next lot of metal, but now his priority was feeding his family, not settling a debt. Soon Ahmed returned pushing the now empty *trokolica*. He handed Bekim 1,000 dinars ($10.50) but this would be split with Harun. Upset at how little they received, Bekim lamented that the price of metal was only decreasing. Like paper, metal recycling relied on market forces and international flows of capital and materials, making it inherently unstable. In 2013 a kilogram of iron fetched 17 dinars (18 cents), but three years later it was worth only 11 dinars (12 cents). The precipitous decline had a significant impact on scavengers. Because Ashkali bought most of their metal, this narrowed an already slim profit margin. These struggles drove daily life. Couches reserved for chatting with neighbors were destroyed to provide a family with negligible income. Even prison could be cast positively, given that inmates received identification that was almost impossible to obtain otherwise. Polje's residents had no choice but to mold their sociality around external economies.

THE UNCERTAINTY OF MARKETS

Ashkali preferred to sell raw materials to recycling consolidators because these transactions were reliable and provided a relatively guaranteed return. However, there was another method of transforming garbage into cash: hawking it at street markets. While Ashkali generally eschewed this type of work, some Roma, like Dragomir and his siblings, survived solely from vending clothes, household goods, and other everyday items. They could earn a living as trash merchants because, once again, it was the act of being thrown away that created garbage, not an inherent loss of usefulness. Dragomir's goods received value from their continued utility, unlike paper or metal that required industrial processes to resurrect their public worth. A pair of shoes or a purse, although worn or scuffed, could be immediately reused. Although vending at the market appeared to be economically straightforward, these transactions were socially complex and suffused with uncertainty, as Endrit would discover.

Given Dragomir's success, Endrit hoped the market would provide an income to counterbalance the falling price of metal. He began scavenging a wider range of items and, after two months, had amassed a considerable cache. His stockpile consisted mainly of clothing: used skirts, trousers, shirts, and sweaters as well as several unopened packages of pantyhose and brand-new boys' soccer jerseys. In addition, Endrit possessed nine purses, eleven pairs of shoes, two dozen books, a dozen dolls and stuffed animals, two car radios, an assortment of small tools, three keyboards, an iron, an antenna, and a few notes of foreign currency. Lastly, there were a number of partially filled bottles of body wash and perfume. Although Endrit had found them nearly empty, he skillfully diluted each with water to increase the volume. His cache was a testament to the bountifulness of the trash, but its value would only be determined when and if it was sold.

Endrit planned to set up a stall at the smaller of the two neighboring markets. Although it saw fewer customers, there was one clear advantage: it was legal and police raids would not occur. At four o'clock one morning, Agim and I loaded Endrit's bulging bags onto a waiting vehicle and departed for the market. We arrived at a large dirt lot sandwiched between a tram depot and a small settlement. Six days of the week, the block was deserted but now it was bustling with vendors. There were at least thirty-five merchants, half of whom appeared to be Roma or Ashkali. Their products varied considerably, ranging from the extremely worn to brand-new. One stall displayed only new toothbrushes and socks while another had a motley assortment of communist memorabilia, old locks, and foreign currency. Rather than use tables, everyone simply placed their wares on sheets on the ground. Agim found a vacant space and laid down a tarp to claim it. We quickly arranged Endrit's goods, trying to ensure that everything was visible.

Several minutes later an older Serbian man walked by and asked the price of the jerseys. Agim replied that they were 200 dinars ($2.10) each. The man immediately shook his head and began to leave. Unwilling to lose the sale, Agim requested a counteroffer. The man proposed half that amount and Agim readily agreed. This pattern was repeated each time a shopper inquired about a price. Regardless of the item, Agim initially asked for 200 dinars. When the customer refused, he took whatever they were willing to pay. Because negotiations were quick and simple, we spent the vast majority of our time waiting for customers. Agim soon became bored and, ceding his sales responsibilities to me, left to wander around the market. Upon his return, Agim reduced the opening price to only 50 or 100 dinars. It was getting late and he hoped to move as much as possible. At seven o'clock, as the market was ending, I mentally listed our sales: two packages of pantyhose, two children's jerseys, two bottles of perfume, three purses, the iron, the antenna, a copy of *The Little Prince*, two dolls, a pipe wrench, three pairs of shoes, and all of the currency. We earned 2,300 dinars ($24.25) in two hours.

Cold and impatient, Agim wanted to leave but we had only sold a fraction of Endrit's wares. I assumed we would be returning the following week and began packing up. Agim, however, told me to stop. He called to a neighboring Romani vendor and offered him the remaining merchandise for no cost. The man agreed, and without another word Agim blithely walked away from our stall and headed toward the bus stop. When we returned to Bekim's shack, everyone was still asleep so Agim and I slipped under the covers for a rest. A couple of hours later I awoke to the sound of Endrit berating his son. Noting that the items took weeks to amass, Endrit yelled at Agim for blithely abandoning his goods. Fatime and Bekim tried to calm Endrit, telling him that Agim had acted appropriately. If an article did not sell immediately, it never would. Everything of value, they reasoned, had gone. Therefore, Agim would have only retrieved worthless dregs. Although Endrit remained unconvinced, Agim's actions were the norm. Ashkali and Roma routinely discarded all of their merchandise at the end of the day. They saw no reason to pack and carry heavy bundles because this stock was easily replaceable. Dumpsters supplied an endless amount of potentially profitable commodities. When ex-trash could not be sold, it easily became trash once more.

While Ashkali attended the small weekly market, Polje's Romani residents did not. They preferred the much larger market that sprawled along a major thoroughfare. It operated six days a week and ran from early morning to late afternoon. Items for sale included the usual recycled trash as well as secondhand watches, televisions, DVD players, plumbing supplies, and cellphones. On a busy day, well over fifty stalls were operating. The variety of wares, central location, and frequency drew many shoppers but hawking here was risky. Despite its size, the market was illegal. Community police routinely arrived each morning and ordered vendors to leave immediately. Those who did not comply faced losing their goods and receiving a fine of 6,000 dinars ($63). On rare days police confiscated everything without warning, compelling traders to surrender valuable merchandise. But for Polje's vendors, the financial opportunity outweighed the fear of raids. Nikola, Dragomir, and his brother-in-law all peddled their wares at the market between four to six days a week. Dragomir and his brother-in-law hawked dumpster goods, but Nikola resold used watches and cellphones that he obtained from Roma in other parts of the city.

Dragomir sought to get to the market early each morning but wanted to avoid the predictable police raid. To maximize his time and minimize his risk, he often asked a fellow vendor to phone him as soon as the police departed. He then packed his items and walked to the closest tram stop. Polje's residents all rode public transportation to the market, which lay approximately five kilometers from the settlement. Dragomir preferred trams because they provided more space for his large bags. Serbs, however, resented having to navigate these obstacles and habitually stared at Dragomir. He ignored acrimonious glances but ticket checks were another matter. Transport workers randomly entered trams and buses to ensure everyone possessed a valid ticket. Anyone found to be traveling without one was immediately ejected and fined. While Serbs were always asked to present their tickets, settlement residents were often disregarded. It was assumed that *cigani* were traveling illegally but lacked the cash to pay a fine. Indeed, Polje's residents refused to purchase tickets and invoked popular stereotypes of poor *cigani* if they were ever confronted. During one interaction I listened as Nikola recited a litany of woe: He lived in a shack. He did not have electricity. He had no access to water. Finally, Nikola asked how he could afford a ticket when even basic necessities were unattainable. With a look of resignation, the inspector moved to the next person. After disembarking, Nikola told the story to Dragomir, who broke out in laughter. See, Dragomir said, there was no need to buy a ticket.

On some mornings Dragomir did not arrive until after ten o'clock and by then most of the prime positions were occupied. If the market was particularly crowded, the entire street could be filled with stalls. But Dragomir knew the importance of having a central position so he consistently asked a friend to reserve a bay for him. Once he claimed the space, Dragomir laid down a sheet and displayed his merchandise: shoes, electronics, toys, books, purses, toiletries, office supplies, and bric-a-brac. Unlike some other vendors, he never sold clothes because they were heavy, awkward to transport, and rarely in demand. Consumers were far more likely to purchase new clothing from a nearby Chinese shopping center, where some items were cheaper than those in the market.[10] Consequently, Dragomir focused on other products.

Although the market provided Polje's residents independence from the corporations that oversaw recycling, scavengers were still subject to the flow of international trade. On one hand, the production of goods in China constrained Ashkali and Romani activities in Serbia. Not only did scavengers lose customers to Chinese wholesalers, men like Dragomir altered their labor strategies in an attempt to compensate. People decided what to take or leave in the dumpsters based, in part, on the presence of cheap transnational commodities. On the other hand, Chinese goods were liberating. This merchandise would, sooner or later, be discarded, scavenged, and resold. Romani vendors might lose some sales to Chinese businesses but eventually Chinese goods would become recycled goods. In fact, most of the items Dragomir hawked were made in China. Yet again, economic integration created a niche for scavengers while pushing them further into the margins.

Once Dragomir's wares were displayed, he waited patiently until he was asked for a price. Like Agim, Dragomir generally started at 200 dinars ($2.10) for most items. The potential buyer often indicated that this was too high, leading Dragomir to solicit a counteroffer. If it was at least 100 dinars, Dragomir invariably agreed. The negotiation process was quick and predictable but each day's revenue was not. Despite years of experience, Dragomir remained unsure of what goods would sell and I could certainly do no better. One day I watched as customers snapped up a broken motherboard and small wooden elephant with a missing trunk but showed no interest in new bottles of moisturizer. Given this inherent indeterminacy, Dragomir's income fluctuated from 3,000 dinars ($31.50) on a good day to 1,000 dinars ($10.50) on a bad one. Nevertheless, he felt this was the best and most reliable way to earn money. He avoided the difficult physical labor of hauling paper or large amounts of metal and, once sales began to dwindle, Dragomir simply abandoned his merchandise and went home.

As in Polje, Roma established reciprocal relationships with one another. Standing by his stall waiting for customers, Dragomir chatted and joked with those around him. Conversations about the weather, the economy, and politics abounded, as did wry observations about the market's denizens. These interactions were bolstered through economic transactions. Hawkers carefully examined neighboring stalls for bargains and often gave discounts to their fellow merchants. Whenever a fellow Rom expressed interest in an item of Dragomir's, he would ask less than half what he charged Serbian customers. However, the most common purchase made by vendors was not goods but refreshments. A number of Serbian and Romani individuals roamed the market with small carts laden with hot drinks, soda, alcohol, snacks, and cigarettes. They did a brisk business serving vendors and shoppers alike. Dragomir preferred to get his coffee from an elderly Serbian woman, who consistently stopped by his stall throughout the day. However, purchasing refreshments significantly diminished his profits. On slow days we could spend half of our meager earnings on drinks. Dragomir, though, viewed this as a mandatory expense. He said he needed the caffeine and conversation to remain alert. At the market, like in Polje, the economic, physical, and social realms were all intertwined.

Given Dragomir's seeming success, Bekim decided to sell at the larger market for the first time. He began by purchasing three bags of merchandise

for 800 dinars ($8.40) on the day of his move. Most of the items were cloth-
ing, although shoes, toys, and purses were also included. In addition, Bekim
had an iron and small vacuum that he had found while searching the dumpsters. Confident he would make a reasonable profit, Bekim departed for the
market in the late morning and I accompanied him. Unfortunately, our
arrival coincided with a police raid. We stood on the sidelines while vendors
reluctantly packed their goods. But as soon as the police left, the sellers rapidly reclaimed their spaces along the roadside. We walked up and down
trying to locate an unoccupied area but were unsuccessful. Finally, Bekim
found a small gap between two stalls but their proprietors shooed him away,
saying there was not enough room for him. Frustrated, Bekim spotted
Dragomir and requested his assistance. Dragomir approached the traders,
whom he knew, and argued Bekim's case. Their friendship with Dragomir
motivated a change of heart and Bekim was allowed to set up his stall. But
when Bekim brought over his bags, the vendors retracted their offer and
told him to leave. We continued searching for a space and walked farther
and farther from the market's center. As Bekim was becoming increasingly
agitated, Dragomir whistled to him. A small section of pavement nearby
was being vacated and Bekim quickly claimed it. At last, Bekim said, he
would start earning money.

A number of people walked by Bekim's stall and examined his wares
but they made no purchases. He eventually became bored and left to
browse the market. While he was gone, I sold a pair of shoes for 50 dinars
(52 cents) but this only irritated Bekim. He said I should have gotten
more money, considering what he paid for the merchandise. Finally, his
luck seemed to improve when a Serbian man stopped and inquired about
the iron and vacuum. To drive up the price, Bekim escorted the man to a
nearby shop with electrical outlets to prove that both items were functioning. Several minutes later, Bekim appeared alone and without the iron or
vacuum. The man had agreed to purchase both for 600 dinars ($6.30).
Bekim had hoped to get more, but given the lack of sales he was desperate.
The man, however, had yet to pay. Claiming to have no cash, he left to find
an ATM and promised to return shortly with the money. But as Bekim
waited, there was no sign of the Serb. Soon Bekim became anxious. As
minutes stretched into an hour, it was clear that the man would not be
coming back. Extremely angry, Bekim vowed to find and beat him. It was

at this moment that the police arrived for another raid. We quickly gathered everything into a bundle and prepared to flee. However, this was not necessary. Within fifteen minutes the police departed and we were able to unpack. Still seething, Bekim left to search for the man. Thirty minutes later, he returned even more upset. Meanwhile, I was unable to make any additional sales. Having lost any hope of turning a profit, Bekim announced that we were leaving. He had spent 800 dinars but only made 50. Cursing, Bekim vowed never to sell at the market again.

Bekim's experience illustrates that vendors were visible and vulnerable in a way that paper and metal recyclers were not. The already complex relations of scavenging were augmented with riding trams, escaping police raids, and negotiating with hard-bargaining customers. Consequently, hawkers spent a great deal of time navigating public spaces and interactions. Dragomir mitigated this risk through his Romani networks. Much like in Polje, sellers created bonds out of necessity to ensure mutual survival. Individuals who lacked these connections were far more susceptible to failure. Bekim's expertise with recycling consolidators was not transferable to the marketplace. Markets, like paper and metal, required a distinct set of skills, affiliations, and tolerances. While Dragomir was freed from the set prices of junkyards, his daily income oscillated considerably. It was impossible to predict which, if any, items would be in demand. Scavenging was already precarious, and hawking only added another layer of uncertainty. Bekim's quest to find a more profitable alternative to metal was, on this occasion, unsuccessful.

WAGE LABOR AND BEGGING

Although scavenging was the norm, Polje's residents occasionally pursued other sources of income such as wage labor. Serbs considered these jobs to be real work, unlike scavenging. In fact, Serbs often stated that *cigani* would only escape indigence through legal employment. Successful citizens took home paychecks, not trash. Consequently, the Serbian government's recent action plan for Romani inclusion stresses the need to increase participation in the formal labor market.[11] NGOs echo these aims. The European Union Agency for Fundamental Rights comments,

"Equal and full access to employment is key to furthering social inclusion and combating poverty."[12] Wage labor—real jobs—were the means to Romani progress.

In reality the line between formal and informal employment was not difficult to cross. Serbs viewed *cigani* as a pool of cheap, unskilled labor and hired them to complete a variety of physical tasks, including washing dishes in cafés, stacking cabbages at the farmers' market, or hauling boxes in and out of stores. Scavenging was the norm for Polje's residents but most also had a history of wage labor. Dragomir, for instance, spent two years stocking merchandise at the Chinese shopping center, while Bekim worked at a café for a few months. However, both men complained about their working conditions. Bekim felt his wage of €10 ($12.50) a day was too low. Scavenging would yield more, he said, and concluding that the job was simply not worth his time, he quit. For Dragomir, work was socially awkward. Although he occasionally ate with his Chinese coworkers, and even learned to use chopsticks, interactions were limited. Dragomir criticized his employers for focusing on business and never joking. At the market he was able to be among friends, exchange gossip, and earn a similar amount. Thus, Dragomir also resigned and returned to scavenging.

While a number of jobs were available to Ashkali and Roma, those at junkyards were preferred. Larger consolidators relied on a sizeable staff to sort and process the items they received each day and scavengers familiar with the metal trade were ideal labor. When one junkyard actively recruited workers from Polje, Bekim and several others signed on. These positions, like most for *cigani,* had unique features. First, they were temporary: workers were required to phone the junkyard each morning to determine if they were needed that day. In addition, crews were separated by ethnicity—Serbs, Bayash, and Yugoslav Roma—to ensure the diverse workforce would not come into conflict with one another. But as was the norm, Ashkali were misrecognized as Roma. Consequently, the supervisor placed Bekim in a team with Harun, Miloš, and Aleksander's son. Their crew spent hours unloading trucks, separating metal, and stacking large pieces of scrap. These tasks were extremely taxing and workers often described being sore in the evening. Bekim commented that hauling grimy materials and sweating all day made him feel particularly filthy. The physical demands of the job were compounded by its long hours. Bekim worked six days a week from seven o'clock in the morning to six o'clock in the evening. While onerous, the job offered a generous salary and benefits. Bekim was paid 2,000 dinars ($21) a day, which was more than he normally earned from the dumpsters. In addition, the supervisor provided lunch and beverages for his workers. Bekim described him as a generous man who would not tolerate racial slurs or insults.

Despite Bekim's praise, most of Polje's residents failed to keep their jobs at the junkyard. Over time, some workers began taking unauthorized breaks, others socialized rather than sorting metal, and a few even stole scrap. In an effort to curtail this behavior, the company installed surveillance cameras and fired the offenders. A short time later the Bayash crew was accused of stripping cable too slowly and every member was dismissed. Only Bekim's crew remained and they did not last much longer. One day the supervisor purchased beer to reward exemplary service. Rather than waiting until the end of the day, they began drinking almost immediately. Soon, everyone became too inebriated to finish the shift. The next morning the supervisor told them he no longer needed their assistance. Although most of the men were eventually invited back on a trial basis, they quickly abandoned these intermittent jobs. Bekim left for Kosovo while Harun and Miloš resumed collecting metal from the villages. Aleksander's sons, however, remained in their positions and, after months with no further incidents, were offered permanent employment. Although these new jobs took them away from the settlement for extended periods, the steady income allowed Aleksander to quit scavenging and concentrate on raising his livestock.

As Aleksander's sons earned their wages at the junkyard, their wives and children were on the streets begging. Members of every Romani family in Polje had begged at least once over the past few years and many did so regularly. Able-bodied men were expected to work but women, children, and disabled men would stand on corners with their hands outstretched. For Serbs this was the antithesis of paid labor. If employment demonstrated economic and social citizenship, panhandling signified unrepentant Otherness.[13] Serbs circulated stories of abusive begging syndicates, female beggars drugging their children, and child trafficking. In Polje, however, begging was neither a socially sanctioned practice nor an exploitative one. Although many people begged, it was considered a shameful source of income. Ashkali, in particular, derided panhandlers as lazy and greedy. Accordingly, these families were among the few in Polje who resolutely refused to beg. While Romani residents routinely engaged in these activities, they seldom admitted to doing so. Nevertheless, neighbors could easily identify beggars loitering at nearby traffic lights or by the small bills that they used to repay loans. Thus, begging was an embarrassing but open secret in Polje.

Those willing to discuss their actions blamed severe financial hardship. Milica said she had vowed never to stoop so low as to ask strangers for money but then, after the birth of her first son, Nenad, her husband could not support the family. Feeling she had no other choice, she began standing by the side of the road, clutching her newborn, and imploring passersby for help. Ten years later Nenad and his younger siblings were begging in her place. After school he rode the tram to an intersection in front of a nearby mall. Walking up and down the line of cars waiting at the traffic lights, Nenad asked for spare change. The mall was an ideal location because it received a constant flow of traffic while giving Nenad access to drinking fountains and toilets. Although he was deemed old enough to beg alone, children between five and seven years old worked in teams and did not stray further than two blocks from the settlement. These shifting groups ranged from four children from unrelated families to siblings. For instance, Harun's son begged with his elder sister on some occasions and with Bogdan's son on others. To pass the time, the children often engaged in a friendly competition to collect the most money.

In contrast to women and children, the only men who could beg successfully were those with, or at least appearing to have, a disability. For example, Dragomir's other brother-in-law, Danilo, was born with severe physical deformities and could only walk with the aid of crutches. Rather than scavenging, he spent a couple of hours each day panhandling. Danilo often took the bus to wealthier neighborhoods in hopes of earning more money and avoiding the confrontations that occurred near Polje. However, Stanislav and his son Jakov preferred to remain closer to home. Anyone passing the neighboring traffic lights consistently saw Stanislav perched on a pair of crutches, his hand outstretched, wearing a red T-shirt emblazoned with an image of Che Guevara. Stanislav's gait resembled Danilo's but it was the result of deception, not disability. Once safely within the confines of the settlement, Stanislav began to walk normally, carrying the crutches that he shared with his son. All three men earned roughly the same amount of money: three hours standing at the traffic lights netted between 1,000 to 2,000 dinars ($10.50 to $21).

The actions of men like Stanislav and Jakov contributed to the opprobrium associated with begging. Dragomir was furious that they chose to forgo an honest career of scavenging in favor of trickery. He was adamant that begging should be only for the truly disabled or destitute. For instance, when Dragomir was hospitalized, his wife temporarily panhandled. But as soon as he recovered, Dragomir returned to work and her begging ceased. He added that the same could not be said of other families. Many continued to panhandle despite receiving other income. Both Harun and Miloš scavenged metal and their wives collected welfare payments yet their children routinely begged. The ease of begging, Dragomir claimed, became addictive. He pointed out that even families with new cellphones and rural homes sent their wives and children panhandling. He found it ironic that Ashkali, the poorest members of the settlement, were the only ones who repudiated begging.

Earning an income was a moral project. Polje's residents and Serbs alike regarded begging as shameful and, at times, dishonest. But opinions of scavenging diverged. For Serbs, scavenging was not only the antithesis of real work but akin to begging. Furthermore, both scavenging and begging were indelibly associated with chronically destitute *cigani* appropriating the resources of others. Whether it was trash or alms, Serbs believed *cigani* had not truly earned their income. Conversely, wage labor was praised. It denoted participation in the economy as well as citizenship. Consequently, Serbs invoked formal employment as an ideal tool to ease poverty and facilitate Romani integration.

In contrast, Polje's residents classified both scavenging and wage labor as work. From an Ashkali perspective there were numerous similarities between these tasks. First, both were physically demanding. Searching dumpsters was just as exhausting as sorting metal. Second, neither offered any hope of advancing beyond manual labor. Ashkali could find jobs stacking boxes but they would never work as store clerks or waiters. Third, Polje's residents were effectively confined to the settlement and its surroundings. Both wage labor and dumpster work occurred within a three-kilometer radius of Polje, reflecting the spatial marginalization of *cigani*. Fourth, each required engaging with Serbs—with recycling consolidators, customers, supervisors, and the police—and Serbian attitudes toward *cigani*. In this respect, formal employment was the more challenging because individuals lacked the circumscribed autonomy of scavenging. Finally, scavenging and wage labor were constrained yet indeterminate. Whether selling paper to consolidators, hawking goods at markets, engaging in wage labor, or begging, residents' income never comprised more than 1,000 to 2,500 dinars ($10.50 to $26.25) per day. In fact, there was no guarantee that any money would be earned at all. Ashkali could not predict a dumpster's contents, the price of metal, whether merchandise would sell, or if a formal job would appear. Work was ultimately a gamble with a limited payout.[14]

Despite Serbian and NGO narratives lauding wage labor, it was comparable to dumpster work and did not liberate scavengers from poverty or the periphery. Consequently, Polje's residents saw little reason to hold formal jobs. At least scavenging provided a measure of independence. Whether through collecting paper, metal, or merchandise, men like Endrit and Bekim saw themselves as entrepreneurs, constantly on the lookout for better opportunities. However, their hopes relied not on formal employment but their unique ability to resurrect countercommodities. Whereas sorting through dumpsters was physically revolting, such actions also could be considered revolting in another sense—they allowed Polje's residents to meaningfully create their own economic sovereignty, albeit one impacted by global capitalism, stereotypes of *cigani*, and marginalization. Rather than attempting to escape the abject, Ashkali embraced it as they embraced the safety of segregation. In an environment of exception, inhabiting the world of trash, stench, and pollution was a purposeful survival strategy.

4 Constrained Aspirations

After years of living in Belgrade's settlements, Bekim concluded that his normal economic strategies were insufficient. To improve his prospects, he looked to his neighbors. Bekim often commented that Romani residents had consistently higher incomes than Ashkali and were better off as a result. Harun and Miloš, for instance, bought beer on the weekend. Aleksander possessed several horses while his sons owned cars. Bekim attributed this relative wealth to two factors that distinguished Roma from Ashkali: access to welfare and exclusively recycling metal. This chapter follows Bekim as he attempted to improve his family's lot by mimicking these tactics. However, this would require reworking his political and social identities.

First, Bekim sought state aid for his family. While a few men collected disability payments, the vast majority of beneficiaries were mothers claiming monthly child support stipends.[1] Every Romani family relied on this income. Jovana revealed that she earned nearly €400 ($500) a month for herself and her five children, one of whom had epilepsy. With Fatime pregnant and his family about to swell to six members, Bekim was hopeful that they would be awarded a similar sum. However, obtaining welfare was not a simple task. It required numerous documents and negotiating a complex Serbian bureaucracy. Through this process, individuals not only gained access to state funds but also demonstrated their right to citizenship. While identity cards ostensibly verified an individual's legal status, one's ability to navigate the system was equally important.

Consequently, welfare was a biopolitical project that extended state control over the lives of its subjects through technologies of governance. This was not only a regulatory regime but also one that included "truth discourses," which normalized particular identities and behaviors.[2] As *cigani*, Ashkali were deemed illegitimate and their claims on the state were routinely refused. National narratives portrayed *cigani* as morally corrupt abusers of welfare funds, which hard-working Serbs desperately deserved. In addition, bureaucratic barriers, such as requiring a legal title to property as proof of address, further excluded Ashkali. For Fatime to successfully enroll in welfare, she and Bekim would need to refashion themselves as citizens and, in so doing, temporarily become subjects of the state, not residents of a space of exception.

Although welfare provided an important revenue, it could not support a family. Harun commented that while €400 might appear to be a great deal of money, it only lasted his family for two weeks or less. To make ends meet, he collected metal in the rural villages surrounding Belgrade. The majority of Polje's Roma practiced this method of scavenging, but given the distances covered, a *trokolica* was inadequate for the task. While a few Bayash utilized trucks or boats, other residents relied on horses.[3] In the afternoons, Harun, Miloš, and Aleksander's son, Radmilo, could be seen returning to the settlement with their carts laden with scrap. Metal fetched a much higher price than paper, leading Bekim to speculate that these men earned as much as €50 ($63) a day. With a horse, he said, success was guaranteed.

Aleksander agreed that his family's income was greater than that of Ashkali residents, but reported that his sons made appreciably less than Bekim imagined, about €10 ($13) per day. Nevertheless, metal yielded more profit than paper while requiring less effort. Whereas Bekim spent the day pedaling a *trokolica*, breaking down boxes, and stacking cardboard, Radmilo sat on a cart. Aleksander added that he would never have the stamina for paper, and even if he did, it would be impossible to feed his large family on such meager pay. While Aleksander espoused the benefits of collecting metal, he was clear that it required skill. A scavenger needed to be familiar with the roads and villages, know an item's value, and build a rapport with clients. These were competencies, he said, that Ashkali simply did not possess.

Like others in Polje, Aleksander linked work and ethnicity: Roma were associated with metal while Ashkali were associated with paper. While a specialization in metal or paper reflected, in part, the contemporary categories of a global recycling industry, labor divisions have pervaded Romani communities for centuries.[4] An individual may first and foremost identify as a Rom but numerous other labels further divide Romani peoples. In the Balkans, ethnonyms have often been tied to specific trades and occupations, such as Kardaraši (cauldron makers), Zlatari (gold dealers), and Ludari (miners). However, over time, groups abandoned some professions and adopted others. Not only were these labels fluid; they did not always correlate to a group's actual activities.[5] As individuals pursued social and economic advancement, they assumed new ethnonyms to reflect their changing circumstances. Consequently, Bekim's desire to collect metal, although motivated by the promise of greater income, would impact his identity as Ashkali. If obtaining welfare required negotiating state sovereignty, working with horses entailed traversing a localized Romani sovereignty.

While Bekim attempted to remake his relationship with the state and his neighbors, entrepreneurship ultimately depended upon trash. Embracing a new scavenging routine gave Bekim access to new materials and geographies, but he remained limited to the discards of others. Nevertheless, he did have one advantage: the line between commodities and garbage was fluid and conventional. For Bekim to truly succeed, he needed to transform merchandise into trash. Instead of simply pulling items out of dumpsters, he could endeavor to actively create the detritus on which he relied. Consequently, Bekim was not merely revising his own identity; he hoped to rework the identity of objects as well. In following his quest to obtain welfare and scavenge metal, this chapter illustrates how individuals pursued their aspirations within the context of Polje's material, economic, and social confinement.

A BUREAUCRACY FOR DISPLACED PERSONS

Throughout Europe, state benefits such as unemployment payments, child support, and pensions are tied to citizenship. This social safety net theoretically covers Romani nationals, but in practice many European governments have erected legal barriers that make it difficult if not impossible for Roma to claim government aid.[6] In Serbia, for example, many Roma and Ashkali lacked the identity documents necessary for not only welfare but also citizenship.[7] This was the result, in part, of the breakup of Yugoslavia.[8] Fleeing violence in newly created states, over three hundred thousand refugees and IDPs flooded into Serbia.[9] The legal status of the forty thousand Roma, Ashkali, and Egyptians from Kosovo was structured by the ongoing political struggle over the region's independence. Because Serbia steadfastly refused to recognize Kosovo's sovereignty, those escaping the war were officially classified as IDPs, not refugees.[10] Unlike refugees, IDPs received limited benefits but were recognized as Serbian nationals and therefore technically eligible for state aid in the form of unemployment, child support, and welfare payments. However, claiming these benefits required a series of documents—a birth certificate, citizenship certificate, and national identity card—that many Ashkali IDPs did not possess.[11]

Birth certificates formed the basis for citizenship and all subsequent forms of identification. Municipalities stored birth records and, after the war, the Serbian state declared Kosovar documents invalid. To be legally recognized, individuals needed to get new Serbian-issued identification.[12] The government chose to decentralize the process and paired Kosovar towns with Serbian ones. Based on their place of birth in Kosovo, document seekers would need to visit one of seven Serbian cities. Belgrade, however, which hosted the largest population of IDPs in the country, was not on this list. Its residents would not only need to pay for the documents but would have to shoulder travel expenses as well.[13] While Serbian IDPs were able to navigate these procedures, they posed a significant challenge for many Ashkali.

Not only did Ashkali IDPs struggle to obtain identification, so too did their children born in Serbia. Unlike in many other countries, Serbia did not automatically register births. Hospital staff only recorded basic information such as the parents' names, child's name, and sex. An official birth certificate was only issued when parents submitted their identification cards at the state registry office. If parents lacked these documents or failed to present them within thirty days, their offspring remained undocumented. Amending information or registering births after the deadline were serious legal issues that could take several months. This was made even more difficult if the parents' or child's name was recorded incorrectly, which occurred for a number of reasons. Pregnant Ashkali women routinely believed they would only be admitted to the hospital if they possessed valid identification so, during childbirth, they presented the health care documents of family or friends. In other cases, Romani mothers feared that the state would remove their children and provided false information to hide their identities and place of residence. In these instances, the marginalization of Ashkali and Roma resulted in inaccurate data, further compounding already challenging administrative hurdles.

A lack of identification was chronic for many Ashkali IDPs, but in recent years this has been changing. While Bekim still lacked an identity card, Fatime was able to acquire one and register the births of her children. However, she had yet to receive welfare. This would require negotiating a series of intricate bureaucratic steps designed to demonstrate, both explicitly and implicitly, one's status as a citizen. While these procedures were onerous, Bekim and Fatime felt the promise of additional income outweighed the impending struggle. So, early one morning, they prepared for a day of navigating Serbian officialdom. Fatime washed her face, combed her hair, and donned her cleanest clothes. She strove to look as respectable as possible to dissuade Serbs from treating her as a dirty *cigan*. For Bekim, though, it was like any other day and he saw no reason to alter his appearance for Serbian officials. While Fatime finished getting ready, Bekim reached between the boards in the shack's ceiling and retrieved Fatime's documents. Finally, Fatime placed their young daughter, Luljeta, into a stroller and we headed out of the settlement. Rather than registering with the local municipality, we were traveling to a neighboring suburb, where Fatime's sister and brother-in-law owned a home.

After a thirty-minute bus ride, we disembarked in front of a large BMW dealership. The shining new cars were a reminder of Belgrade's increasing affluence, but the city's entrenched poverty was also on display. Nearby stood a dilapidated building ringed with shacks, trash, and paper recycling containers. This former school, with classical columns and decorative flourishes, had been converted into a temporary shelter for Ashkali IDPs during the Kosovo War. Fifteen years later, families were still occupying classrooms, while toilets were few and proper kitchens nonexistent. The building had become a tenement and a site of permanent displacement. As in Polje, Serbs relegated Ashkali to a circumscribed geography, which was simultaneously remarkable and taken for granted. The school visibly stood out from its surroundings but was dismissed by Serbian passersby as simply another *ciganski* slum.

Bekim, Fatime, and I walked past the school and up a hill to a small commercial precinct. The first step in registering for welfare was to obtain proof of unemployment. The municipality boasted several government offices and Bekim was unsure of where to go. He began approaching Ashkali or Roma, requesting directions. But after two Romani men were unable to help, Bekim turned to Serbs and was eventually able to locate the National Employment Service. Upon entering the office, we faced a maze of numbered counters. Bekim found what appeared to be an information kiosk and asked about obtaining the necessary documents. The clerk replied that he must begin by purchasing a working book from a stationery shop and validating it at a nearby counter. These passport-sized documents certified an individual's employment eligibility and provided a record of job history. The clerk handed Bekim a form before directing him to a neighboring store. We quickly walked to the shop, purchased the working book for 90 dinars (95 cents), returned to the office, and waited in line at the appropriate counter.

When our turn arrived, Bekim presented Fatime's identification card, the blank form, and working book. But the clerk refused to process the paperwork because Bekim had failed to fill in the form. She gruffly sent him away, saying he should not return until it was completed. This, however, presented a problem. Bekim could not read the form, let alone fill it in. While he was able to decipher some words in the Latin script, the form, like all government documents in Serbia, was written in Cyrillic. It was completely unintelligible to Bekim. Furthermore, his writing skills were almost nonexistent. Even phone numbers were too difficult for him to jot down. Fatime could do no better. Approaching another counter, Bekim obliquely said he needed help, too ashamed to acknowledge his illiteracy.

The clerk was indifferent and told him to return to the first counter. Bekim did not want to face the stern woman again; unsure of what else to do, we stood in the center of the main room.

Although Fatime had made every effort to appear like those around us, our presence felt fundamentally conspicuous. On one hand, Bekim and Fatime's skin color marked them as different. On the other, they were utterly confounded by a bureaucratic process that Serbs seemed to have mastered. I also lacked this knowledge and could do little to assist Bekim and Fatime. While I could read and write in Cyrillic, I was still unsure about how best to fill in each box. The opaqueness of the process itself—what window to approach, what form to complete, what information to provide—barred the uninitiated from participation. Ultimately, it was not Bekim and Fatime's skin color that posed the greatest hurdle but rather their ignorance of the Serbian bureaucratic system. By linking membership in the state to a specialized knowledge, people like Bekim and Fatime were functionally excluded without reference to their identity as *cigani*.[14]

After several minutes, a security guard approached and asked if there was a problem. Bekim showed him the form and embarrassingly explained that he was unable to read or write. Without saying a word, the guard took the paperwork and Fatime's identification card, walked to the information desk, and began filling out the document. He occasionally had the clerk confirm that he was entering the information correctly but never spoke to us. Once the form was completed, the guard handed it to Bekim and walked away. Returning to the counter, Bekim gave the papers to the clerk. Seemingly satisfied, she placed Fatime's identification card into a reader. Looking at her computer screen, the clerk informed Bekim that Fatime's official residence was in Kosovo. Without a local address, she would be unable to proceed. But Bekim expected this response.

In Serbia, identity documents were a necessary but not sufficient condition of belonging. An equally important requirement was an official address. A holdover from the socialist era, formal housing was equated with personhood. Because settlements were unlawful, their inhabitants lacked addresses and hence were unrecognized as residents of Belgrade. This was another mechanism through which *cigani*—including those with citizenship and documents—were excepted from the nation. Amid growing calls from NGOs and human rights organizations, the Serbian government attempted to amend this requirement. Legislation was introduced in 2013 that allowed settlement residents to use the address of a relative or a Center for Social Work, but this has not always proved effective. When Dragomir provided one such center's address, he was denied. Some clerks were unaware of the change while others ignored it. In addition, Polje's residents were migrants and refugees so few had family members in Belgrade with enough means to own a home. Consequently, addresses remained a critical mechanism of exclusion.

Luckily, Fatime's elder sister, Edona, and her husband, Naim, did own a home. Bekim explained to the clerk that this was where they were living. She informed him that to change Fatime's address, they must visit the local police station with the title for the property. Unfazed, Bekim retrieved Fatime's papers and led us out of the building. He immediately phoned Naim, who agreed to provide the required documents. But to get them, we would need to go to his home, which lay a few kilometers away. We returned the way we came, marching down the hill and past the repurposed school, before stopping in front of the BMW dealership. We boarded a bus and disembarked several stops later. After walking a few more blocks, we arrived at the side of a divided six-lane highway. Without saying a word, Bekim hoisted the stroller over the crash barrier and I suddenly realized that he intended for us to cross. We waited on the shoulder and the instant a small break appeared in the oncoming traffic, Bekim sprinted across with Luljeta while Fatime and I dashed behind them. We reached the median only seconds before a truck barreled past. Traversing the grass strip, we repeated the exercise once more and again barely avoided being hit. When I noticed several Roma making the same crossing, Bekim commented that a settlement lay nearby. This route, although dangerous, offered the best access to the city.

Once on the other side of the highway, we followed a dirt path into a dense stand of trees. The trail ran approximately three hundred meters through the forest before it emerged onto a small lane flanked with houses. Naim's home was only a couple of blocks further. Unlike the Ashkali residents of Polje, Naim's family relocated to Belgrade well before the start of the war. He was born in the city and grew up in a house. His current home was made of brick, sported a large yard, and was surrounded by a low fence. As soon as Naim spotted us walking down the lane, he came out of the house and ushered everyone inside. We sat in the main room, which contained a television, two large couches, and a small stove for preparing hot drinks. Edona served tea as we discussed the day's events. Conscious of the time, Bekim and Fatime did not stay any longer than politeness dictated. The moment everyone finished their tea, Bekim requested the necessary documents and we departed. Retracing our steps, we crossed the forest and freeway, caught a bus back to the BMW dealership, and walked up the hill to the municipal buildings.

This time we entered an adjacent police station, which was smaller and had fewer clerks assisting people. We joined the longest queue and I counted eight people in front of us. Over an hour later, we approached the counter. Bekim handed the clerk Fatime's identification card and Naim's deed, explaining that he needed her address changed. The clerk took a cursory glance at the documents before declaring that the title was only a copy and therefore unacceptable. Bekim would need to produce the original legal document. Frustrated, he left the counter and phoned Naim, who was quickly able to locate the correct papers. To save time, Naim promised to bring the title to us but after thirty minutes elapsed, he had still not appeared. Bekim was irritated and called Naim again, only to be told that the documents would arrive soon. Another fifteen minutes passed and Bekim phoned a third time. As earlier, Naim promised he would be at the station shortly. Impatient and angry, Bekim suggested that he and I meet Naim at the bus stop. Yet again, we trundled down the hill. Not long after we arrived, Naim stepped off the bus clutching a bundle of paper. Bekim quickly took the documents, uttered a perfunctory thank you, and hurried back up the incline.

When we reentered the police station, the line had dissipated and within a few minutes Bekim was handing the title to the clerk. She declared that the new papers were sufficient and produced a form for Fatime to complete. Quietly, Fatime said, "I can't," and Bekim awkwardly explained that they were illiterate. Without saying a work, the clerk filled out the paperwork. The next step was to pay the fee: 380 dinars ($4) at the counter and an additional 380 dinars at a neighboring bank. This procedure took us another half an hour. With the receipt in hand, Bekim, Fatime, and I waited twenty minutes before facing the clerk for the third time. She inspected everything in detail and announced that the application was almost complete. The last, and seemingly easiest step, required

Fatime to sign her name on two documents. But Fatime said this was impossible. Looking at Bekim, the clerk asked if he could do it for her. He shook his head. The clerk informed them at without a signature, they could not proceed. After a long pause, Fatime said that she would try to sign. With an unsteady hand, she hesitantly printed her first name in large Latin letters. Finding this satisfactory, the clerk stamped the papers. It had taken five hours to change Fatime's address.

We returned to the National Employment Service office tired and annoyed but cautiously optimistic that the working book would be certified at last. Bekim presented all of Fatime's documents along with the form and the working book. Without hesitating, the clerk processed everything. Finally, Fatime could apply for welfare. At last feeling a sense of accomplishment, we left the building and walked one block to the Center for Social Work. We entered the office and approached the clerk at the information desk. She informed us that Fatime would need to submit duplicates of all her documents, but unfortunately their photocopier was broken. Facing another delay, we went back outside and Bekim asked passersby for the location of a stationery store with a photocopier. We soon located a shop but Fatime had accidentally mixed up her own papers with those of her children. Because these documents were in Cyrillic, she could not identify which needed to be duplicated. I pointed out the relevant papers and the store clerk copied them. With everything in hand, we walked back to the welfare office. It was late in the afternoon and only four people were waiting ahead of us. Bekim was extremely stressed and left to smoke on the street. He returned just as Fatime was called to the counter. The office would be closing in ten minutes.

The clerk carefully examined Fatime's documents before disappearing to speak with her supervisor. She reemerged several minutes later and explained that because Fatime was a registered IDP, evidence of her status needed to accompany the application. Could Fatime produce these papers? Fatime replied that she did not have her IDP certification, which would take days to obtain. Becoming upset, she argued that her residence was now in Belgrade so her IDP status should be irrelevant. But the clerk refused to relent, calmly stating that further documentation was required. After a long day of laboring to surmount a string of bureaucratic hurdles, it seemed as if Bekim and Fatime were ultimately going to be unsuccessful. Dejected,

Bekim turned to leave but Fatime refused to go. She angrily marched into the supervisor's office and asked why the woman hated IDPs. The supervisor claimed she was only following protocol. In response, Fatime shouted that they had obeyed every rule but were still denied. As Fatime repeatedly accused the supervisor of discrimination, Bekim stood quietly in the main hall looking extremely uncomfortable. It was only after the staff began locking the doors that Fatime relented and we left the building.

Bekim and Fatime's experiences illustrate the lived reality of being excluded citizens. Fatime possessed identification as well as an address yet she was unable to register for welfare. Her identity as a *cigan* and IDP not only limited her ability to participate formally in the state apparatus; it suffused the day's events. Fatime, conscious of Serbian responses to her appearance, combed her hair and donned clean clothes but she nonetheless stood out on the street, on the bus, and in the municipal offices. She also traversed a bifurcated geography including an abandoned school adjacent to a BMW dealership and *cigani* dashing across a potentially deadly freeway. Finally, she could not even read her name on identity documents, let alone fill out the requisite forms. Consequently, exception was not confined to settlements such as Polje. It was embedded into the landscape of Belgrade, the bodies of its inhabitants, and the knowledge they possessed. While difficulties in obtaining documents reflected the status of Ashkali IDPs, they were also emblematic of the material, semiotic, and lived worlds of a marginalized population.

For many, these barriers were virtually insurmountable. A few days after our encounter at the Center for Social Work, Bekim and Fatime visited the Commissariat for Refugees and Migration to have her IDP papers reissued. However, this request could not be processed immediately and it took weeks before the certification was finalized. Because of their liminal status, refugees and IDPs were not a priority. Eventually, Fatime was able to register for welfare but received significantly less than she had anticipated: only €50 ($63) a month, a fraction of Jovana's allowance. Bekim explained that because his two boys did not attend school, the family's payment had been reduced. Yet again, legal requirements ensured that those deemed illegitimate citizens—in this case, families who refused public education—were barred from obtaining full benefits. Despite Bekim and Fatime's best efforts, they were unable to demonstrate their status as normative biopolitical subjects. Incapable of escaping the margins, they could not realize their dream of economic advancement through welfare.

ROMANI HORSES

Given the seeming capriciousness of the state, Bekim, like others, believed the only way to improve his position was through the trash. Consequently, he decided to pursue the other avenue through which Polje's Roma seemed to prosper: horses. With a horse, Bekim said, collecting would be easier and more profitable. Instead of straining to pedal a *trokolica*, he could sit in a cart, letting the horse do the work. In addition, he would transport larger and therefore more profitable items such as refrigerators, boilers, and stoves. Finally, a horse would allow Bekim to expand his geographical range considerably. The villages surrounding Belgrade were rumored to be excellent sources of pipes, appliances, and machinery that fetched sizeable returns at junkyards. But Bekim acknowledged that a horse came with challenges. The villages lay many kilometers away and the long commute meant scavengers could spend up to twelve hours a day working. Furthermore, he would need a supply of cash to purchase metal. In short, success required efficiently managing time and money.

When Bekim vowed to buy a horse, his Ashkali neighbors were uniformly dismissive. A horse, they said, would not increase his income. Rajim commented that Roma did not profit as much as Bekim supposed. Villagers charged quite a bit for metal and even large piles would not yield a great return. In addition, Bekim was too impoverished to afford even a small amount of scrap, let alone a horse and cart, Rajim declared. And he doubted anyone would be foolish enough to loan Bekim the €700 ($875) to upwards of €1,000 ($1,250) needed to purchase one. But the costs did not end there: horses required constant care. Endrit predicted that Bekim would have to choose between feeding his horse or feeding his family. Moreover, many Ashkali thought that Bekim lacked the skill needed to scavenge metal. Gazmend pointed out that Bekim had no experience collecting in the villages and no idea where to start. Those with horses, he added, were certainly not going to help him. Roma jealously guarded their routes in an effort to restrict competition. Valon noted that metal collectors established strong and exclusive relationships with their clients, making it difficult if not impossible for Bekim to break into the trade. Endrit believed it was much better to own a *trokolica* and work hard. Gazmend and Rajim agreed, saying that paper was quite profitable if one was industrious. Even Dragomir endorsed this assessment. He saw no need for an expensive horse when trash could be collected with nothing more than a bicycle.

Despite constant discouragement, Bekim maintained a horse was the solution to his family's problems. This was because a horse not only promised economic advancement, it bestowed cultural capital. Bekim would be admitted into an elite group of residents who were, by Polje's standards, prosperous. The few men who owned horses formed a unique social unit that shared strategies of equine care and traded animals, much as others swapped cellphones. Crucially, this was a Romani network. Aleksander believed that Roma were raised for metal work in a way that Ashkali were not. Horses were a powerful expression of identity in Polje. In dismissing Bekim's ambitions, Ashkali were also rejecting what they saw as a Romani way of life. But Bekim hoped to embrace it and, in so doing, escape the disapproval of Gazmend and Endrit.

It was not long before Bekim realized his dream. One day, with little fanfare, he drove into the settlement on a cart pulled by a brown gelding. Bekim could not have looked prouder. At last, he said, he would be able to earn enough money to purchase a house. But before he could begin saving for his family's future, Bekim needed to pay for the horse. He agreed to a price of €800 ($1,000). The previous owner, a Romani man who lived in the fields behind Polje, had required an initial installment of €300 ($375) and expected the balance to be repaid within three months. However, Bekim lacked the cash for the down payment so he arranged a loan from Gazmend, who was extremely reluctant. Bekim conceded that making enough money to repay both men would require significant work, but he was confident that he now had the means to succeed. Convinced that his new purchase would be an unparalleled asset, Bekim, who knew only a few English words, christened the horse Lucky.

As the weeks passed, it became clear that many of people's predictions—both positive and negative—were accurate. There was no doubt that Lucky revolutionized Bekim's life and that of his family. Routine tasks were suddenly much easier. We could carry significantly more water and, when the hydrant was locked, ride farther afield in search of unmonitored taps. Bekim commented that this alone was worth €800. But as Endrit anticipated, Lucky also required a great deal of care. While the horse facilitated water collection, most of our payload was for him. To cut down the time consumed filling bottles at a hydrant, Bekim and others obtained water from the stagnant canal in the rear of the settlement. In addition, feeding Lucky was not only laborious but costly. The grazing ground around Polje was insufficient, forcing owners to devote a portion of each day to cutting grass from vacant fields and road medians. During winter this resource was unavailable and bales of hay were purchased from farmers. For nutrition, this feed was supplemented with corn, an additional expense. Bekim could spend almost 1,000 dinars ($10.50) a day on Lucky's diet. Furthermore, keeping the horse healthy caused stress and inconvenience. Concerned that Lucky might fall ill, Bekim refused to go scavenging in the rain. However, a day without work was also a day without income. Lucky was simultaneously beneficial and burdensome.

Despite Bekim's earlier vow to scavenge in villages, this did not occur. As many Ashkali expected, he lacked the knowledge and the resources to do so. But this was of little concern to Bekim, who assured everyone that he would learn the metal trade once his debts were settled. For the time being, he continued to follow his usual route through the city. Although it was now possible to haul much more, Bekim could no longer work alone. Lucky became skittish on the busy streets and, if left unattended, would bolt. Even the few minutes it took to rummage through a dumpster was too long. To solve this problem, Bekim brought Fatime and me. He waited with Lucky while we searched the dumpsters. However, this strategy also required taking the children with us, as there was no one at home to watch them. The boys were often bored, having little to do but look at photos in the magazines we found. On the occasions that they attempted to help, I was their mentor, teaching them to break down boxes. Fatime, though, had a particularly difficult time. Her pregnancy was now in its seventh month and she was already enduring significant physical discomfort. Bending over dumpsters and pulling out boxes aggravated her back pain while stench caused constant nausea. At least once a day, I saw Fatime vomiting next to the cart. Sighing after each incident, she stoically wiped her mouth and continued to the next dumpster. Bekim insisted on working long hours to pay off his debt but his industriousness affected the entire family; by dinner, everyone was exhausted.

As the days progressed, Ashkali looked on with skepticism. No one thought Bekim had made a good choice. One evening, Agim gestured to a boiler sitting in his *trokolica* and asked why it took six of us to get boxes when he was able to procure metal all on his own. Conscious of these remarks, Bekim was determined to show that Lucky could access areas unavailable to other Ashkali. Consequently, he decided to visit a large open-air greenmarket situated on the outskirts of town. Even though he had never scavenged there before, Bekim was confident that the volume of cardboard would dwarf our usual supply. Assuming we would require assistance, he asked Fatime's two younger sisters, Quendresa and Elona, to accompany us. We set off at midday and planned to arrive just as the market was closing.

When we pulled up, I saw an expansive but half-vacant lot dotted with produce stalls. The vendors were clearly packing up and, as Bekim predicted, they had discarded a wealth of boxes into the surrounding dumpsters. While he stayed with the horse, Fatime, Elona, Quendresa, and I walked past a boom gate into the market. A few vendors glanced at us but most ignored our presence. As usual, I began pulling boxes out of dumpsters and piling them on the ground. Quietly, Fatime instructed me to break down each box as soon as I removed it, lest we appear to be littering. Before long, we had each amassed a reasonable pile. Fatime retrieved a few abandoned packing ties and strapped the cardboard together. I dragged the bundle to the next group of dumpsters where we added to it. By the third set, the bale had swelled considerably and could barely be moved. With the help of a crude harness fashioned out of the packing ties, Quendresa and I eventually towed it back to the cart. While Bekim began loading, we returned and started the process again. It took almost three hours to visit all the dumpsters. The final bundle was so large and heavy that it required four of us pulling in unison to get it back to the cart. We were tired and sore but had managed to gather far more cardboard than was possible around the settlement. It seemed Bekim had found an untapped source of recyclables and one that could only be exploited with a horse. But as we were about to discover, this was not the case.

As Bekim was piling the last of the cardboard onto the cart, two security guards arrived. Calmly, Bekim asked if there was a problem. The men informed him that scavenging was prohibited in and around the green-market. Bekim replied that we only took items from the dumpsters and did not pilfer anything. But the security guards disagreed. They told Bekim that the marketplace sold its cardboard to a recycling consolidator. Taking the boxes, they said, was stealing. Bekim and Fatime immediately pleaded ignorance. Unmoved, the men instructed us to unload the cart and leave the cardboard. In this instance, what appeared to be trash was actually a commodity. Although the boxes had been discarded, they were not stripped of value, giving them a unique identity. Once again, garbage was relative and could easily move between categories. As a result, what Bekim had regarded as scavenging was transformed into theft.

Bekim and Fatime began pleading with the guards, while Elona, Quendresa, and I stayed silent.[15] Bekim said that they had worked hard and were just trying to earn a living like everyone else. Fatime kept repeating, "Just let us go. Let us take it." With the security guards still unmoved, she added that they had three children at home who were hungry and needed to eat. Touching her belly, Fatime added that another was on the way. For good measure, she stretched out her hands and asked the men to observe how dirty and sore they were. This was proof that she was a hard worker, not a criminal. Simultaneously, Bekim reiterated that he only wanted to support his family, not steal from others. Fatime entreated them to examine her hands once more. Finally, the guards agreed to let us depart with the cardboard if we left immediately. Bekim, Fatime, and I quickly piled the remaining pieces on top while the guards surveilled our every move. As soon as everything was secured, we drove away. We would not return.

During this exchange, there was a stark contrast between Bekim's aspirations and the guards' responses to them. Using a horse and cart to gather cardboard at the greenmarket was both economically and socially entrepreneurial. Bekim was attempting to earn money, refute Ashkali allegations, and align himself with an exclusive Romani group. However, upon leaving Polje, his positionality changed. To Serbs he was simply a *cigan*, consigned to rummaging through the dumpsters. Even then, scavengers were only permitted to profit from trash when Serbs did not. To effectively navigate this environment, Ashkali enacted the very stereotype that circumscribed their identity. When Bekim and Fatime were threatened, they invoked their suffering, hunger, and vulnerable children. Like Nikola on the tram, they played the role of destitute *cigani* because there was no other option available to them. Ironically, this was a productive strategy. The security guards allowed us to leave because Bekim and Fatime appeared to be typically impoverished *cigani*, not uniquely entrepreneurial Ashkali.

As we drove back to Polje, contrasting notions of prosperity and indigence were again on display. Although the authorities curtailed our activities, the cart was overflowing with cardboard. This would not only provide Bekim with a reasonable income, he could brag that Lucky was worth the effort and expense. Overall, it had been a successful day. Bekim took pride in our accomplishments and it seemed as if his fortunes were finally on the rise. Then, while Lucky waited at a traffic light, a Serbian woman pointed her cellphone at us and took a photo. At that moment I became aware of how we must have looked to Serbs. We were dirty and tired, sitting in a wooden horse cart that was brimming with trash. What Ashkali saw as good fortune was, for Serbs, an embodiment of the stereotypical *cigan:* abject and poor. There was no way for Bekim to be anything else.

CLEANING UP

After the episode at the greenmarket, Bekim resumed his usual route in an effort to avoid further clashes with Serbs. Nevertheless, he remained on the lookout for unexpected opportunities. Late one afternoon as he and Fatime were returning from purchasing hay, they saw workers removing debris from the lower story of a small industrial building. The façade was stained black and the front windows were shattered; clearly a fire had occurred. Bekim stopped to ask if they were discarding any paper and learned that it was a warehouse owned by Chinese importers. Instead of receiving paper, Bekim and Fatime were offered jobs. The supervisor needed workers to clear out the building and he promised the damaged merchandise as payment. Bekim immediately agreed. Chinese businesses were renowned for disposing of products that scavengers viewed as perfectly usable. At a settlement near Polje, merchants occasionally left boxes of new shoes, sunglasses, clothes, and paper, all of which were hawked at local markets. Residents were able to derive a significant income from this charity, leading one Ashkali woman to comment, "The Chinese keep us alive."

The growth of Belgrade's Chinese population was the result of war and the state's subsequent neoliberal shift, the same factors that produced Ashkali displacement. Chinese migration began in earnest during the disintegration of Yugoslavia in the 1990s.[16] As the conflicts severely reduced foreign trade, Serbs and Roma smuggled in cheap Chinese goods from Hungary. Because the Serbian state was preoccupied with waging war, it ignored these illicit activities. By 1996 Serbia relaxed its immigration laws for traders, hoping to court Chinese investment.[17] At this time the economic and political environments were ideally suited to import activities. A market for Chinese goods was established, but Serbia possessed weak links to global trade. Within this "economy of scarcity," Chinese merchants faced minimal competition and government oversight.[18] Rather than hindering opportunities, Serbia's decline and isolation actually spurred migration. A similar pattern occurred in other central and southeastern European countries—including Hungary, Bulgaria, and Romania—as they sought to attract international investment and commodities.[19] Economic necessity prompted these nations to adopt a graduated sovereignty, in which state authority and citizenship became flexible.[20] Although the number of Chinese nationals in Belgrade swelled, they remained isolated from mainstream Serbian society and were largely invisible.

As Bekim surveyed the outside of the warehouse, he realized that the task would require more than two people. While Fatime stayed to ensure that the owners did not make a similar arrangement with other scavengers, he sped back to Polje for assistance. When he arrived, Agim, Fadil, and I were helping Endrit wet his paper. Bekim insisted that we come immediately but Agim and Fadil refused to abandon their task. However, I agreed and we returned to the warehouse. As we pulled up, I saw Fatime picking up charred glass and burnt papers while five Chinese men chatted nearby. We joined her and began removing small pieces of debris from the exterior. Once the front was cleared, two men escorted us inside.

A spacious central room was replete with large boxes, most of which sported charred, gaping holes. Walking with care, we picked our way through the blackened merchandise that littered the floor. The men began inspecting boxes in one section to identify which wares were salvageable and which were not. We then loaded the designated boxes onto a waiting truck, while being watched closely. Finally, the supervisor told us to dispose of anything left in the area. We could deposit these damaged goods in a nearby dumpster or transport them to Polje. At this point, Fatime took charge and sifted through the remaining detritus. Separating everything she wanted to claim, she scooped loose merchandise into the makeshift containers constructed from box fragments. I brought these bundles outside to Bekim, who stacked them on the wagon. Before long, the bed was filled to capacity and he departed for Polje. Given the amount of time it took to clear only a section of the warehouse, I realized that hours of work lay ahead of us. Fatime, however, was undeterred.

Sorting, packing, and cleaning were strenuous activities and I soon became exhausted. We were constantly stooping over, rummaging through broken glass, sweeping up debris, and hauling heavy loads. Despite being eight months' pregnant, Fatime worked intensely and sweat poured off her brow. Her efforts were keenly observed by the Chinese workers, with one commenting that he rarely saw a woman labor so tirelessly. He hoped to find a wife who was just as industrious. I was also impressed with Fatime's abilities but concerned that she was overexerting. At my repeated urging, she eventually agreed to take a short break. As we sat on a pile of trash, she said her stamina was not a choice. Children, she mused, did not ask to be fed; they must be fed. However, Fatime confided that she actually enjoyed working. Because most Ashkali women were confined to the settlement or their homes, she was simply grateful for an opportunity to be outside.

Sighing, Fatime pulled out a cigarette and lit it. It was then that I noticed her hands. They were stained black with soot but her fingernails were painted bright red. This seemed to encapsulate so much of her life. Fatime sported the normative trappings of womanhood even as she was consigned to filthy labor. Furthermore, her existence as a woman was so fundamentally constrained that even arduous chores were, in a way, liberating. Men's lives were circumscribed but women's were even more so. In Polje, Fatime was the subject of sexual jokes and here she attracted the gazes, and comments, of Chinese workers. Ashkali men were surveilled by store workers and police officers but Ashkali women were watched by everyone. While Bekim avoided entering supermarkets and shopping malls,

Fatime could be confined to the settlement for days at a time. Clearing the warehouse might have been exhausting, but it was the only way for her to spend a day away from Polje. Fatime was still smoking when one of the men complained we had been sitting for too long and gruffly instructed us to get back to work.

By this point, we had established an efficient routine. One of the two Chinese supervisors examined a section of the warehouse and identified the recoverable boxes, which we took to the truck. Then we packaged the remaining goods for Bekim and disposed of the debris in the dumpsters. As soon as we cleared an area, our work was inspected and, if it was deemed suitable, we were escorted to a new sector. Every time we repeated this process, Fatime employed a number of tactics to increase our allotment. She quickly learned that each man possessed differing opinions regarding a box's salvageability. Whereas the one gave her most items, the other was far stricter. As subtly as possible, Fatime attempted to deal only with the former while positioning her body to obstruct the latter's view. Whenever she was given a box in relatively good condition, Fatime had me immediately take it to our pile outside. She wanted these items out of view lest the stricter individual see what his colleague was discarding. Also, Fatime simply assumed that she could remove any unclaimed merchandise such as loose items strewn on the floor and any boxes that the workers overlooked.

These interactions and maneuvers were actually establishing the boundary between commodities and garbage. A complex knot of motivations, strategies, and visibility structured how and when trash was socially created. On most occasions scavengers were bystanders to this process, but in this case Fatime could actively negotiate an object's identity. As she appropriated goods, Fatime was making trash. Because taking discarded items was work and not theft, labeling an object as garbage morally justified her actions. Consequently, Fatime was not only producing waste; she was constituting her own identity as a scavenger. Once more, the biographies of Ashkali and the biographies of garbage were linked. However, Fatime's efforts could not be sustained. The Chinese supervisors eventually realized her strategy and began inspecting our cache for items they may have missed.

By the time Bekim reappeared, Fatime and I had a large stack of goods ready for him to load. As soon as everything was on the wagon, he departed again. But when he returned, the pile had grown considerably. Seeing that only a third of the warehouse was emptied, Bekim realized that he did not have enough space on the wagon to transport everything. To solve this problem, he phoned Aleksander's youngest son, Zlatko, who owned a van. Normally, Ashkali would never ask Roma for assistance but Bekim had grown close to Zlatko over the past few weeks. After many late nights drinking together, the two men vowed to become blood brothers. Bekim hoped that this bond would ensure Zlatko's participation but, to be certain, offered to pay for gasoline. Several minutes later Zlatko pulled up to the warehouse. He and Bekim quickly filled the van and sped back to Polje. When the men returned, two of Zlatko's brothers, each holding a large bottle of beer, accompanied them. The Romani men did not offer to help and instead chatted with one another while Fatime and I carried boxes out to the van.

On the following trip, Zlatko's brothers were replaced with Agim and Fadil, who had finished preparing Endrit's paper. Unlike the others, they immediately joined Fatime and me in the warehouse. Bekim's relationship with Polje's other Ashkali residents might have been strained but the norms of reciprocal labor remained inviolable. With Agim and Fadil lifting, sorting, and sweeping, we began to make considerable progress. But the two men were less disciplined than Fatime. When they found several boxes containing sunglasses with LED lights on the rim, they paused to try them on and snap selfies. Enamored with the sunglasses, Fadil waited until the supervisors looked away before quickly stuffing a pair in his pocket. A few minutes later, Agim followed suit. Neither man was caught but the supervisors were clearly suspicious and redoubled their inspections. Although Ashkali publicly decried thievery, Agim and Fadil viewed the sunglasses as a reward for their labor.

It was nine o'clock at night when we at last finished. By that time Bekim had made a total of two trips with the horse and another four with the van. Even so, the last load barely fit in the vehicle. Bekim and Fadil sat in the cab with Zlatko while the rest of us were wedged in the back. Every time the van turned a corner, hit a bump, stopped, or accelerated, merchandise tumbled down on us. Once we were safely back in Polje, I discovered that Endrit had been busy unpacking and sorting the products. The floor of Bekim's shack was a mosaic of knickknacks: Jonas Brothers and Hannah Montana bags, playing cards displaying photos of naked women, dice depicting different sexual positions, heart-shaped notepads, imitation Rubik's cubes, large sheets of temporary tattoos, mugs, Mickey Mouse keychains, small foam penises, red knotted Chinese wall decorations, children's backpacks, and several multicolored candles. Unfortunately, almost every item was singed, torn, or broken. Nevertheless, Endrit was confident that the majority could be rehabilitated.

Over the next two days, Fatime, Drita, and Agim's wife, Emine, spent hours cleaning the merchandise. Their efforts yielded amazing results and almost everything emerged looking like new. Once the weekend arrived, Bekim and I took approximately half of the stock to the small legal market. Our wares contained ashtrays, keychains, scissors, mop heads, gloves, gift bags, Christmas mugs, decks of cards, dolls, mirrored boxes, and small rubber balls. As we waited for customers, I noticed that far fewer vendors were present than when I visited eight months earlier with Agim. Nevertheless, our wares proved to be quite popular and, in two hours, we earned 4,000 dinars ($42). This was a significant amount of money yet only a small fraction of the total inventory had sold. Several Roma offered to purchase the entire lot for between 4,000 to 5,000 dinars ($42 to $53) but Bekim refused, saying the bids were too little. While it would take days to sell everything, I calculated that Bekim could potentially make as much as 25,000 dinars ($263). However, this was not to be. With the market ending, a Romani man approached Bekim and offered to buy the remaining merchandise for 2,000 dinars ($21). Bekim readily agreed. On the ride back to the settlement, I told Bekim that I thought he could have gotten more. Bekim replied that he was happy to have made 6,000 dinars ($63). If we went to the market again, he mused, maybe nothing would sell. Bekim reasoned that it was better to accept a low price now rather than endure uncertainty.

A few days later Bekim received a call from the Chinese merchants. They needed another section of the warehouse cleared and Bekim quickly volunteered. The next morning we arrived at nine o'clock, hoping to be finished by lunch. A supervisor escorted us to a large yard littered with charred, broken ceramic bowls and told us to dispose of everything. The bowls were in such bad condition that Fatime decided nothing was worth salvaging. As we began shoveling the rubble into old bags destined for the dumpsters, Bekim realized yet again that Lucky's cart was insufficient for such a large undertaking. He phoned Zlatko and Miško but both claimed to be busy. Finally, Bekim called Fitim. Fitim not only brought his small tractor, he was accompanied by Endrit and Fadil.

While the men worked outside, Fatime and I were led into the warehouse where another large expanse of incinerated goods was in need of removal. Seeing the extent of the damage, I knew that our task would once again require more time and effort than I originally expected. Nonetheless, the compensation for cleaning was substantial. The supervisor pointed to over thirty boxes of merchandise, which would be ours at the end of the day. A cursory inspection revealed that they contained a wide variety of goods including machines for rolling cigarettes, decorative bags, plastic puzzles wrapped in mesh, UNO cards, cards, tea candles, small glass boxes for tea candles, mugs, wooden blocks, puzzles, and small plastic photo albums. However, the supervisor was adamant that we were forbidden from taking anything until our assignment was completed.

Suspicion and conflict pervaded our work at the warehouse. Throughout the day the supervisor carefully monitored our activities. I often looked up from sweeping to see him staring at us. When we took breaks, he became impatient and, after only a few minutes, instructed us to return to work. However, Fatime refused to comply and routinely asked for more time to finish smoking. The supervisor was visibly annoyed but acquiesced. On other occasions, though, he was less amenable. A wheelbarrow stood next to the door but the supervisor forbade us from using it, insisting that we transport everything by hand in torn, singed, or wet boxes. In an effort to construct sturdier containers, Fatime requested packing tape to seal holes and join cardboard scraps into functional containers. Eventually, the supervisor handed her a small roll with the proviso that it be utilized sparingly. But after Fatime applied a few strips to a single box, he said she had used enough and confiscated the tape. While Chinese merchants also occupied marginal positions within the city and relied on scavengers' labor, they regarded us with detached opprobrium. These two groups were separated by a chasm even wider than that between Serbs and *cigani*.

Alongside the Chinese employees, three Serbs were also working in the warehouse. Unlike the supervisor, they did not attempt to surveil our activities and seemed unconcerned about the potential theft of Chinese merchandise. Nevertheless, we were treated as *cigani*, with a typical mix of disdain and familiarity. As occurred on supermarket loading docks, the

Serbs never handed items directly to us. When we bent over to gather broken pots from the ground, a Serbian worker "helped" by kicking stray
shards at us. Several narrowly missed hitting us in the face. However, the
Serbs took more interest in conversing with us than with their Chinese
coworkers. One man loudly called Bekim a *cigan* before asking how many
children he possessed. Bekim, not wishing to discuss his family after being
insulted, replied he had three children and quickly walked away. Another
Serb pulled out a folding chair displaying a woman's thong and asked
Fatime if she liked to wear such garments. Fatime remained silent. These
interactions mirrored those that occurred on the city's streets and in
Miško's truck. Although Ashkali were marginalized, they belonged in a way
that the Chinese did not. Scavengers' ordinariness made them approacha-
ble. Consequently, Ashkali were aggressively confronted by Serbian perceptions of *cigani* but were too fearful to repudiate them. The Chinese supervisor might have scrutinized Bekim's behavior, but the Serbian workers called
him a *cigan* and made sexually suggestive comments to his wife.

As the day wore on, we settled into a fatiguing routine of scooping up
debris, hauling deteriorating boxes to the dumpsters, sweeping floors, and
piling our items outside. By one o'clock, my back and arms were in constant pain. Numerous cuts adorned my hands, inflicted by the broken
cups and pots that I was collecting. Bekim, Fatime, and Endrit were hurt-
ing just as much as I was. Weary, Endrit returned to the settlement with
Fitim. By this time all four dumpsters were filled but a significant amount
of debris still needed to be removed. With no other receptacles available,
Bekim and I piled additional rubbish on the adjacent ground. Late in the
afternoon Bekim was allowed to begin transporting merchandise to Polje
while Fatime and I continued laboring in the warehouse. Soon, the
Serbian and Chinese workers left for the day and only the supervisor
remained. Although we were exhausted, he would not allow us to depart
until the building and its surroundings were cleaned to his satisfaction.

It was almost six o'clock when the supervisor declared that our work
was completed. However, we still needed to dispose of several boxes of
trash and transport a significant amount of merchandise to Polje. Wanting
to get home, Bekim was determined to make a single trip. He packed the
cart to overflowing and hung bags of items on its sides. The final boxes of
debris were placed on the bench and then, with no place to sit, we walked

Lucky to the dumpster. Once the trash was deposited, Bekim and Fatime took their seats. There was no room for me in the front so I gingerly scaled the mountain of merchandise and splayed my body over its summit to establish a firm perch. Bekim slowly urged Lucky forward in an effort to keep the boxes and myself in place. But instead of driving directly to Polje, he stopped in front of a *prodavnica*. We had worked the entire day but, between us, had eaten only a single packet of chocolate wafers and drunk two bottles of soda. We were famished. Bekim bought a limited number of cheap staples: soda, cheese, cold cuts, bread, ketchup, mayonnaise, and yogurt. Sitting under a shady tree, we ravenously shoveled the food into our mouths. Our hands were stained black with dirt and before long a dark film covered the cheese, meat, and bread.

No sooner had we filled out bellies than Bekim's cellphone rang. It was Endrit. Two loan sharks had arrived at the settlement and were impatiently awaiting Bekim's return. They expected him to make a substantial payment toward his debt. Instead of cash, Bekim intended to trade the merchandise. Informing Endrit that he would return shortly, he urged us back onto the cart. During the twenty-minute trip to the settlement, Endrit phoned another five times, stressing that the men were upset at Bekim's tardiness and could become violent. Bekim responded calmly and made no effort to speed Lucky's careful gait. When we finally entered Polje, a Romani boy shouted a greeting and disappeared behind the cart. Bekim, believing the boy was pilfering goods, told me to watch the cargo closely. Bekim and Fatime were returning home after an exhausting day of labor, filth, hunger, surveillance, and stigmatization but the settlement offered little respite: others were waiting to appropriate their earnings.

Pulling up to the shack, I saw Endrit, Drita, Agim, Emine, and Fadil waiting outside with two men. Bekim stepped down from the cart and exchanged curt pleasantries with the visitors while everyone else stood tensely on the sidelines. Clearly, this was not a friendly visit. As soon as Endrit and I began unloading the cart, the men broke off their conversation with Bekim and, without seeking permission, began inspecting the contents of each box. Their scrutiny was so intrusive that Emine surreptitiously raised her hands over her head and silently screamed in exasperation. Endrit nervously motioned for her to stop lest the men see her and take offense. Once everything was off the cart, a heated negotiation ensued. The loan sharks insisted that the merchandise was worth a pittance, while Endrit and Bekim argued the opposite. To demonstrate the potential value of the items, Drita quickly cleaned a few teacups, saucers, and ashtrays. After more haggling, they reached an agreement. Bekim would receive a credit of 10,000 dinars ($105) for the entire lot. Later, he confessed that the price seemed fair but, in reality, Bekim had no choice but to accept the offer. Yet again, his aspirations were constrained.

Considering the effort Ashkali usually expended to secure even a small income, Endrit felt that netting almost €100 for a single day's work was a bonanza. Indeed, I never again saw Bekim and Fatime earn so much money in such a short period. This largesse was only possible because of Chinese trade, the disposability of their mass-produced goods, and, crucially, war. The conflicts that displaced Ashkali also precipitated a neoliberal order in which Chinese merchants could prosper as independent entrepreneurs, who in turn created opportunities for scavengers through trash. The low cost of Chinese goods ensured that they were expendable in a way that other commodities in Belgrade were not. Consequently, these objects supplied Serbs with cheap merchandise and scavengers with an additional income. But as much as our work at the warehouse represented a significant windfall for Bekim's family, it had a negligible effect on their lives. Bekim's debts were reduced but he still owed over €900 ($1,125). Thus, there was no rest for Bekim or Fatime. The next day they were once again scavenging through the dumpsters.

While the Chinese merchandise provided a fleeting income, the materiality of these wares persisted. Fatime decorated the shack with stickers and ornaments from the warehouse. She saved wooden blocks and puzzle pieces to stoke the stove. In a gesture of goodwill she gave several mugs, ashtrays, and bags to Romani neighbors. Weeks later, Petra served me coffee in these cups. In most cases, though, the gifts were quickly discarded in front of shacks and along the lane. For months to come, I passed Jonas Brothers bags, UNO cards, and Christmas mugs strewn around the settlement's landscape. In a marginal space such as Polje, disposable commodities were remarkably enduring. Scavengers retrieved item after item from the dumpsters and these goods were routinely abandoned in and around the settlement. But Polje was not simply suffused with trash; its trash had a history. In this case the Jonas Brothers bags, UNO cards, and

Christmas mugs were decaying yet lasting reminders of our work at the Chinese warehouse. Because garbage was inescapable, it marked the passage of time and memory in a world where other resources were ephemeral. Ultimately, trash lived in Polje, sharing spaces, potentialities, and biographies with its Ashkali neighbors.

IMPERFECT TRANSFORMATIONS

Despite Bekim's hopes, owning a horse did not result in prosperity. The family often went hungry and, on some nights, dinner consisted of nothing more than rice, bread, and salad. On a few occasions they lacked even the cash for soda. To survive, Bekim borrowed more and more money from Gazmend and Fitim. When he failed to make payments on time, they threatened to take Lucky. Desperate, he traded Lucky for a smaller mare and received €150 ($188) in compensation. While this allowed him to repay some of his debts, Bekim was still financially overburdened. Within a few months he was struggling even more than before. As soon as Bekim began receiving threats from loan sharks, Gazmend proved unwilling to help further. Having no other choice, Bekim sold his horse. The next day, he bought a *trokolica* and went back to pedaling from dumpster to dumpster.

Losing Lucky severely strained Bekim's relationships with other Ashkali. Gazmend, for instance, grew exasperated with Bekim's chronic insolvency. On the increasingly infrequent occasions that they spoke, Gazmend lectured Bekim about his responsibilities to Fatime and urged him to be more industrious. These reprimands infuriated Bekim, who complained that Gazmend's wealth came from his children in Germany, not hard work. Eventually, Bekim ceased all communication with Gazmend. Gazmend attributed these actions to selfishness, saying Bekim had no interest in a relationship that did not benefit him financially. Accepting the new status quo, Gazmend remarked that he was not going to force anyone to talk to him. As the conflict wore on, Fitim, Endrit, and Rajim sided with Gazmend. Rajim often observed that Bekim was incapable of managing his finances responsibly. He wryly commented that even if Bekim was in the middle of a bank vault, he would still be penniless. Meanwhile, Bekim claimed that his Ashkali neighbors were like politicians, lying to get what they wanted.

Frustrated, he vowed to withdraw from Ashkali social life. Bekim's estrangement only intensified as more and more Ashkali left Polje. Endrit, Drita, Agim, and Emine returned to Kosovo while Fadil and his family departed for asylum in Germany. Within a few months, only Bekim's family, Gazmend, and his wife remained in Polje. Bekim's shack, which had been a hive of Ashkali activity, now seemed desolate.

With his Ashkali neighbors gone, Bekim decided to move his family into the center of the settlement and purchased Harun's former shack. In the past Bekim remained aloof from Romani residents, but now he courted them. Only a year earlier he refused to invite Roma to his daughter's birthday party, saying they were dirty and lecherous. But once in his new shack, Bekim and his family were gradually incorporated into the Romani social world. Bekim began purchasing and reselling metal with Harun and Miloš. If he needed advice, Bekim turned to Aleksander, not Gazmend. Meanwhile, Fatime struck up a close friendship with Jovana. On hot summer days Bekim's family accompanied their Romani neighbors to the riverbank where they picnicked under shady trees, drank beer, and swam in the cool water. In the evenings Roma invited Bekim and Fatime to their parties. When the hosts served pork, Bekim consumed it with gusto, unconcernedly flouting Muslim prohibitions. Fatime also rejected Ashkali norms by expressing a desire to have her children's names tattooed down her arm.

Rajim and Gazmend were shocked by Bekim and Fatime's new behavior. Gazmend wondered how they could spend so much time with people of another religion who possessed such different values. He was particularly concerned that Bekim was impoverishing his household by purchasing alcohol for Romani parties. Annoyed, Gazmend declared that Bekim had become a lazy Rom. Rajim shared this perspective. After discovering Bekim relaxing by the river with Roma, he shook his head and wrinkled his nose. Bekim, he said, was dirty just like a Rom. To drive his point home, Rajim added that Bekim's shack was strewn with filth and stank. Although Bekim had few interactions with Ashkali, he was aware of their censure. He attempted to rebut these accusations by stating that Harun, Miloš, and Aleksander were more accepting and, most importantly, more successful than Ashkali.

Ultimately, Bekim hoped that his friendships with Roma would result in economic opportunities. Despite losing his horse, he still aspired to learn the village metal trade. Harun and Miloš repeatedly promised to form scavenging partnerships with Bekim, but joint expeditions never materialized. As Gazmend observed months earlier, Roma had no desire to share their routes. Nevertheless, an opportunity presented itself when Miloš agreed to take me scavenging in the villages. Bekim assumed he would accompany us and made an agreement with Miloš: the men would pool their cash, collect and buy metal together, and split any profits at the end of the day.

On the appointed morning Bekim and I arrived at Miloš's shack at nine o'clock. He had emerged from bed moments before and was wearing a T-shirt that declared, "I'm a Legend in Japan." After drinking a quick cup of coffee, he harnessed his gelding and we drove out of the settlement. As we passed Gazmend's shack, I noticed Fitim, Valon, and two other Ashkali men sorting metal. They looked up at us but failed to offer a greeting or even a wave. This was a blatantly discourteous act and reflected the extent to which Bekim's relationships with other Ashkali had deteriorated. Once on the main street, Miloš urged the horse on, kicking him until the desired speed was achieved. Soon we passed the greenmarket where the security guards confronted Bekim, Fatime, her sisters, and me. Then, without the slightest hesitation, Miloš steered the cart onto the shoulder of a busy freeway. Cars sped past us but neither he nor his horse appeared concerned. Finally, he took an offramp and turned onto a small street lined with a few shops. We followed this road for several minutes before Miloš declared we had arrived at our destination. Our surroundings were more reminiscent of a rural suburb than a village. A series of small lanes ran between modest two-story homes. A few shops—a bakery, *prodavnica*, butcher, and small clothing store—dotted what appeared to be the main road. In one direction, train tracks delineated the border between the village and fields beyond. In the other, a few of Belgrade's high-rise apartments were visible on the horizon.

Miloš pulled the cart off the road, dismounted, and removed a car battery, loudspeaker, and microphone from the rear. He placed the battery under the seat and affixed the loudspeaker to a wooden stick tied to the cart's frame. Taking the exposed wires from the loudspeaker, he gingerly tied them around the battery's terminals. As soon as he heard a loud crackle, Miloš plugged in the microphone. Ready at last, he urged the horse down a small street flanked with homes. Driving slowly, he spoke into the microphone: "Old iron, old refrigerators, old batteries, old radiators, old boilers, we are buying." Miloš had raised the volume to its highest setting and his entreaties blared across the neighborhood. When we reached the end of the street, he made two right turns, and repeated the process in the parallel lane. Although Miloš encouraged him to use the megaphone, Bekim demurred, clearly uncomfortable at being so visible. Unlike dumpster work, our success here depended upon our conspicuousness.[21]

We drove up and down for an hour before a man whistled at us from his yard. He disappeared inside a small shed and emerged with a rusted bed frame. We received the item for free but it would fetch very little money at the junkyard. Frustrated at our lack of success, Bekim suggested abandoning this area for another closer to the settlement. However, Miloš firmly refused and continued along the road. Our next interactions occurred over an hour later, as we drove past a row of small shops. A visibly intoxicated Rom offered to sell us a small water heater for 400 dinars ($4.20). Miloš refused, saying it was worth no more than half that price. While we were still stopped, a Serb hailed us and produced a heavily dented wheel rim with a flat tire still in place. Again, Miloš declined to pay money for the item, this time because it was too damaged. Clearly, the villages did not contain the plethora of metal that Bekim had imagined.

Hungry, we decided to take a lunch break. After purchasing bread, soda, bologna, buttermilk, and spicy peppers from a *prodavnica*, we pulled down a small lane and stopped under a shady tree. As we ate, Miloš reminisced about his life and family. He had arrived in Polje at the age of ten and learned to scavenge metal soon thereafter. He was now thirty-three years old and had three siblings: Jovana, who was married to Harun, another sister, who was living in Germany, and a brother, who was serving time in prison for theft. Families like this were typical in Polje. For many, the only real options included remaining in the settlement, incarceration, or seeking asylum in the EU.

While Miloš talked, Bekim's phone began to ring. It was Fatime and she was upset. Nikola was demanding the immediately repayment of a 2,000 dinar ($21) loan. Bekim told her that he could not return to the settlement and, anyway, he lacked the cash. Given our dismal yield thus far, he was certain that we would not earn this amount by the end of the day. Irritated, Bekim told her to sell the phone and use the proceeds to pay

Nikola. Hanging up, he shrugged. What else could he do? Bekim might have left Polje but his social and financial responsibilities were inescapable and unrelenting. Luckily, Fatime was resourceful. She convinced Stanislav to pay Nikola and assume the debt, giving them four more days before the money was due.

With lunch finished, we resumed driving back and forth through the neighborhood. This time, a Serb on a bicycle offered to sell a pile of scrap metal and two refrigerators. For the first time all day, Miloš was excited by the prospect of a sizeable haul. Refrigerators' metal exteriors were not worth much but their motors commanded a high price. We began driving to the man's home only to have a cart filled with Bayash overtake us. Competition among scavengers in the villages could be fierce and Miloš was concerned that these men would claim the refrigerators first. Fortunately, they turned off the road, bound for a different destination. Breathing a sigh of relief, Miloš pulled up in front of a small house. But upon inspection the stockpile failed to meet expectations: the refrigerators were small and lacked motors while the loose metal was negligible. Miloš proposed 200 dinars ($2.10) but the man insisted on 300 ($3.15). Refusing to negotiate, Miloš was preparing to depart when Bekim urged him to reconsider. But Miloš remained resolute, saying he knew what metal was truly worth. At this point, the man relented and we collected the items.

It was now late afternoon and Miloš decided we should depart for home. But the detour to find the refrigerators had disoriented him. Unsure of the exact route, he began looking for familiar landmarks. We had not gone very far before encountering a group of Bayash who had previously lived in Polje. After exchanging pleasantries, they agreed to let us follow them home. Unlike Miloš, the Bayash avoided driving on major roads, opting for rural routes instead. As we rode behind them over dirt tracks and through fields, I noticed the contents of their cart. They managed to find a boiler, a few scraps of iron, and a couple of meters of metal fencing. They fared no better than us. Contrary to Bekim's assertions, it was clear that working in the villages did not predictably yield vast amounts of metal.

Finally, we emerged at a familiar intersection and Miloš, confident he could continue alone, bid farewell to our escort. Bekim suggested that we make a small detour to his brother's home, which was nearby. Miloš readily agreed, parked the horse under a tree, and followed us to Ezgon's house.

Although Miloš and Bekim had been acquaintances for a decade, neither knew much about the other's background or family. Their relationship was rooted in the present: a shared experience of Polje and a desire to earn money. This, and the stark divide between Ashkali and Roma, was on clear display as Ezgon invited us to sit outside and chat. In the past I had always been asked indoors, but today Miloš's presence barred us from entry. Ezgon did not want a Rom inside his home. When Miloš casually inquired about the house, Ezgon instructed me to recount its history. Clearly, this was intended to demonstrate that a foreigner knew more about Bekim's family than did his supposed Romani friend. As soon as the coffee was finished, Miloš was ready to leave. We were saying our farewells when Bekim spotted a woman pushing a wheelbarrow full of metal objects that included a DVD player, a coffee maker, pots, knives, pans, cans, and a sink. Bekim asked for a price but she demurred, telling him to bid first. Unsure, Bekim glanced at Miloš, who offered 500 dinars ($5.25). She agreed and we loaded everything onto the cart.

On the ride back to the settlement, Bekim's mood improved dramatically. Pleased that we had finally obtained a reasonable amount of metal, he began playing music on his cellphone and then held it up to the loudspeaker. The cart blared Balkan Beats as we drove through the suburbs. Using loudspeakers in populated areas could draw police attention, but on this occasion Bekim and Miloš did not care. Despite their merriment, there was little to celebrate. The scrap netted only 600 dinars ($6.30) for each man. Tellingly, they found the largest portion of their haul not in a village, but in front of Ezgon's home. Bekim had hoped that canvassing the villages would provide an income of €50 ($63) a day but he discovered otherwise. Whether Polje's residents were recycling paper, metal, or goods, they were economically constrained. As we arrived back in the settlement, Miloš explained that metal, like every other form of scavenging, was uncertain.

In a circumscribed space, financial aspirations produced intractable and unstable socialities. Bekim's poverty prompted his public realignment. His desire for economic advancement drew him closer to Roma while his inability to repay Gazmend pulled him away from Ashkali. Crucially, he could not survive on his own. Abandoned to a space of exception, Polje's residents relied on symbiotic relationships for essentials such as loans, labor, guidance, and friendship. As Bekim's ties to Ashkali frayed, he had little choice but to look to Romani men like Miloš. He continued to share a language and history with other Ashkali but they increasingly called him a dirty Rom. Meanwhile, Roma invited Bekim to their parties but they did not significantly involve him in their scavenging enterprises. Although Bekim became ethnically liminal, his identity as a *cigan* remained fixed. His position was insecure within Polje but intractable without. Paralleling this shift was Bekim's struggle to expand his access to trash including boxes from the greenmarket, Chinese merchandise, and metal from villages. In each case he attempted to negotiate the identity of garbage, for instance with security guards or Chinese merchants. But as with his own identity, this was hampered. Although Bekim strove to alter his status, he could not overcome the social and economic boundaries that circumscribed his life in Polje.

Bekim's precarity was profound and led to a major crisis. A few days after we visited the village, he began to suspect that Fatime was having an affair with Miloš. The evidence was unsubstantiated but Bekim was nevertheless convinced. Livid, he wanted to confront them but could not. Leveling such an accusation would destroy his fragile social web. Harun was tactlessly mocked for Jovana's extramarital affairs and Bekim did not want to be the subject of jokes or pity. Having few palatable options, he remained silent but distanced himself from Miloš and aggressively monitored Fatime's movements.[22] Nevertheless, this tension eventually erupted into public view. When Nikola made an offhand remark about Fatime's lack of virtue, Bekim lost control. Instead of alleging sexual impropriety, he accused Miloš of spreading malicious gossip. This quickly escalated into a physical confrontation, with Bekim running inside his shack, grabbing a knife, and attacking Miloš. The scuffle was intense but brief. Other residents immediately separated the men and Bekim soon returned to his home cursing loudly. No one was physically injured but other damage was done. Bekim's aspirations of building a new and valuable social world had collapsed. Angry and disillusioned, he sold his shack and left Polje.

5 Relocations

The day after his argument with Miloš, Bekim packed his belongings and moved into a small brick home not far from Polje. It lay next to Rajim's house and was surrounded by fields and pastures. The walls of the illegal shack-sized structure were erected by a Serb in less than a month but he failed to add a roof. Rajim purchased the house and then sold it to Endrit, who wanted a part-time residence in Belgrade. With the help of Valon, Fitim, and other Ashkali, Endrit constructed a roof from an amalgam of recycled materials including a box from the US embassy in Jakarta and a tarp emblazoned with the UNDP logo. Knowing that Endrit was in Kosovo and the house was unoccupied, Bekim offered to buy it for €250 ($313). Endrit agreed, concerned that his daughter might not have a roof over her head otherwise.

On the morning of the move, Bekim, Fatime, and I entered the house to find "Agim" spray-painted on one wall, old moldy clothes strewn across the concrete floor, and a multitude of flies buzzing through the stale air. The two small windows could not be opened. Outside, a refrigerator's Styrofoam skeleton lay in a yard of overgrown grass and trash. Fatime and I began clearing the interior of debris while Bekim and Harun transported the family's belongings from Polje. Soon, Harun bid us farewell and

Fatime prepared lunch, a simple soup containing scavenged tomatoes. Once we had eaten, Bekim and I gathered the detritus in the yard, formed it into a pile, and set it alight. Indoors, Fatime laid rugs over the floor, positioned the chest and couches, displayed family photos, and suspended wall hangings depicting mosques in Istanbul and Mecca. Finally, Bekim pulled the derelict refrigerator under the shade of a tree and we rested on this makeshift bench. Before long, Rajim appeared carrying a cable. It took him less than thirty minutes to connect the electricity and depart.

As the sun began to set, I was struck by the silence. In Polje, families would be standing outside discussing the day's events. Here, there was no one. Fatime desperately missed the activity of the settlement and complained that the house was miserable. Any shack was preferable to this, she said. Once the lights came on, we headed inside and, with nothing else to do, watched a series of movies: a black-and-white drama about the Second World War followed by a Jackie Chan comedy. Around midnight, Fatime and the children curled up on the couches and fell asleep. After unscrewing the light so they could sleep, Bekim began discussing the day's events. The move had taken an emotional toll. Not only was he in conflict with a man he had considered a close friend, Bekim was cut off from the settlement's sociality. With his face dimly illumined by the glow of the television, he veered between threating to hire thugs to assault Miloš and steeling himself for the loneliness of the next several weeks. Despite his feelings of isolation, Bekim believed the house was a positive step for his family. He was ready to escape the gossip, dirt, and crime. Unlike a shack, he thought this house could provide security for his family. Or maybe, Bekim quietly mused, they would leave Belgrade altogether and apply for asylum in Germany. Either way, he said, his life would be better soon.

Bekim's departure from Polje was unexpected but not unusual. The population of Belgrade's settlements was always in flux. Some families resided in Polje for years or even decades, but countless more came and went. A few, like Bekim and his brother Ezgon, moved into permanent structures that they believed would provide the stability and legitimacy that a shack could not. Others, dissatisfied with the meagre income earned through the trash, chose to travel to the EU, register as asylum seekers, and collect social benefits until their cases were adjudicated. A third group returned to Kosovo, taking possession of newly constructed homes funded by NGOs and foreign governments. While many of these relocations were voluntary, some were forced. As the Serbian government continued to tear down settlements and evict their inhabitants, Ashkali and Roma were unambiguously managed by the state. Occupants of bulldozed shacks were either housed in metal shipping containers or, in rare cases, placed directly into social housing. A mix of state strategies and scavengers' aspirations propelled settlement residents throughout the EU, Kosovo, Serbia, and Belgrade. Nevertheless, Ashkali and Roma continued to inhabit excepted spaces including refugee centers, rural villages, and container communities.

Governments created detached geographies for *cigani* and transferred people between them by employing biopolitical strategies to delineate space and reinscribe national identity.[1] European nations endorsed minority rights, but principles of equality were ignored in these contexts.[2] Crucially, when the state positioned Ashkali and Roma on its margins, it often separated them from the resource upon which they most relied: garbage. Not only were scavengers socially and spatially isolated, they were effectively denied even a precarious income. Because they were unable to resurrect commodities in their new homes, most relocated families maintained ties to settlements out of necessity. Even those with apartments in Belgrade or houses in Kosovo continued to frequent Polje. Consequently, state efforts to resettle Ashkali and Roma did not sever their ties to settlements; rather, it reinforced them. Polje's residents might move out of their shacks, but a reliance on trash ensured that they would be perpetually displaced among multiple zones of exclusion.

FROM SHACKS TO HOUSES

Many of Polje's residents would live in shacks during their time in Belgrade, but a few were able to move into houses. A number of Romani neighborhoods existed throughout the city and this is where most Ashkali and Romani settled. Unlike container settlements, social welfare apartments, or homes in Kosovo, these houses were not funded by the state or NGOs. Reports indicate that family-financed homes are one model for improving Romani housing, but they concede that most settlement residents are unable to afford this option.[3] Indeed, independent homeownership required significant financial resources to purchase land and an edifice. Those with less cash sought to offset this handicap with ingenuity. Individuals could reduce costs by procuring materials and building their own structure. When I asked one Ashkali man how he learned masonry, he replied, "When you live like we do, you have to know." Although homeowners no longer lived in shacks, many were still responsible for constructing their abodes and were limited to spaces reserved for *cigani*. These constraints can be illustrated by examining Rajim's, Ezgon's, and Goran's transitions from shacks to houses.

Rajim's decision to build a house was the result of necessity and opportunity. He commented that although he disliked living in a shack, Zgrade was at least populated with friends and kin. His parents and brother's family were residents and provided a support system for him, his wife, four daughters, and two sons. This abruptly ended when Zgrade was razed. While his relatives decided to return to Kosovo, Rajim was determined to remain in Belgrade. But he was unwilling to move his large family to a resettlement center and did not relish living in a shack surrounded by Roma. Fortunately, Rajim had managed to save a bit of money and he purchased a plot of land in the fields behind Polje. He was adamant that the deed was legal but admitted that one of his neighbors disputed this. There was no question, however, that his house was illegal and constructed without permits. Rajim simply bought the necessary materials and began the work himself, although he did employ a mason to assist him from time to time. The house was built in stages, beginning with a single room. As Rajim earned more money, he added to it. By the time I first visited, the structure was almost finished and only a small gap in the roof remained.

Around half of the house's area was devoted to a large multipurpose room. It abutted an open kitchen and sported a china cabinet displaying several sets of immaculate plates, platters, cups, and saucers. On the top shelf stood a metal statue of four horses that Rajim had found in a dumpster. Three smaller rooms were used for entertaining guests and sleeping. One of these served as a living room and boasted a television and computer. However, these devices only functioned in the evening, when the streetlights were operating. The house was not supplied with electricity or water so Rajim utilized an illicit cable. Smaller appliances, such as fans, were powered during the day using a car battery. On the walls, Rajim's daughters had displayed posters of Ronaldo and Neymar. To further high-light their devotion, the girls hung banners with the players' names writ-ten in Cyrillic script. Unlike Bekim's children, Rajim's were literate and attended school. Nevertheless, they did not view education as a priority. Altin, Rajim's son, enjoyed learning English but anticipated dropping out as soon as he turned fourteen and could work full-time.

Rajim's home, with its computer, Cyrillic banners, and china cabinet, stood in stark contrast to Polje's shacks. Although he regularly visited the settlement, Rajim distinguished himself from its residents. At the crux of his narrative was the notion of entrepreneurship. Rajim asserted that his house was the result of hard work. He assured me that only lazy scavengers were poor. As proof, he pointed to a pile of metal that Altin had collected during his school's spring break. Rajim concluded that if a child could gather this in his spare time, an adult should be able to do much better. Unlike many other Ashkali, Rajim seldom scavenged paper and supple-mented his income completing odd jobs for his Serbian and Romani neigh-bors. His daughter bragged that he was a master of many trades and able to repair engines, electronics, and a range of small machinery. One week he was being paid 6,000 dinars ($63) to overhaul an engine while the next he was getting 7,500 dinars ($79) to tow a broken-down car. With the suc-cessful completion of each job, Rajim's reputation grew, allowing him to amass a loyal client base. Nevertheless, collecting and trading items from the dumpsters continued to be a prominent feature of his family's life.

Rajim's shift from a settlement to a house was not unique. Bekim's elder brother, Ezgon, also made the transition but under different circum-stances. After Zgrade's destruction, Ezgon moved his family into a shack in Polje, where he lived in close proximity to his brother. However, Ezgon quickly became frustrated with his Romani neighbors, complaining that they were either cheating someone or stealing from them. When the wheels of his *trokolica* disappeared, Ezgon had enough. He and his family rented a small home in another municipality for over a year while he saved money and solicited his in-laws for financial assistance. Finally, he paid €2,500 ($3,125) for an existing house in a suburban neighborhood. At last, he said, his family had a permanent home.

Although Ezgon had security, he still inhabited a segregated and con-cealed space designed to house *cigani*. On my initial visit Bekim led me through a quiet Serbian suburb, where trees shaded single-family homes and the streets saw little traffic. We stopped at a small bridge spanning a narrow gully dug for a decommissioned railway line and Bekim pointed downwards. Ezgon's house lay sixteen meters below. But from the bridge I could discern no sign of it. Bekim escorted me to a concealed set of stairs and we began the descent. Eventually, we intersected a muddy road that provided access to Ezgon's small community. Arriving at the bottom, I saw that the gully's floor was lined with a row of houses. At first, I was certain that this was another illegal settlement but, as I came to discover, this was not the case. The community's roots dated to the 1970s when building was strictly controlled and illegal edifices were rarely tolerated. The original Romani residents had obtained permission from the municipality to settle here and, as a result, many of houses were legal and had official addresses. More recently, however, newcomers built shacks alongside existing structures, causing the population to swell. Nonetheless, the community remained confined to the gully and largely unnoticed by the Serbs living above.

As I approached Ezgon's yard, I saw it was littered with items to recycle: plastic bottles, paper, and metal. His house was made of brick and the exterior was unpainted. Inside, a narrow hallway opened into a large windowless room with a kitchen niche on one side. At the very rear, a smaller bedroom sported two windows. All of the interior walls were painted lilac and trimmed in white, while the doors and windows were adorned with valances. Unlike Rajim, Ezgon had legal access to the power grid and was able to run his television and electric range during the day. The house lacked interior running water but there was a spigot in the yard.

Although Ezgon and his wife, Ajshe, possessed more amenities than did settlement residents, she observed that a Serbian family would never live in these conditions. Conscious of the entrenched disparities circumscribing their lives, Ajshe had become resigned to marginality. Unable to improve her family's overall prospects, she focused on the house. Ajshe was pregnant with their second child and she worried that the current structure would be too small to accommodate the growing family. In response, Ezgon secured a loan from his father-in-law and purchased bricks, cement, and drywall. A few weeks later, Ezgon had added a room. When I told him that I was impressed with how much he did in a relatively short period, Ezgon shrugged. It changed very little, he said, but at least they had more space than before.

As with Rajim and Ezgon, Polje's Bayash residents achieved homeownership through a mix of aspirations, resources, and unexpected events. Although they had already built houses in their village, its distance from the city and lack of economic opportunities ensured that they would never permanently settle there. Belgrade, Goran said, was their real home. After spending a generation living as squatters, they wanted the security that only legal ownership could provide. Furthermore, several families possessed the means to do so. Decades of scavenging metal allowed some individuals to accumulate significant monetary resources that Polje's other residents did not have. But ultimately it was two tragedies that finally pushed Bayash families out of the settlement: a shack burned down, killing three children, and then the settlement was flooded, damaging homes and destroying possessions. Rather than be surrounded by trash, bad memories, and uncertainty, they bought property, built houses, and removed their shacks from Polje.

Bayash families approached home ownership as they did the recycling trade: collectively. First, monetary contributions from each family were combined to purchase land near the settlement. They paid €30,000 ($37,500) for five acres, a high price that no other group in the settlement could have afforded. The parcel was approximately one kilometer from Rajim's home and lay between a small road and shallow creek. Most importantly, this location still provided Bayash with ample access to their income source: the trash just beyond Polje's boundary. With the deed signed, families began erecting houses. Because of its rural setting, the property lacked municipal services. Rather than rely on illicit connections as Rajim had done, Bayash paid to have power and water lines extended to the lot. Soon they relocated the mountains of scrap and machinery from Polje and the new compound was bustling with activity. Sitting in front of his house, Goran spoke positively about the move. With permanence, he said, came more responsibility. Residents no longer littered and instead made an effort to beautify their surroundings. Parents also began sending their children to school in greater numbers. But in the midst of these changes, some things remained the same. Given the difficulty navigating state bureaucracy, only one Bayash man was an official resident of Belgrade. Everyone else remained registered in their village.

Although Bayash families now owned the land upon which they lived, only six could initially afford a house. Bayash cooperated, but economic differences suffused the group. Goran, one of the wealthiest individuals, spent €6,000 ($7,500) on property alone and was able to construct one of the largest homes in the compound. In contrast, Veljko paid €1,000 ($1,250) for his plot but lacked additional cash to fund a permanent structure. Consequently, he and his wife, Jelena, erected a shack but planned to build in brick as soon as they could find the means to do so. Even though Veljko's family was still living in a home of recycled materials, he said their life was significantly better. Not only would they never face the threat of eviction, he possessed a reliable connection to the energy grid. Homeowners with legal electricity strung cables to their neighbors' shacks, ensuring that everyone had power. In return, Veljko and the others paid for their usage each month. However, a couple of households were unable to afford even this cost. Bogdan's family, for example, rarely possessed funds for electricity, let alone land. In an act of charity, his *kum* shouldered this expense.

Certainly the biggest determinant of homeownership was wealth. Goran routinely recycled a considerable amount of metal, Rajim possessed valuable skills, and Ezgon had prosperous in-laws. Consequently, houses were much more than dwellings; they functioned as cultural capital. All three men routinely stressed that they were unlike those inhabiting shacks. Rajim often crinkled his nose in disgust while remarking that he could not live like people in Polje. His children echoed these views, dismissing those in the settlement, including Bekim's sons, as dirty and uneducated. On one hand, there did seem to be a stark difference between Rajim's home and Bekim's shack. When I visited Rajim, we drank hot tea in matching glasses while soberly discussing current events. Occasionally, Altin asked for help with his English homework. In many ways this seemed a world away from the dirt, trash, cursing, and noise of Polje. On the other hand, it was not. Rajim no longer lived in the settlement but he was not far away. His family still inhabited an illegal structure in circumscribed space that lacked electricity and running water. Ezgon's and Goran's homes were similarly segregated. Crucially, all three men continued to rely on garbage. One of Rajim's most prized possessions, his horse statue, was from a dumpster.

Although Ezgon was able to leave Polje, his brother was not. The day after Bekim's family moved into the small house, he and Endrit began to fight. Bekim accused Endrit of inflating the price and attempting to sell the home to another buyer, while Endrit worried that Bekim would not pay him as promised. Endrit was particularly wary, recalling that Bekim had cheated him before. Bekim's estrangement from the Ashkali community coupled with his inability to make a monetary deposit further complicated their negotiations. While the two men attempted to reach an agreement, Bekim and Fatime grew ever more restless. They missed the unceasing activity of Polje and, despite Bekim's feud with Miloš, visited as often as possible. However, if Bekim was working, Fatime was housebound. Due to concerns for her safety and the difficulty of managing four children alone, Fatime could not walk to the settlement without an escort. Although she had felt confined in Polje, Fatime at least had the ability to socialize with others. Now she was completely sequestered and it immediately began taking a toll on her emotional well-being. When Endrit accused Bekim of "holding his dick all day" instead of working to pay for the house, Bekim marched into Polje and bought Sara's old shack for 5,000 dinars ($53). He moved his family back to the settlement the next morning. They had only spent four nights in the house.

Bekim's brief attempt to relocate elicited sardonic comments from Gazmend and Rajim. They said that he loved Polje, and Roma, too much to leave. Certainly settlements exerted a strong pull on their residents. Bekim and Fatime relied on Polje's social and economic networks. Without these connections the family was isolated, particularly given its rupture with other Ashkali. Rajim and Ezgon were successful in their relocations, in part, because they forged relationships with their new neighbors. In contrast, Bayash did not need to establish new bonds because they moved their entire community. But in each case, none of these families completely left the settlements. Rajim's house and the Bayash compound were next door to Polje, whereas Ezgon inhabited a space that strongly resembled a settlement. Crucially, trash remained a central feature of their lives and this would never change. In the end, the limited social and economic opportunities circumscribing Ashkali existence were more impactful than the type of structure that they inhabited. For Bekim, a brick house alone could not replace the tug of Polje.

STATE REMOVALS, STATE RESETTLEMENT

Zgrade's destruction motivated Rajim and Ezgon to find houses, but most of their neighbors were unable to afford permanent accommodation. When settlements were razed, almost all of their inhabitants were resettled by the state. As a result, Ashkali and Roma were increasingly subjected to government bureaucracy and oversight. Amnesty International estimates that from 2009 to 2013 over 2,500 people were evicted from settlements in and around Belgrade.[4] Removals, as the Serbian government dubbed them, followed a similar pattern. In many cases, the city delayed informing residents of their settlement's demolition to forestall legal action.[5] Then, on the appointed day, bulldozers appeared and flattened every structure, while residents watched from the sidelines. Ashkali and Roma not only lost their homes; any belongings that they could not carry with them were also destroyed. Generally, inhabitants with legal residency in Belgrade were taken to container settlements on the margins of the city. These rehousing centers consisted of little more than a series of intermodal freight containers that lacked insulation. Meanwhile, individuals registered elsewhere in Serbia were returned to their hometowns and villages.

Two removals received significant press coverage in Serbia and abroad: the demolition of 175 households in the Gazela Bridge settlement in 2009 and 257 households in the Belville settlement in 2012.[6] At Gazela the eviction occurred without any international legal safeguards and residents received no compensation for their loss of personal property.[7] The site was cleared to facilitate the refurbishment of the bridge, which had become a bottleneck on the Pan-European Corridor X that ran from Salzburg to Thessaloniki. Given that the project was viewed as critical for European social and economic integration, the construction work and resettlement were funded by transnational agencies: the European Bank for Reconstruction and Development and the European Investment Bank. Economic factors also doomed the Belville settlement, which lay adjacent to one of the wealthiest malls and urban housing tracts in Belgrade. A desire to further expand the site and preserve its property value motivated the settlement's removal.

The Serbian government has argued that these resettlements benefited residents because they eliminated unhygienic shacks and provided families with access to electricity and water. The Directorate for Human and Minority Rights described one removal as "an example of good practice," while the Protector of Citizens noted that Roma have "incomparably better living conditions" in containers.[8] Drawing from long-standing assumptions regarding *cigani*, government agencies portrayed settlements as a threat to the health and well-being of their inhabitants. The solution was to clear these polluted areas and place Ashkali and Roma in camps specifically designed to house unsanitary subjects.

These governmental narratives were fiercely contested, however. NGOs reframed relocations as forced evictions and human rights violations.[9] Kilibarda argues that container settlements were part of a continental project to create circumscribed spaces with limited economic opportunities.[10] He writes, "Instead of empowering the Gazela Roma, the policy seems designed to produce a docile Roma subject dependent on formalized market networks of finance, credit and consumption, in a context of precarious short-term work, official surveillance, racialization and peripheralization."[11] As an alternative to container accommodation, advocates and human rights organizations have urged the government to house Roma in state-subsidized apartments alongside Serbian families. Whereas containers were cast as inferior and dehumanizing, apartments signaled Romani integration into Serbian society via the public aid network.

Relocations were certainly a mechanism of governance, but they were driven primarily by nongovernmental entities. Even as media coverage and NGO reports have focused on the state's role in evictions, the Serbian government simultaneously allowed settlements to flourish. The removal of Gazela and Belville attracted attention, but Belgrade was home to more than a hundred other settlements.[12] The ailing Serbian economy, coupled with the shift from state socialism to neoliberalism and the subsequent retreat of the social safety net, severely limited the government's ability to provide housing for its impoverished citizens.[13] Consequently, the state preferred to abandon Ashkali and Roma to settlements, where they were visible yet forgotten. But this situation was complicated and contested by private and international interests. Wealthy landowners, who could leverage economic investment into political power, increasingly pressured the government to facilitate the development of profitable parcels, like at Belville. Similarly, the EU, when funding improvements to a transportation corridor, could proscribe the resettlement of a Romani community living in its shadow.[14] Evictions were the result of a graduated sovereignty in which land tenure was negotiated among the state, corporations, and foreign governments. Consequently, all three of these groups played a role in consigning Ashkali and Roma to containers and geographies of exception.

These dynamics had profound consequences for Ashkali scavengers, as the destruction of Zgrade and the resettlement of its residents demonstrates. As with Gazela and Belville, land development prompted Zgrade's demolition, but it drew much less coverage because only about thirty families were affected. Nevertheless, grief and uncertainty pervaded the process. Winter weather caused delays and residents had no idea where they would be sent once the bulldozers actually arrived. Authorities concealed the relocation sites, in part, to forestall Serbian protests and reprisals. When the eviction finally occurred, the majority of Zgrade's inhabitants, including Albin and his family, were placed in a container settlement twenty kilometers away. It lay in a depression excavated to supply slate for the building trade and was ringed by industrial land, factories, and smokestacks.

The settlement consisted of approximately thirty-five shipping containers arranged in neat rows on a barren expanse of cement.[15] Each unit measured two meters by six meters, with a door positioned on the longest side and a window on the shortest. Socially, the center resembled the ethnically divided space of Polje: Zgrade residents received containers in the same area of the yard, while Roma occupied the remaining domiciles. Although Albin was acquainted with his Romani neighbors, he claimed not to know any of them well. But as in Polje, symbiotic networks were established through buying and selling merchandise, arranging loans, and occasionally stealing from one another.

Albin, reflecting on the three years he spent in the container, commented that in many ways it was preferable to a shack. His unit was no smaller than his shack had been and here he received free power and water. A reliable supply of electricity was used to run a refrigerator and an electric stove, both provided by the state, as well as his television and computer. To keep his family entertained and connected to relatives in the EU, Albin purchased a cable package featuring 125 channels and broadband internet. In winter, space heaters ensured that his family was warmer than they ever would have been in a shack. Outside, a string of ablution blocks held toilets, showers, and sinks. Most importantly, Albin said, there were no rats. However, there was one significant problem. Given the location, it was impossible to collect recyclables anywhere in the vicinity. Residents were forced to search farther afield so they relied on bicycles or automobiles, not *trokolice*. This largely restricted scavenging activities to metal. Consequently, only a few *korpa* adorned the margins of the container settlement. To find suitable recyclables, Albin and many other Ashkali commuted to Polje. While the trip was onerous, it did allow them to maintain ties with their former neighbors from Zgrade.

Albin was broadly satisfied with his family's accommodation but his Romani neighbors had different opinions. Victor, for instance, was upset at being relegated to a container. He became a resident after his shack was destroyed in the flood a year earlier. Viktor contended that the city illegally funneled funds to rehouse Roma into projects benefiting Serbs. Gesturing to the containers, he declared that Serbs did not live like this. Viktor just wanted to leave and considered claiming asylum in Germany. However, he eventually abandoned the idea, reasoning that there was no place where he could escape being treated like a *cigan*.

While Viktor was angry about his situation, Nikola was resigned to his. He had lived in a container for six years and doubted his family would ever dwell anywhere else. Unlike many of the other residents, Nikola held a wage job at the water board, where he earned 25,000 dinars ($263) a month. With this money, he attempted to transform his container into a permanent home by furnishing it with a large television, a new couch, pristine rugs, and two china cabinets filled with elegant plates and cups. It could easily be mistaken for a room in a middle-class Serbian home. In addition, Nikola built an entryway onto the front of his dwelling, which not only provided shelter and a small storage space but also helped to reduce the road noise and the smell from the adjacent sewer. His wife jokingly added that it also offered additional security against their crazy Ashkali neighbors. Living in a container was far from ideal, she said, but it was an improvement over a shack.

A common topic of conversation around the container settlement was apartments. Residents were told that sooner or later they would be relocated to a residential building. While this process was indeed occurring, as evidenced by the steadily declining population, it was slow. Eligibility was determined by strict criteria such as households with socioeconomic vulnerability, a single parent, an elderly member, a disabled child, a severely ill family member, or a victim of domestic violence.[16] Because the number of available apartments paled in comparison to the volume of applicants, individuals who were simply poor—which included most of the residents of settlements and containers—were placed at the bottom of the list. Families with ailing and disabled members had the best chance of receiving a space in social housing. For instance, Drita's sister's husband, Bajram, suffered a series of health crises while living in Zgrade. First, a stroke left him mentally impaired and unable to work, then he was diagnosed with the early stages of cancer. Knowing this would improve their ranking, Bajram's wife, Aferdita, labored for months to obtain legal identity documents and establish proof of her family's hardships. By the time the bulldozers arrived at Zgrade, Aferdita lodged an application, and six months later the family moved from their container into an apartment. She commented that this was not the result of luck but rather hard work and tragedy.

Ironically, the family's new home was in a building on the former site of Zgrade. Although the majority of the new high-rises were rented and sold at market prices, two were devoted to social housing. Residents included Roma and Ashkali as well as several Serbian families. These edifices lay at the far end of the complex, where they abutted empty greenspace. Anyone approaching could immediately see that these properties were different from the others. Whereas the privately owned structures were painted orange and yellow, the social housing units were gray and dark blue. Most conspicuously, they were ringed by *trokolice*. Aferdita's apartment was considerably larger than her former shack and contained two bedrooms, a kitchen, a bathroom, and a spacious living area that opened onto a small balcony. The kitchen was equipped with a refrigerator, two freezers, and an electric stove, while the living room contained a television, china cabinet, and large sectional couch. The white walls were artistically speckled with black paint that continued upward onto the fringes of the ceiling.

Unlike containers, this housing was not free. The family spent approximately 17,500 dinars ($184) a month to cover rent, electricity, cable television, and internet. While Bajram's disability payments helped defray much of the cost, they still needed money for food and other expenses. To make up the difference, Aferdita and her eldest son, Valon, scavenged. Hoping to avoid competition from other recyclers, Aferdita frequently visited the dumpsters at midnight. This was a dangerous time to be a female *cigan* alone on the street but she felt there was no other option. Concerned for her safety, Aferdita's neighbors routinely waited for her return each evening. Residents looked after one another, she said, because everyone struggled. Almost all of the buildings' Romani and Ashkali families supplemented their welfare payments with income earned through recycling. Given the lack of storage space in the apartments, most scavengers exclusively focused on metal or items to resell at the market. However, Aferdita and Valon, with their connections to Polje's Ashkali, had another option: they secured a plot of land in the settlement to store paper. Nevertheless, the family often found themselves straining to make ends meet. When Aferdita and Valon were unable to earn enough income to cover the electric bill, their power was disconnected. Others in the building faced similar difficulties. In the worst cases, families were evicted for failing to pay rent. On one occasion, a family voluntarily turned in their keys and moved back to a shack. Many more, frustrated at their inability to succeed even with state assistance, left for Germany. Consequently, Valon reported that there was a high turnover of residents in the building. Despite winning the struggle to get an apartment, few people kept them.

The costs associated with apartments dissuaded many Ashkali and Roma from pursuing this option. Viktor desperately wanted to leave the container settlement but worried that he could not afford social housing. Although Romani rights advocates endorsed state-sponsored accommodation as an ideal alternative to shacks and containers, in reality this was not the case. Apartments might have been subsidized but they were still a financial burden. This was compounded by a lack of storage space, which limited scavenging. Consequently, some residents embraced living in containers. When Albin was eventually offered an apartment, he refused, commenting that it was simply too expensive. A container, he said, was the best possible choice. But no matter where the state placed Ashkali, they continued to rely upon the conveniences found in and around settlements. Albin needed an urban base from which to scavenge, while Aferdita and Valon required a plot for their paper products. In each instance, eco-

nomic marginalization, the recycling trade, and the spatiality of trash permanently tethered Ashkali to settlements. Even if families were relocated
to containers or apartments, they could never truly leave Polje.

YOU CANNOT EAT A HOUSE

Whereas most of Zgrade's former residents acquiesced to resettlement in
containers, a few rejected this option, choosing instead to return to
Kosovo. Since the cessation of hostilities, the Serbian and Kosovar states
have encouraged repatriation but the success of these efforts has been limited. Over ten years after the war, estimates indicate that 35,000–40,000
Roma, Ashkali, and Egyptians resided in Kosovo, less than a quarter of its
pre-conflict population.[17] Supporting this trend, a 2011 survey found that
only nine percent of Roma expressed a desire to return to Kosovo.[18] To
incentivize resettlement, international governments, NGOs, the UNHCR,
and UNDP funded programs to build new homes for eligible returnees.[19]
From 2005 to 2015, 510 domiciles were constructed for Roma, Ashkali,
and Egyptians.[20] Furnishings, temporary stipends, and occasionally trac-
tors were also provided.[21] Focusing resettlement policy on homes allowed
organizations to demonstrate tangible outcomes that appeared to meet
pressing needs while invoking narratives of humanitarianism.[22] The
Serbian Commissariat for Refugees embraced these programs and, in an
effort to decrease Belgrade's IDP population, proactively recruited from
the settlements. On a few occasions, Ashkali found a representative standing outside their shack asking if they would like a home in Kosovo. In
contrast to the wait to obtain an apartment, getting a home usually
occurred rapidly, sometimes in only a matter of weeks.

   During removals, these offers could appear particularly attractive. With
his shack slated to be bulldozed, Endrit initially considered remaining in
Belgrade. But after visiting a container settlement, he remarked that its
remote location and shabby appearance made it utterly inadequate as a
home. Instead, he and four other families chose to return to Kosovo. When
I saw Endrit in Belgrade several months later, he was overjoyed. His new
house, he reported, was wonderful. He owned the land, the structure was
permanent, and he had access to electricity and water. After years living in

the limbo of settlements, he was finally able to settle down and even take a shower. Endrit added that his new surroundings were free of trash and rats, unlike Polje. Best of all, the cost of living in Kosovo was significantly cheaper. Adamant that the move had dramatically improved his family's life, Endrit portrayed Kosovo as the antithesis of settlements: clean, stable, and civilized. However, I soon discovered that this description was not entirely accurate.

I first traveled to Kosovo with Bekim, Naim, and their families for the wedding of Endrit's daughter, Quendresa. Given Bekim's lack of documents, the trip was long, expensive, and tense.[23] We began by taking a seven-hour bus ride to Kosovoska Mitrovica, the largest city in the Serb-majority area of Kosovo. Although the adjacent border was considered the most dangerous, it was also the least regulated. When our bus arrived at the checkpoint, immigration agents admonished Bekim for not possessing an identity card or passport but they ultimately allowed him to proceed. Soon we were disembarking in Kosovoska Mitrovica, where Agim was waiting in a taxi. We now needed to drive from the Serbian sector to the Albanian one but this could make us a target. To ensure the vehicle was not identified as originating on the other side, its license plates had been removed. Weaving our way through back streets and skirting around impromptu barricades, we finally crossed the Ibar River and entered the Albanian area. With the license plates back in place, we stopped to purchase refreshments. As Agim exited the store, he spotted a group of Albanian men and crossed the street to avoid them. Whether in Serbia or Kosovo, Ashkali constantly navigated the hostilities that accompanied their status as *cigani*.

We drove for another forty-five minutes before arriving in Endrit's village. Turning off the paved road onto a dirt lane, we saw that a recent downpour had transformed the street into a quagmire. The taxi driver, nervous about becoming bogged in the mud, made us walk the last hundred meters. Finally, after hearing so much about his new home, I was able to see it for myself. As I stepped through the front door, Endrit proudly greeted me and immediately provided a tour. The entry corridor gave access to a small bedroom, two large multipurpose rooms lined with couches, and a bathroom. Endrit explained that during the day he entertained guests in the large rooms but in the evening used the couches as beds. In one of the rooms, a curtained alcove concealed a narrow countertop, sink, stove, and oven. It was here that meals were prepared and served. Lastly, Endrit showed me what he said was one of the best features of the home: a bathroom containing a sink, toilet, and shower. As we sat down to eat, he bragged that the tomatoes in the salad were grown in their small garden, which produced a variety of vegetables including peppers, beans, and zucchini. Endrit noted that in Kosovo their food was either homegrown or purchased at the store, not scavenged from the dumpsters as in Belgrade.

Endrit espoused the benefits of returning to Kosovo but he and his family faced significant hardships there. His home was on the margins of the margin. The village contained little more than a small recreation center, two *prodavice*, and a derelict rain line. The nearest banks, cafés, and grocery stores were five kilometers away in a neighboring town. Although there was a bus service, it was infrequent and almost exclusively utilized by ethnic Albanians. Ashkali either took an expensive €4 ($5) taxi ride or walked along the train tracks. Consequently, traveling to town was not an everyday event. Even within the village, Endrit's home was isolated. His family occupied the penultimate house two kilometers from the small center. Buying a bottle of soda required a twenty-minute walk down a road shared by pedestrians, cars, and livestock. On one side, overgrown fields stretched to the horizon. However, the view in the other direction was far less bucolic. A massive power plant with belching smokestacks and radiating electric lines loomed in the distance. Despite being in close proximity to the plant, Endrit's village experienced numerous power outages, sometimes lasting several hours each day. On quite a few nights we ate by candlelight. When the power was off, so was the water. Endrit was not linked to the municipal sanitation system; an electric motor pumped wellwater into the home.

Endrit also occupied the economic periphery. His village was profoundly distanced from most resources. Emine commented that there was nothing in Kosovo: "no jobs, no money, and no food." Unlike in Belgrade, Endrit and Agim could not scavenge. There was simply no trash in the rural regions because widespread poverty ensured that goods of value were seldom discarded. Even Pristina, the Kosovar capital, lacked the large population, developed economy, and prolific garbage of Belgrade. Consequently, far fewer scavengers roamed the streets. Whereas Belgrade was dotted with settlements, Pristina was not. To survive, Endrit's family gleaned their income from welfare payments and sporadic wage labor. Occasionally, Agim was able to find temporary employment but this could pay as little as €5 ($5.25) a day, little more than a single taxi-ride into town.[24] Without work, Endrit and Agim had little to do and were virtually confined to their home.[25] Endrit's family owned a house but they had difficulties affording even basic necessities such as food.[26] Summing up this situation, Ashkali often remarked, "You cannot eat a house." To put food on the table, Endrit not only cultivated a garden, he chose to return to Polje. Both he and Agim spent several months each year working in Belgrade to fund their lives in Kosovo. As I made more visits to Kosovo, I discovered that this pattern of migrant labor was a necessity for many returnees.

Not far from Endrit's, past a cemetery and a low field that functioned as an impromptu toilet, stood the home of Rajim's brother and parents. Their house was also built after the destruction of Zgrade and was slightly larger than Endrit's. While Rajim had no desire to live in Kosovo, his brother, Burim, felt this was the best place for his wife, four sons, and two daughters. He proudly remarked that all of his children went to school. Opening an old refrigerator used to store important documents, Burim withdrew his eldest son's report card, showing me the boy's high grades in English, Albanian, math, and science. The only problem with Kovoso, Burim observed, was the dearth of jobs. So like Endrit, he traveled to Belgrade to work. Staying with Rajim for one to two months at a time, he earned between €500 ($625) and €600 ($750) before returning to Kosovo, spending a few weeks with his family, and then beginning the cycle again.

Burim and Endrit could not escape the pull of Belgrade's trash economy nor their marginalization as *cigani*. Returnees were placed in segregated spaces with little access to resources. Moreover, the skills that guaranteed their survival in Belgrade—trash-picking—were rendered useless in Kosovo. Endrit now had a house with water and electricity, but he was even more isolated and impoverished than in Polje. Yet this was ignored by the Kosovar state, international governments, and NGOs, which portrayed resettlement programs as success stories. Not only did focusing on house construction disregard the larger economic context of Kosovo, it impacted the state's response to Ashkali. If foreign governments and NGOs provided accommodation for *cigani*, then the Kosovar government was seemingly exempted from doing so. Sigona notes, "A corollary to the compartmentalisation of RAE [Roma, Ashkali, and Egyptians] in a human- and minority-rights discursive and policy frame is their de facto exclusion from citizenry, with the Kosovo authorities feeling legitimised in not treating RAE as Kosovo citizens and political subjects, but rather as an issue for the international community to deal with."[27] International anxieties about equality in Kosovo exacerbated views of Ashkali as the Other and simultaneously reinforced their precarity. Tied to a house but needing an income, Ashkali would be perpetually in flux and unable to settle permanently anywhere. Ashkali characterized their contrasting lives in Kosovo and Serbia with a simple dichotomy: a house without food or food without a house.

Although many people like Endrit and Burim returned to new houses in Kosovo, this was not the case for families who either lacked land or the ability to purchase it. Muhamet's family, for instance, had also lived in Zgrade but, without a plot to build upon, were placed in a small container settlement not far from Burim's house. Muhamet initially resisted moving here but received assurances that it would be temporary. However, four years later, the family was still waiting to leave. Although identical in size to Albin's container, Muhamet's differed in every other way. In place of a stove and oven, there was only a single gas cooking element. The walls and floor were stained and the structure was in visible disrepair. To make ends meet, Muhamet worked odd jobs, his eldest sons collected cans from around the neighborhood, and the family received a modest amount of welfare. Frustrated at his situation, Muhamet opined that in life, no one helps you: not mothers, not fathers, not brothers, not sisters, and not God. He complained that there was no work in Kosovo but, unlike Endrit and Burim, he could not travel to Belgrade. The Serbian authorities had issued a warrant for his arrest. If Muhamet returned, he would be imprisoned. Without a house and effectively barred from Serbia, he struggled considerably more than people like Endrit. Endrit might have lived in a segregated space and been unable to reliably feed his family, but he was still better off than some other Ashkali in Kosovo.

In stark contrast to those placed in containers, Gazmend owned a home not far from the center of Pristina. Whereas most of Zgrade's other residents were relocated after the settlement's destruction, he was not. Because his home survived the war intact and in his possession, Gazmend was ineligible for aid. But unlike Endrit, Burim, and Muhamet, he did not inhabit a zone of exception. Gazmend lived on a busy street in a row house, with three rooms accessed via a hallway that ran the length of the dwelling. Prior to the war, approximately 250 Ashkali had resided in the neighborhood but now only ten remained. Before the war he would not even ask directions from an ethnic Albanian for fear of assault. Now physical violence was rare but every once in a while a passerby shouted *cigan* at him.[28] Gazmend remarked that the hatred unleashed during the war was now channeled through religion and, to prove his point, produced a newspaper clipping describing a suicide bombing perpetrated by a Kosovar Albanian in Iraq. Gazmend shook his head in distaste and wondered if the United States now regretted supporting Kosovo's independence. He vowed that if Serbia abandoned its claim to Kosovo, he would never return. It was only the presence of Serbs and the UN, he believed, that prevented Kosovar Albanians from expelling Ashkali once again. Consequently, Gazmend preferred his shack in Polje to his home in Pristina. As spaces set apart from the national project, segregated communities also acted as refuges from nationalist intolerance. Gazmend's perceived vulnerability came from his home's integration within Pristina's primarily Albanian urban core.

While Gazmend was apprehensive around ethnic Albanians, Zgrade's returnees could also feel uncomfortable around other Ashkali. Years living in Belgrade's settlements spawned a normativity that was distinctive from that in Kosovo. Consequently, Ashkali from Serbia, particularly younger individuals who had spent most of their lives outside of Kosovo, often behaved differently from those who remained. Bekim and his eldest sister, Vlora, illustrated this divergence. When Bekim's father took his family to Serbia, Vlora did not accompany them. She was married just prior to the war and her husband, Ismet, chose to stay in his rural village, where his family had lived for two hundred years. The couple now has five children and resides in a three-room home in the *mahala*. These neighborhoods were established during the Ottoman era as segregated spaces. This particular *mahala* consisted of a jumble of densely packed houses cut off from the rest of the village by a stream on one side and walls on the others. While the village's Albanian residents owned large plots of land and relied on agricultural income, Ismet earned money through odd jobs. These ranged from construction work to playing in a wedding band. To find enough work, Ismet traveled throughout Kosovo and could be absent from the village for weeks at a time. The family constantly struggled to put food on the table and two of the children exhibited signs of malnutrition and stunted growth.

Each time I visited Vlora with Bekim, Fatime, and their children, I noticed significant differences between the two families. First, there was language. Although Bekim's family spoke Albanian at home, years of living in Belgrade had limited their linguistic competence. Ismet, on the other hand, was the only member of his household who spoke Serbian. Consequently, there were times when the cousins had difficulty understanding one another. On these occasions, Bekim translated into Serbian for his children. As the youngsters interacted, it was also clear that they experienced divergent upbringings. Vlora's children were all learning English in school and the eldest hoped to become a lawyer. They bathed every day, sat quietly when adults were speaking, and always used polite language. In contrast, Bekim's children wore the same clothes for days at a time, ran through the house, jumped on furniture, yelled at each other, and occasionally swore. While this behavior was customary in Polje or even at Endrit's house, it was conspicuous here. Embarrassed, Bekim shouted at his children to calm down, saying that this was not their home and Kosovo was not Belgrade. But his outbursts also elicited stares. The boisterous exchanges of the settlement were considered offensive here, and Bekim was careful not to curse. Jokes about having sex with other men's wives were strictly forbidden.

Ismet and his family, like many in Kosovo, were more socially conservative and religiously observant than those in Belgrade. Ismet made a point of praying each day, celebrating Muslim holidays, and fasting at appropriate times. Bekim was conscious of this difference and attempted to alter his public behavior accordingly. He never mentioned eating pork and refrained from introducing me as his children's godfather, a role associated with Orthodox Christianity. When Ismet peppered his speech with a few Arabic phrases, Bekim and Fatime could only understand one of them, *Allahu akbar*, and privately made jokes about how funny it sounded. On one visit, Fatime arrived in the village wearing leggings, which Vlora insisted she cover with a skirt. Later, Fatime complained that the extra clothing hid her figure and made her look ugly.

Although Bekim and Vlora cherished their time together, these tensions demonstrated the lasting consequences of displacement. The *mahala* and Polje were both areas reserved for *cigani*, but these were disparate spaces. Ismet commented that Bekim, who only knows how to recycle paper, would never be able to earn a living in Kosovo. Indeed, individuals who possessed these skills elected to temporarily return to Serbia. In so doing, men like Endrit maintained their ties not only with settlement residents but with their sociality as well. Rather than abandoning the settlements, returnees brought them to Kosovo, complicating notions of belonging. The war, its aftermath, the economics of trash, and the international politics of humanitarianism not only forged Ashkali identity, they fractured it.

As time progressed, Ashkali in Belgrade increasingly shed their connections to Kosovo. Older men like Endrit, Burim, and Gazmend returned, but the younger generation was much less prone to do so. Gazmend remarked that none of his children wanted his house in Pristina. Although Albin was born in Kosovo, he had not returned since the war. He told me that Kosovo meant nothing to him. Rajim's children, Valon, and Naim echoed this sentiment. They complained about the lack of work in Kosovo and considered Belgrade to be far more comfortable. Bekim agreed, adding that he would rather live in a shack in Belgrade than a house in Kosovo. However, Ashkali who remained in Kosovo held different opinions. Vlora commented that Belgrade was a loud and dirty city while others cast it as a fundamentally immoral space. But it was the settlements that attracted the most derision. When Endrit's younger brother was in Belgrade for a medical procedure, he visited Polje for a single night, interested to see it for himself. His curiosity, though, quickly turned to disgust. Appalled at the omnipresent detritus and smell, he vowed to never return. Noting that Ashkali in Kosovo would not tolerate these conditions, he said, "I am black but I am clean."[29] Later that evening while dancing around a bonfire, he proudly yelled "Kosovo!" Without hesitating, Fatime retorted, "Serbia!"

SEEKING ASYLUM

Fatime may have praised Serbia in relation to Kosovo but she, like everyone else in Polje, was dissatisfied with her family's economic position.

While residents acknowledged that it was possible to earn adequate money scavenging, they also asserted that this was a laborious, tedious, and uncertain process. An alternative financial strategy, which promised greater returns in a shorter amount of time, entailed migrating to the EU. Germany and Sweden were renowned for providing refugees with housing and financial assistance. Hoping to access these resources, Polje's residents routinely discussed making the trip to Germany, the preferred destination. Even as Bekim extolled the virtues of his small house, he contemplated migrating abroad. Whenever Rajim complained about the falling price of metal, he also vowed to leave the country. The very first time that I met Aleksander's son, Radmilo, he told me that I might not see him again because he planned to depart for Germany within a matter of days. At the container settlement, Albin instructed families on crossing the Hungarian border clandestinely. In Kosovo, Muhamet spoke at length about his desire to reach the EU.

These statements were not simply daydreams; Ashkali and Roma went to Germany in large numbers. Almost everyone either had relatives in the EU or had been there themselves. Most of Gazmend's and Albin's children were in Germany, as were many of Bekim's and Rajim's siblings. Endrit, Ezgon, Ajshe, Ismet, and Danilo had all resided in Germany. Jovana had lived in Sweden while Bekim and Fatime were in Austria. So many of Burim's neighbors were absent, he joked that half of Kosovo's Ashkali were in Germany. It seemed as if the same could be said of Belgrade. As the weeks passed, Polje's population noticeably shrank as families—including Fadil's, Imran's, Petra's, and Naim's—left the settlement bound for the EU. Although individuals declared that financial gain was the only consideration motivating their departures, another factor was also at play. As *cigani* relegated to the state's periphery, Polje's residents lacked durable ties to nation or place, thus encouraging transnational movement.[30] Ashkali and Roma were pushed to leave as a result of their marginalization. Hence, narratives extolling Germany were also implicit acknowledgments of *ciganski* precarity in Serbia.

Asylum seeking began in earnest during the Yugoslav wars in the 1990s. Many of the Roma displaced by the conflicts found shelter in Serbia but others journeyed to the EU. Initially, border regimes hindered this movement as citizens of Serbia, Bosnia, and Kosovo required visas to enter the

Schengen area. This changed in 2009, setting off the most recent phase of Romani migration. In the following year 17,715 Serbian citizens lodged asylum applications in the EU, a 76 percent increase.[31] By 2014 a new record was set as more than thirty thousand Serbian asylum seekers entered the EU, of whom between 85 and 90 percent were Roma.[32] As relations between Serbia and Kosovo were normalized, Kosovar citizens began traveling overland to the EU via Serbia, further swelling the number of asylum seekers. It is estimated that between summer 2014 and spring 2015 approximately four thousand Roma, Ashkali, and Egyptians left Kosovo, which represented 10 percent of their total population.[33] The influx prompted Germans to debate whether these individuals were persecuted refugees in genuine need of aid or economic migrants unfairly exploiting state benefits.[34] As in other EU nations, popular narratives often focused on the exceptional nature of Roma—their presumed criminal status and nomadism—rather than their exclusion from national agendas.[35] The European Commission officially condemned discrimination but nevertheless exerted pressure on Serbia to halt the flow of Roma. Serbia subsequently tightened its border and adopted policies that ultimately limited Romani mobility, which was the opposite of the commission's stated goals.[36] Similar to the demolition of the Gazela Bridge settlement, the Serbian state invoked international directives to justify its disregard of Ashkali and Romani rights.

Examining the steps Polje's residents took to reach Germany illustrates the resources and perseverance needed. The journey entailed significant bureaucratic and financial obstacles. First, crossing the border legally required a passport. The documents, costs, address, and knowledge needed to obtain a passport was a challenge. Fatime, who struggled to qualify for welfare, was skeptical that Bekim would ever have an identity card, let alone a passport. Likewise, Jovana dreamed about leaving for Germany but acknowledged that Harun's lack of identification was an almost insurmountable hurdle. However, an alternative did exist. Individuals without passports could hire human traffickers to smuggle them across the border. Bekim and Fatime employed this method several years earlier when they took their family to Austria. They paid €150 ($188), but the price has steadily risen as Serbia and Hungary tightened control of the frontier. When Bekim began contemplating making the trip again, he was told it could cost €300 ($375) per person. For his six-member family, Bekim would need upwards of €1,500 ($1,875), which was well beyond his means. Whether traveling legally or illegally, entry to the EU required resources and planning. Consequently, not everyone could make the trip. The poorest families were often confined to Serbia and Kosovo, demonstrating that migration was a product of marginalization as much, if not more so, than poverty.

Those who did arrive in Germany safely reported the asylum process was simple: walk into a German police station or government office and utter the word *Asyl* (asylum).[37] Once registered, applicants were housed in reception centers for three months. These centers varied in size and condition from city to city. In Kassel, Naim's family shared a unit with one other family, while in Berlin, Imran's family lived in a large building with an estimated three hundred people from Syria, Kosovo, Afghanistan, and Africa. Both men recalled that this was the most unpleasant period of their stay in Germany. Sharing facilities with strangers was stressful and space was limited. Each person was legally allotted only seven square meters and inhabitants were subject to entrance controls.[38] Imran described relentless disagreements between asylum seekers, who were occasionally prone to violence.

When Naim's and Imran's families were eventually moved to their own apartments, their conditions improved. They not only gained more privacy, they also received greater financial benefits. Because meals, clothing, and heating were provided at reception centers, the monthly stipend was lower. Once settled into individual units, this amount was increased.[39] The challenge for asylum seekers was to minimize expenses and conserve their stipends. Accustomed to surviving with very little, Ashkali and Roma were able to save a significant portion of these funds. Naim, who had four children, reported being able to set aside as much as €1,000 ($1,250) a month. Given the money at stake, Ashkali sought to stay in Germany for as long as possible; however, legal and emotional challenges hampered their longevity.

As the years progressed, the German government streamlined and accelerated the asylum process for Balkan citizens. By 2012 what had taken months was, in some cases, reduced to weeks or even days. These changes were driven by the assumption that the majority of applicants would be denied permanent residency and repatriated.[40] Indeed, in 2014 only 1.4 percent of Serbians and 5.5 percent of Kosovars were granted refugee status.[41] Once their applications were rejected, individuals lost their preliminary residency permit and received a suspension of deportation (*Duldung;* literally "toleration"). Those with *Duldung* status would eventually be required to leave the country but were allowed to remain temporarily. These permits could be granted for short periods of time, only a few months, and needed to be constantly renewed. Furthermore, there was no way to predict when, at last, the permit would be denied. The constant uncertainty that accompanied *Duldung* further destabilized people's lives.

Ashkali were well aware that their chances of being granted asylum were small but nevertheless worked to delay their deportation. When their application was rejected, Ashkali used a portion of the money they saved to hire lawyers and appeal the decision. Bekim's eldest brother paid €800 ($1,000) for legal aid, which allowed him to remain in Germany for an additional eight months. However, this tactic also came with risks. I was told stories of lawyers who overbilled and neglected their clients. A family could spend a large sum of money for legal representation and still be sent home weeks later. Mounting a defense consumed a family's financial resources, was a constant battle, had an unpredictable duration, and was ultimately prone to fail.

As Ashkali navigated the asylum process, they were socially isolated. Work permits were not issued immediately, which resulted in men spending their days at home interacting only with their families or other reception center residents. Compounding this, most Ashkali were unable to speak German and could not communicate easily with others. As a result, migrants had difficulty establishing relationships like those that pervaded Belgrade's settlements. The lack of work and friends took an emotional toll on many families. Petra characterized her time in Germany as the loneliest period of her life. Similarly, Besnik complained that his children had no playmates and he could not even talk to his neighbors. He said that all they could do was wait. Besnik was frustrated, but because this was his second sojourn in Germany, he knew how agonizing it would be but felt he had no other choice. If they could survive a year or more in Germany, his family would return to Belgrade with enough money for a house.

While Ashkali strove to extend their stay in Germany, almost none wished to settle there permanently. The lack of social networks, higher cost of living, and difficulty of learning German dissuaded many. The EU was a place to earn money but Serbia was home. Most of Polje's former residents voluntarily left Germany once their legal options were exhausted and some did so even sooner. After eighteen months Imran became fed up with constantly waiting in line next to bellicose asylum seekers. Even though his case was still being processed, he packed up his family's belongings and moved back to Belgrade. The money, Imran said, was no longer worth the aggravation. Naim also returned with his family while Edona's application was pending. Shaking his head, Naim declared that he was not sorry to go. His family's life in Germany was just too lonely. Of the many people I knew who traveled to the EU, only Fadil's family were successful in obtaining refugee status and chose to relocate permanently.

When Ashkali departed Germany, they often took a significant amount of money with them. For instance, Naim saved €8,000 ($10,000) during his nine-month sojourn. Upon his arrival in Belgrade, he bought a used car for €2,500 ($3,125) and remodeled his home. Those accruing more time abroad could make even larger purchases. Besnik, who was gone for over two years, had the means to move his family out of their shack and into a house. He paid €9,000 ($11,250) for a three-bedroom home with running water and electricity. Not long after he moved in, Besnik was already making plans to expand the structure. Taking me outside, he pointed to its flat roof, noting that it was designed to support an additional story. Although returnees were able to acquire vehicles and property that were previously unaffordable, they eventually depleted their savings. Within months Naim traded his car for a cheaper model, needing the cash to cover his family's expenses. And approximately one year after his homecoming, the electricity in his home was shut off due to lack of payment. Money earned from asylum claims was transformational but also fleeting. A family might be able to purchase a house, but they would continue to inhabit a segregated space and, most importantly, long-term financial security was still out of reach.

Given the inability to permanently improve their lives in Serbia, some settlement residents returned to Germany a second or even third time.

Statistics indicate that 27 percent of asylum seekers from the Western Balkans have applied on multiple occasions.[42] Hoping to halt this cycle, the German government declared Serbia and Kosovo safe countries of origin in 2014 and 2015, respectively. As a result, new applicants were deported almost immediately and those already in the system were expedited. News of this change quickly rippled through Polje, leading Imran to declare that Serbian citizens were effectively banned. Germany, he said, was now only for Syrians. Suddenly, Polje's population began to grow again as families like Petra's returned. Across the region the number of Ashkali and Romani returnees was swelling dramatically. Germany was expected to expel ten thousand people a year to Serbia and five thousand a year to Kosovo.[43] This high rate of forced repatriation had significant consequences. Some migrants spent ten or more years in Germany and had few links to their homelands. These individuals lacked a place to settle as well as Serbian or Kosovar identification documents. Their children, who were born and educated in Germany, could possess only a limited knowledge of Serbian or Albanian. A Belgrade city official told me that returnees posed a greater challenge for the state than did the proliferation of settlements. Meanwhile, NGOs warned that existing services were inadequate for integrating and supporting an incoming population of this size, particularly in Kosovo.[44]

As the movement of people to and from the EU demonstrates, Ashkali displacement was the result of national and transnational policies. German legislation regarding payments to asylum seekers and the categorization of safe countries structured migrants' aspirations and actions. This was compounded by the marginalization *cigani* experienced in Serbia. Neither country embraced Ashkali, and so they were relentlessly pushed back and forth. This pattern was pervasive and inescapable. Whether living in container settlements, apartments, homes in Kosovo, or German refugee centers, Ashkali were never truly secure. Furthermore, each location lacked access to the resource upon which Ashkali in Serbia's settlements had come to rely: trash. Confined to a single economic niche, scavengers could only survive through state-funded support or resurrecting discarded commodities. Families resettled by the state often faced a difficult but familiar choice: a house without food or food without a house. Consequently, national and international attempts to improve housing only resulted in greater marginalization. Ironically, it was the settlements that provided the most to Ashkali. Although Polje was an illegal and segregated geography that lacked basic services, it was also a space in which people could earn a living and exercise a degree of sovereignty because it was a domain of trash.

Conclusion

JEBEM TI ŽIVOT

No sooner had Bekim moved back into Polje than rumors of its impending destruction began to circulate. Well aware that the city was razing settlements, residents were vigilant for signs that theirs would be next. It appeared as if this moment had come when trucks began dumping dirt, broken concrete, and other rubble in the former Bayash area. This continued day after day without explanation. With a vehicle arriving as frequently as every thirty minutes, Polje was transformed. The piles of trash left behind by Bayash residents were quickly covered by dusty fill. Soon, bulldozers arrived, flattening the mounds of sand and creating a level path for the trucks to drive further into the settlement. After a couple of weeks, the debris had raised the rear of the settlement by three meters. The bulldozers were now pushing dirt close to existing shacks. Unable to obtain reliable information about the source of the rubble or the reason it was being deposited, residents assumed their forcible removal was imminent. Some worried about their future, while others, like Gazmend, were resigned. Everything must end, he said. The settlement, with its dirt, trash, and shacks, had lasted long enough.

The lives of Polje's residents were inextricably tethered to the detritus that was abandoned around them. Serbs equated *cigani* with filth and degradation; scavengers were trash. Like the dusty rubble carried by the trucks, Ashkali and Roma were dumped in Polje. They were stripped of their humanity just as garbage was stripped of its worth. But as Endrit and Bekim could attest, trash was valuable. Regardless of popular perceptions, the act of being discarded did not erase an item's usefulness. Ashkali were surrounded by trash, but they were able to resurrect these spent commodities and give them a new existence. Likewise, within the confines of Polje, scavengers were able to salvage their own personhood. Here Ashkali were invisible and, as a result, exercised their own, albeit limited, sovereignty. It was through an existence of exception that they saw a path to autonomy and success. Marginalized geographies forged novel ways of being-in-the-world. Belgrade's settlements refashioned identity and belonging while simultaneously restructuring social and material lives.

Ultimately, however, this Other world was in perpetual crisis. Polje's residents lived in fear of eviction and the arrival of the dump trucks only confirmed their anxieties. Hunger, pain, and death suffused the settlement. Scavengers returned home at night chronically sore from long hours spent in the dumpsters. Parents struggled to feed their children. Every day brought new misfortune, but this was simply how life seemed to work in Polje. When faced with yet another catastrophe that was unexpected yet predicable, Bekim exclaimed, *"Jebem ti život!"* or "Fuck life!" Perhaps more than anything else, this statement reflected the frustration and resignation that pervaded Polje. It bluntly acknowledged obscene adversity while simultaneously dismissing it. People suffered but this was ordinary. To illustrate the normality of distress and its impact on people's lives, I conclude by examining the events surrounding my final weeks in the settlement and the changes that occurred after my departure.

SQUEEZED

Like other aspects of life in Polje, the dump trucks and their cargo were not only a threat; they were also an opportunity. Residents quickly discovered that the debris contained metal objects such as pipes, rebar, and wires. While only scraps could be found, it was still significantly more than the dumpsters yielded. Soon, the site was peppered with Ashkali and Roma waiting for the next truck. Fitim, Valon, Agim, and Bekim spent most of their days there. Scavengers sat under trees to avoid the sun's heat and seldom socialized with the other groups. Once a truck arrived, individuals took up positions on the edge of a steep embankment. The driver, ignoring the throng of people surrounding the vehicle, backed the truck into place, raised its open-box bed, and spilled the contents down the incline. It was then that ten to fifteen people, including men, women, and children, rushed forward and swiftly grabbed anything that looked remotely metallic. With a wave of rubble cascading from the truck, scavengers had to avoid tripping over one another, being covered in debris, or falling down the slope. Once the truck had discharged its contents, a bulldozer leveled the mound, revealing additional objects. Men, desperate to outmaneuver each other, darted through the small space between the bulldozer's treads and its blade to snatch items. The driver never spoke to residents but routinely paused for a few seconds, allowing people to briefly scavenge.

Amidst the uncertainty, Polje's residents continued to lead lives pervaded by an unpredictable mix of mirth and violence. This was epitomized one afternoon, when residents were socializing next to the lane. While their parents chatted, several children were kicking a ball back and forth. Harun spied Jakov returning from begging and decided to have some fun. He took the ball from the kids and hurled it at Jakov, who expertly caught it and tossed it back, narrowly missing Jovana. Harun immediately returned fire, causing two other onlookers to duck out of the way. These volleys and feints quickly morphed into an impromptu game of dodgeball. Harun and Jakov threw the ball back and forth, trying to hit the six adults standing between them. As the children watched, their mothers and fathers bobbed and weaved to avoid being struck. Jovana was particularly good at dodging. After a while, Miloš came to investigate the commotion and jumped into the game. Bekim, who had been watching from the sidelines and cheering on several of the participants, refused to acknowledge Miloš. Bekim was still furious but, as often occurred when men were in conflict with one another, he chose to avoid Miloš instead of confronting him. Instead, Bekim vented his anger on Fatime.

The day before, Fatime had briefly left her infant unattended in the lane, where Bekim found him. She was only absent momentarily but Bekim flew into a rage. He rang Agim, demanding that Fatime be disciplined. It was during the dodgeball game that Agim appeared. Seeing the merriment, he instantly joined in. Jovana, tired of dodging, traded places with her husband and began pelting balls at Miloš and Agim. Bekim quickly grew impatient and summoned Agim and Fatime into their shack. As Jovana and Jakov hurled the ball back and forth, the players could hear Agim yelling loudly. A few moments later, the shack shook. Agim had struck Fatime, knocking her against the wall. All those outside were acutely aware of the violence occurring just a few meters away. The game continued but its exuberance had vanished. We heard more yelling and the shack shook again. With everyone visibly tense, the match ended and the adults drifted back to their shacks. When Agim and Bekim emerged from the shack a few moments later, Jovana darted inside to console Fatime. Over the next few days, no one would discuss the events of that afternoon.[1] Bekim and Fatime continued to argue sporadically but neither acknowledged that she had been beaten. It almost seemed as if it did not occur.

Then, two weeks later, Fatime had a miscarriage. Three months' pregnant, she awoke with heavy vaginal bleeding and soon passed out. Bekim was frantic. He yelled for help and his neighbors immediately called an ambulance. When it arrived, Jovana wanted to accompany Fatime to the hospital but the paramedics forbade it. Bekim could not go either. He needed someone to look after his four children but trusted no one in the settlement with this task. His only option was to take them to his brother's house and then continue to the hospital. It was only then he learned that Fatime had lost the pregnancy. As Bekim was waiting for her to be discharged, a doctor emerged and bluntly asked if he had hit his wife and caused the miscarriage. Bekim vociferously denied assaulting Fatime and was eventually allowed to take her home.

That evening Naim drove his new car into Polje. While Fatime rested inside the family's shack, Bekim discussed the situation with him outside. Nonchalantly, Naim commented that it was better to have a miscarriage than another child. Bekim and Fatime already had four and, how, he asked, were they going to look after one more? Naim admonished Bekim to wear condoms and admitted that he had paid €150 ($188) for his wife to have an abortion. Bekim just nodded and bid Naim farewell so he could purchase bread and bologna for his family's dinner. Later, as Bekim fed the children, Fatime remained curled in a ball on the couch, clearly in pain. But Bekim appeared unconcerned. Once the lights came on, a Romani neighbor, Andrej, arrived with a case of beer and a set of speakers. Fatime remained motionless while the men blared music and drank.

Ashkali were labeled as *cigani* by Serbs and then either ignored or assaulted, but women like Fatime were additionally vulnerable to the men who lived with and around them. Polje's male residents joked about having sex with her as her husband laughed. She could not leave the settlement without a male escort and spent her days singlehandedly taking care of four children. This was so confining that the grueling labor of scavenging was preferable to staying at home. When Bekim was angry, he could vent his hostility on Fatime and was often supported by the male members of her family. And these episodes were never publicly acknowledged. As Agim assaulted Fatime, those outside remained silent. Her pain was similarly unrecognized. After her miscarriage, Naim casually characterized it as a positive event and later Bekim became drunk and listened to music. If the embodied struggles of Ashkali were disregarded by Serbs, the struggles of Ashkali women were disregarded by Ashkali men. Fatime was constrained not only as a *cigan* but also as a woman.

Just before midnight, Andrej departed and Harun appeared, cryptically telling Bekim it was time to go. Bekim instructed me to look after Fatime before disappearing into the night. Fatime and I sat silently in the shack, watching an old Arnold Schwarzenegger movie. At one point a large rat crawled across the window. An hour later Bekim and Harun returned pushing a *trokolica* filled with an office chair, several scraps of metal, and three pairs of men's shoes. They had just robbed an eighty-year-old Serb. The man's house was situated off a small dark road next to the fields. Assuming the man could neither see nor hear well, Bekim and Harun grabbed every metal item lying around the home's perimeter. As Harun showed off the *trokolica*'s contents to other residents, Bekim took me aside. Elated, he confided that they had actually stolen much more, perhaps 150 kilograms of metal.[2] For security, they had stashed their bounty in the fields, lest it be discovered by the police or pilfered by other residents. Bekim and Harun planned to sell the metal the following day but this did not occur. Once the theft was reported, police began patrolling the surrounding area, making it impossible to retrieve the stockpile. Two weeks later, when Bekim and Harun were at last able to take the items to a junkyard, they earned much less than anticipated: only 1,500 dinars ($15.75), which was split between them. Bekim had hoped to supplement this money by selling the shoes at the market, but before he could do so, they were stolen from his shack.

These events—residents jockeying for metal scraps underneath a bulldozer, Agim beating Fatime, and Bekim's theft—were exceptional. In Polje, life had always been suffused by precarity, disposability, and violence, but this seemed to intensify when the price of metal dropped and the settlement appeared destined for removal. As the years progressed, opportunities to transform debris into profitable commodities were shrinking. With residents economically, materially, and spatially squeezed, there was an increase of violence, risk taking, and theft. If an existence in Polje was already a struggle, it was only becoming more difficult. Furthermore, there was no alternative. Bekim had attempted to leave the settlement but returned within days. People were stuck in Polje and subjected to the vacillations of the state, land developers, and global markets. Scavengers were masters of finding opportunity in the trash but this had limits. As trucks dumped debris next to people's homes and recycling yielded diminishing returns, those limits were glaringly visible. *Jebem ti život.*

SCAVENGING *CIGANI*

As Ashkali and Roma negotiated the confines of Polje's Other world, non-Romani interlopers routinely wandered into the settlement to "document," "understand," or "help" its residents. About once every two months, a journalist, documentary filmmaker, graduate student, or tourist would appear, ask a few questions, and vanish. These individuals all seemed intent on confirming popular stereotypes, not challenging them. This pattern also fit aid workers. Because the Serbian government was absent from the settlements, NGOs and members of the civil society sector filled the void. However, these visits were infrequent, unregulated, and often benefited the organization more than Polje's residents. This dynamic was illustrated two weeks after Fatime's miscarriage.

One afternoon I was walking into the settlement and noticed a group of visitors with a video camera talking to Danilo. Assuming they were journalists, I continued to Jovana's shack, where Fatime and Bekim were sitting outside. Before long, the group approached us and explained they were missionaries from an evangelical church in the United States. Their goal was to assist impoverished Roma by providing food, clothes, and other needed items. Jovana immediately spoke up, revealing that her son had epilepsy. She said her family would gladly take whatever aid was available. One of the men replied that they might be able to deliver a food parcel later. In the meantime he promised that they would pray for her and suggested that everyone bow their heads. Jovana seemed unimpressed but remained silent. Bekim, on the other hand, had enough and suggested that he and I depart. As we walked out of Polje, he told me the missionaries could fuck off. However, they did not.

Over the next few days the missionaries returned to conduct a series of videotaped interviews. Most of Polje's families took part because, as a reward, they received a bundle of food containing potatoes, beans, sugar, coffee, spaghetti, cookies, and seasoning salt. Bekim was disappointed that the parcel did not include meat, but he was particularly vexed that the missionaries were not distributing cash. Nevertheless, he agreed to participate. But as his interview was about to begin, Bekim learned that one of the men was a pastor. He immediately declared that his family was Muslim and would never attend a Christian service. The pastor explained that converting to Christianity was unnecessary and the interview continued as planned. It lasted about half an hour and followed a pattern that was repeated each time the missionaries spoke with a resident on camera.

First, the family was asked to stand in front of their shack. Sometimes children from other families joined in, giving the impression of households that were abnormally large. Once the camera was rolling, the pastor's wife said, in English, that the family had nothing. Shifting to Serbian, she asked a few questions to ascertain the family's history. She then looked directly into the camera and, again speaking English, recounted narratives of anguish: of winters spent in freezing shacks, of making fires on the floor, and of wanting to escape terrible living conditions. Continuing to face the camera, she said, "You might not think you can help but you can. Give today and make a difference." It was at this point that she began to cry. Then, as proof of the transformative power of aid, she distributed the food parcels, provoking an ebullient display of gratitude. These interviews revealed that the missionaries were not in Polje to proselytize. Their primary goal was to elicit donations from their congregation. But Ashkali and Roma were not simply props for an international money-making enterprise; they were, metaphorically speaking, trash. The missionaries were going from settlement to settlement—essentially from dumpster to dumpster—collecting families' images and stories to recycle in America for cash. The pastor and his camera crew were not alone in this endeavor. Charities, NGOs, and international aid agencies participated in the same practice. They earned their money scavenging *cigani.*

When the missionaries finished their last interview for the day, I approached the pastor and introduced myself. His name was Brian and he had been working in Romani settlements with his Serbian wife, Teodora, for fifteen years. Pointing to the woman he had just filmed, Brian declared, "She has nothing. It's terrible." Not only did he characterize settlements as ubiquitously poor, he believed that Roma possessed neither the interest nor ability to improve their standard of living. Gesturing in all directions, Brian commented there was dirt everyplace but no one seemed to care. He added that Roma were invariably either drug users or drug takers. Furthermore, they prioritized purchasing cigarettes over food, allowing their children go hungry. In one settlement, he said, a man had seventeen wives. Brian characterized each of these examples as disgraceful. When Teodora joined us, she echoed his perspective, saying, "Roma children are so beautiful but look at what becomes of them." She asked about my work in Polje and if I had discovered a way to make Roma change their deleterious behavior. I explained that my goal was to understand people's lives, not create a blueprint for altering them. Once it became clear that I could not contribute to their project, they politely bid me farewell. As they left the settlement, I realized that although Brian and Teodora ostensibly sought to aid Roma, the couple ultimately believed that their efforts would be fruitless. *Cigani* were simply immoral people who were incapable of change. However, this did not prevent the missionaries from soliciting money on their behalf.

The next day I asked Milica to share her opinion of the missionaries. Shrugging, she replied that she had none. Identical conversations with others revealed that no one in the settlement gave Brian or his film crew much thought. This was because residents were accustomed to strangers

sauntering into Polje unannounced, snapping photos or conducting interviews, making lofty promises, and then disappearing. Ultimately, Ashkali
and Roma had no control over who entered their community or how they
were represented. But this was of little interest to Polje's residents. They
were far more concerned with avoiding the police, finding valuable trash,
accessing reliable electricity, and just surviving. Given the magnitude of
these struggles, their exploitation at the hands of interlopers was of no
consequence. The missionaries might have been making considerable
money through the videos but this was expected. It was simply everyday
life in a state of exception. At least Brian gave each participating family a
food parcel, which was more than the community obtained from the EU
delegation or the NGO providing flood aid. *Jebem ti život.*

PAPER LIVES

Soon it was my last day in Polje. My bag was packed and sitting in the
corner of Bekim's shack, but for everyone else it was a normal day full of
conflict, joking, tedium, and trash. From a distance Rajim waved to me as
he headed home from work. Then Dragomir passed by and told me to
bring him a voluptuous woman from America. Meanwhile, Harun came
and went, slowly amassing a cache of metal before finally selling it. While
the men went about their business, I also had a task I had to complete:
replacing my cellphone's Serbian SIM card with an American one.
Unfortunately, I lost the narrow metal rod designed for this purpose long
ago. So I did what any of Polje's residents would do—I went to the trash.
Scavenging around Bekim's paper pile, I found a magazine, carefully pried
out a staple, and straightened it. Sure enough, it fit perfectly.

Not only did garbage provide for most basic needs, it also served as a
chronicle of people's lives. Paper caches were collections of tangible memories. Every time I rooted through Bekim's pile, I was reminded of when
and where a particular item was scavenged. For instance, Hannah
Montana and Jonas Brothers bags triggered recollections of the two days
we spent at the Chinese warehouse. I could not forget Fatime, with her
bright red fingernails, tirelessly cleaning the charred remains of mass-
produced trinkets and knickknacks. Then there was the magazine with an

article about Woody Allen, which I read to Besart while we rode on the back of Lucky's cart. On another occasion, I came across dozens of cash register receipt rolls and remembered how, instead of handing them to us, supermarket employees threw them from the loading dock. Or the psychology journals that Agim helped me unload before we left to check the cable. Ashkali, I realized, had paper lives. Their existence was not only embodied in the trash they scavenged; it was fragile.

As the sun set, Bekim, Fatime, their children, and I were sitting in their shack reminiscing about my time in Polje. The settlement had become quiet and I was preparing to leave for the airport. But, as was too often the case, peace was shattered by tragedy. Suddenly, the door was flung open and Jovana yelled that we must come to the street immediately. Leaving the older children to look after the younger ones, Bekim, Fatime, and I sprinted out of Polje. I saw a crowd of people forming a circle on the sidewalk and in the middle, lying motionless on the ground, was Aferdita. Her son was crying over her body while everyone else appeared frozen. Soon, an ambulance arrived and the medics immediately pronounced her dead. But Valon refused to leave her side. Most of Polje's residents were there, lending silent support. I stood next to Nikola, who whispered that she must have had a heart attack. She just collapsed, he said. Bekim and Fatime wanted to comfort Aferdita's family so I returned to the shack to look after the children. When I entered, the infant was crying and Besart was unable to quiet him. Needing help with the baby, he asked for his mother. I carefully explained that she would not be back for a while because his great aunt had unexpectedly died. Besart just nodded and then I helped him rock the baby to sleep. Speechless and grieving, we sat down and watched old Mickey Mouse cartoons on television.

After an hour Bekim and Fatime returned. Fatime was crying loudly, unable to speak. Soon, Rajim entered and said they would need to make plans. It was clear that my assistance was no longer necessary and, if anything, I was an added distraction. So I quietly informed everyone that I would be departing. Bekim nodded and apologized for being unable to escort me out of the settlement. I replied that, given the circumstances, he needed to remain with his family. I stood up and Rajim, Fatime, and finally Bekim shook my hand. Without another word I turned and left. As I walked, the faintly glowing shacks thinned and before long I found myself at the edge of the settlement. Striding forward, I was enveloped in darkness, crossing the boundary into the outside world one final time. Suddenly, I emerged into an imposing geography of tall buildings, bright lights, and blaring traffic. A crowd was still gathered on the street but I did not stop. A few blocks later, I boarded a bus bound for the airport. As I left Polje, my heart ached. Moreover, the chasm between my life and theirs could not have been wider. I would be getting on a plane and going back to my home and job in America. Meanwhile, only a few weeks after having a miscarriage, Bekim and Fatime would be burying a family member. Amidst all of this, they would worry about feeding their family and the potential destruction of their home. There was no security. *Jebem ti život.*

Two years passed before I was able to return to Polje, and it had changed considerably during my absence. First, the settlement's geography had been reconfigured. The area formerly inhabited by Bayash families and then covered in rubble had sprouted grass and scrub. Polje's historic nucleus now appeared as if it had never been inhabited, let alone con- tained over a dozen shacks. The settlement's remaining dwellings were also different. Several new families had taken up residence and, in their yards, large piles of plastic bottles replaced industrial baskets filled with paper. Before, no one had scavenged plastic, but now it was the material of choice. Incoming families further reworked the aesthetics of Polje by erecting fences around their shacks. These barriers were constructed of old doors and couches, like the shacks themselves. Being able to collect or purchase this quantity of building materials marked their owners as rela- tively affluent. I was told that these security measures were necessary because crime had increased significantly. Neighbors distrusted each another and socialized far less. Bekim admitted that the settlement was no longer the convivial space that it had been.

When I began my fieldwork, Bekim's family was one of the settlement's newest but now they were among its oldest. Of the approximately two hundred Ashkali and Roma who called Polje home then, only five house- holds remained: Bekim's, Gazmend's, Aleksander's, Jovana's, and Petra's. Everyone else had departed. Miloš and Milica left for Srem, in hopes of buying a house, but several months later they made their way back to Belgrade, moving into a neighboring settlement. Harun also departed for Srem but did so alone. After a series of affairs, Jovana finally left him for her latest paramour, Andrej. Nevertheless, Harun occasionally came back to the city and visited the settlement. Dragomir also left Polje for another shack in another municipality, but not long afterwards, tragedy struck. One morning Dragomir's lifeless body was discovered on the outskirts of a settlement. The incident was reported in two sentences: "[Dragomir's initials] (36) was found dead in a landfill in the Belgrade suburb of Rakovica. It is suspected that he died of electric shock when stealing electricity." The man who had taught me how to wire a shack had lost his life attempting to access a basic service provided to other Serbian citizens. And the only public mention of his death branded him a thief.

Like Roma, Ashkali also grappled with a variety of difficult and changing circumstances. Burim was still unable to settle down and continued traveling to and from Belgrade in an effort to fund his family's life in Kosovo. Endrit and Agim also made the trip every few months, staying in the small house that Bekim abandoned. Drita, however, lived permanently in Kosovo and, embracing her Muslim faith, began wearing a head scarf. Muhamet's family finally received an apartment after years of waiting and his container settlement was removed. In place of the containers, a plethora of new homes were built, most for returnees from Macedonia. What had been green fields were now covered in almost identical brick structures.

In Belgrade Albin's family remained in their container despite seeing more and more of their neighbors depart. At Rajim's house the posters of Ronaldo and Neymar were replaced with a large tapestry of the Kaaba, while a framed photograph of his eldest daughter's wedding hung on the opposite wall. Rajim supported the match and felt that, at eighteen years old, she was the appropriate age. In contrast, his eldest son, Altin, eloped when he was fifteen. Initially, Rajim was furious but eventually reconciled himself to the marriage. Nevertheless, he felt Altin was too young to shoulder this responsibility. To support his wife, Altin dropped out of school and began working with his father. A few months later his wife became pregnant with twins. But even as Ashkali celebrated new life, they had to mourn. After days of declining health, Gazmend collapsed at home and could not be revived. As he had predicted, Gazmend died in a shack.

Throughout these events Bekim and Fatime remained estranged from other Ashkali and socialized exclusively with a small group of Roma. Bekim still struggled to make money and contemplated switching from paper to plastic, like his neighbors, hoping it would increase his income. His eldest son, Besart, now begged regularly alongside his Romani friends. When Nenad and Besart's younger brother were caught stealing ice cream from a convenience store, Bekim was furious but his son just laughed. Reflecting on the state of her family, Fatime divulged that she was extremely depressed. During my absence she gave birth to another child, had another miscarriage, and was pregnant again. Fatime characterized her life as an endless progression of days spent cleaning a shack that would always be dirty. In this city, she said, it would not get better. Fatime wanted to leave Belgrade and never return. Bekim had also grown exasperated with Polje and hoped to move to Kosovo. His siblings in Germany bought the couple a plot of land near Pristina and a repatriation program vowed to build a house on it. But as yet, nothing has materialized. The family continues to wait, not knowing what the future will bring or where they will be living. *Jebem ti život.*

For Bekim, Fatime, and others who called Polje home, settlements were both temporary and enduring. They, like their residents, came and went, perpetually relocating around the periphery. However, these unstable geographies of displacement were testaments to the intractability of marginality. No matter where they made their home, Ashkali and Roma inhabited segregated, excepted, and precarious communities. At the center of this Other world was trash. It was ubiquitously present yet fundamentally transitional. Through its economy, sociality, and materiality, garbage constrained people like Bekim, and simultaneously, constituted their humanity. The story of Polje was the story of trash.

Notes

INTRODUCTION

1. Because visibility can particularly impact vulnerable populations such as Polje's residents, I have used pseudonyms, disguised the identity of the settlement, and refrained from publishing photographs. These measures were endorsed by Polje's residents.

2. Ljiljana Živković and Aleksandar Đorđević, *General Characteristics of Substandard Roma Settlements in Serbia and a Proposal for Further Development Initiatives for the Improvement of the Living Conditions of the Roma Community* (Belgrade: OSCE Mission to Serbia, 2015), 16.

3. The word *cigan* (*cigani*—plural, *ciganski*—adjective) has its roots in eleventh-century Byzantium. The exact meaning of the term is still debated, but it may refer to a heretical sect that was associated with magic, as were Roma. In contrast, Gypsy was introduced a few centuries later and is derived from the misidentification of Roma as originating in Egypt. Subsequently, the term gypped resulted from stereotypes depicting Roma as criminals. See Angus Fraser, *The Gypsies* (London: Blackwell, 1995), 46.

4. For an analysis of popular tropes, see Kalwant Bhopal and Martin Myers, *Insiders, Outsiders, and Others: Gypsies and Identity* (Hatfield: University of Hertfordshire Press, 2008); Gyorgy Csepeli and David Simon, "Construction of Roma Identity in Eastern and Central Europe: Perception and Self-Identification," *Journal of Ethnic and Migration Studies* 30, no. 1 (2004): 129–50; Alaina

Lemon, *Between Two Fires: Gypsy Performance and Romani Memory from Pushkin to Post-socialism* (Durham, NC: Duke University Press, 2000); Aidan McGarry, "Roma as a Political Identity: Exploring Representations of Roma in Europe," *Ethnicities* 14, no. 6 (2014): 756-74; David Myall, *Gypsy Identities 1500-2000: From Egipcyans and Moon-Men to Ethnic Romany* (London: Routledge, 2004); and Carol Silverman, "Negotiating 'Gypsiness': Strategy in Context," *Journal of American Folklore* 101, no. 401 (1988): 261-75.

5. See Aniko Imre, "Whiteness in Post-socialist Eastern Europe: The Time of the Gypsies, the End of Race," in *Postcolonial Whiteness: A Critical Reader on Race and Empire*, ed. Alfred Lopez (Albany: State University of New York Press, 2005), 79-102; and Nando Sigona, "Locating 'The Gypsy Problem': The Roma in Italy—Stereotyping, Labelling and 'Nomad Camps'," *Journal of Ethnic and Migration Studies* 31, no. 4 (2005): 741-56.

6. Miloš Marjanović, "Encountering the Ethnic Stereotypes about the Romanies," *Facta Universitatis* 2, no. 8 (2001): 433-34.

7. The Decade of Roma Inclusion ran from 2005 to 2015 and involved twelve European nations. For a critique of its goals and outcomes see Christian Brüggemann and Eben Friedman, "The Decade of Roma Inclusion: Origins, Actors, and Legacies," *European Education* 49 (2017): 1-9.

8. V. V. B., "The Plights of Europe's Roma," *The Economist*, May 25, 2012 (accessed January 15, 2020).

9. Scholars draw upon Edward Said's *Orientalism* (New York: Vintage Books, 1979) and argue that similar accounts have defined Roma for generations. See Myall, *Gypsy Identities 1500-2000*; Jan Selling, "Assessing the Historical Irresponsibility of the Gypsy Lore Society in Light of Romani Subaltern Challenges," *Critical Romani Studies* 1, no. 1 (2018): 44-61; and Marco Solimene, "Undressing the Gağé Clad in State Garb: Bosnian Xoraxané Romá Face to Face with the Italian Authorities," *Romani Studies* 23, no. 2 (2013): 161-86.

10. During this initial encounter, a friend translated from Serbian to English. However, I was also able to speak with Endrit in German. I eventually gained the ability to communicate in Serbian and Albanian. Because most of the Ashkali and Roma living in Polje had no knowledge of Romani, I did not acquire proficiency in this language.

11. Eric Wolf, *Europe and the People without History* (Berkeley: University of California Press, 2010).

12. Milan Vučković and Goran Nikolić, *Stanovništvo Kosova u razdoblju 1918-1991* [Kosovo population in the period 1918-1991] (Munich: Slavica Verlag, 1996), 80.

13. Eben Friedman, *Roma in the Yugoslav Sucessor States* (European Centre for Minority Issues, Working Paper #82, December 2014), 5.

14. European Roma Rights Centre, *Abandoned Minority* (Budapest: European Roma Rights Centre, 2011), 18.

15. Any discussion of Romani identity is complex and fraught with scholarly disagreement. See Thomas Acton, "Modernity, Culture, and 'Gypsies': Is There a Meta-Scientific Method for Understanding the Representation of 'Gypsies'? And Do the Dutch Really Exist?", in *The Role of the Romanies: Images and Counter-Images of "Gypsies"/Romanies in European Cultures,* ed. Nicholas Saul and Susan Tebbutt (Liverpool: Liverpool University Press, 2004), 98–117; Ian Hancock, *We Are the Romani People* (London: Hertfordshire Press, 2002); Judith Okely, "Recycled (Mis)representations: Gypsies, Travellers or Roma Treated as Objects, Rarely Subjects," *People, Place & Policy* 8, no. 1 (2014): 65–85; and Michael Stewart, "Roma and Gypsy 'Ethnicity' as a Subject of Anthropological Inquiry," *Annual Review of Anthropology* 42 (2013): 415–32. Consequently, I readily acknowledge that the account I am presenting is open to dispute, as indeed are all explanations of Romani identity. On the range of Romani people inhabiting Kosovo, see Adam Balcer, "The Development of Identities among the Population of Gypsy Origin in Kosovo: Ashkali, Egyptians, and Roma," *Sprawy Narodowos'ciowe* 31 (2007): 247–62; and Rubin Zemon, *History of Ashkali Identity* (Brussels: Council of Europe, 2010). For data on Kosovo's Romani population see European Roma Rights Centre, *Abandoned Minority,* 14.

16. Balcer, "Development of Identities," 254.

17. European Roma Rights Centre, *Abandoned Minority,* 16; Balcer, "Development of Identities," 255.

18. Zemon, *History of Ashkali Identity,* 2; Balcer, "Development of Identities," 253.

19. Sevasti Trubeta, "Balkan Egyptians and Gypsy / Roma Discourse," *Nationalities Papers* 33, no. 1 (2005): 71.

20. Elena Marushiakova and Vesselin Popov, "New Ethnic Identities in the Balkans: The Case of the Egyptians," *Facta Universitas* 2, no. 8 (2001): 467.

21. Claudia Lichnofsky, "Ashkali and Egyptians in Kosovo: New Ethnic Identifications as a Result of Exclusion during Nationalist Violence from 1990 till 2010," *Romani Studies* 23, no. 1 (2013): 35.

22. Claude Cahn and Tatjana Peric, *Roma and the Kosovo Conflict* (Budapest: European Roma Rights Centre, 1999), www.errc.org/cikk.php?cikk = 798 (accessed February 2, 2019).

23. In reality, Serbs in Kosovo had little affection for *cigani.* See European Roma Rights Centre, *Abandoned Minority,* 16; and Trubeta, "Balkan Egyptians and Gypsy / Roma Discourse," 71.

24. Cahn and Peric, *Roma and the Kosovo Conflict;* European Roma Rights Centre, *Abandoned Minority,* 20.

25. See Mary Jean Brown et al., "Lead Poisoning among Internally Displaced Roma, Ashkali and Egyptian Children in the United Nations–Administered Province of Kosovo," *European Journal of Public Health* 20, no. 3 (2010): 288–92; Human Rights Watch, *Kosovo: Poisoned by Lead* (New York: Human Rights

Watch, 2009); and Internal Displacement Monitoring Centre, *Kosovo: Durable Solutions Still Elusive 13 Years after Conflict* (Geneva: Internal Displacement Monitoring Centre, 2012).

26. There is disagreement over the origin of the word Ashkali. Linguists have hypothesized that it is derived from *eshke / ashke,* referring to charcoal used by blacksmiths. This suggests that the name could have originally denoted an occupation rather than an ethnicity (see Balcer, "Development of Identities," 250). Another explanation is that it is derived from Ashkelon, a city is present-day Israel, which is one location from which Ashkali are said to have originated. See Zemon, *History of Ashkali Identity,* 3; Marushiakova and Popov, "New Ethnic Identities," 475; and Elena Marushiakova et al., *Identity Formation among Minorities in the Balkans: The Cases of Roms, Egyptians, and Ashkali in Kosovo* (Sofia: Minority Studies Society, 2001), 15.

27. Marushiakova and Popov, "New Ethnic Identities," 475; Balcer, "Development of Identities," 259.

28. Marushiakova and Popov, "New Ethnic Identities," 465; Trubeta, "Balkan Egyptians," 71.

29. Dejan Šabić et al., "Belgrade Slums: Life or Survival on the Margins of Serbian Society?," *Trames* 17, no. 1 (2013): 61.

30. Governments and NGOs often group Ashkali alongside Roma and Egyptians, resulting in the widely used acronym RAE (Roma Ashkali Egyptian).

31. Carol Bloom, Sunil Sharma, and Ann Neel, *The Current Plight of the Kosovo Roma* (Sebastopol, CA: Voice of Roma, 2002), 21.

32. European Roma Rights Centre, *Abandoned Minority,* 20; International Crisis Group, *Violence in Kosovo: Who's Killing Whom?* (Pristina: ICG Balkans, 1999), 21.

33. OSCE, *Sustainable Solutions for Displaced Roma, Ashkali and Egyptians and Policies to Improve the Reintegration of Repatriated Roma* (Belgrade: OSCE, 2010), 2.

34. For an analysis of how the breakup of Yugoslavia precipitated an ethnicity-based citizenship regime in Serbia see Jelena Vasiljević, "Imagining and Managing the Nation: Tracing Citizenship Policies in Serbia," *Citizenship Studies* 16, nos. 3-4 (2012): 323-36.

35. Snežana Đurđević, "Obstacles for the Integration of the Ashkali Community into the Serbian Society," *Facta Universitatis* 12, no. 1 (2014): 44.

36. UN-HABITAT, *State of the World's Cities 2006/2007* (New York: UN-HABITAT, 2006), iv.

37. Although the couple had been married according to their religious beliefs, they were legally unwed because Bekim lacked identity documents.

38. Liisa Malkki, *Purity and Exile: Violence, Memory, and National Cosmology among Hutu Refugees in Tanzania* (Chicago: University of Chicago Press, 1995), 16.

39. For information on the Romani holocaust, or Porajmos, see Ian Hancock, "Romanies and the Holocaust: A Re-evaluation and Overview," in *The Historiography of the Holocaust*, ed. Dan Stone (London: Palgrave Macmillan, 2004), 383–96; Karola Fings, Herbert Heuss, and Frank Sparing, *The Gypsies during the Second World War: From "Race Science" to the Camps* (Hatfield: University of Hertfordshire Press, 1997); Donald Kenrick and Grattan Puxon, *Gypsies under the Swastika* (Hatfield: University of Hertfordshire Press, 2009); and Guenter Lewy, *The Nazi Persecution of the Gypsies* (Oxford: Oxford University Press, 2000).

40. Scholars using a Foucauldian framework have argued that this unrelenting surveillance is a primary method through which the state exerts biopower over its Romani population. See Isabella Clough Mariano and Ulderico Daniele, "Roma and Humanitarianism in the Eternal City," *Journal of Modern Italian Studies* 16, no. 5 (2011): 621–36; Nando Sigona, "The Governance of Romani People in Italy: Discourse, Policy, and Practice," *Journal of Modern Italian Studies* 16, no. 5 (2011): 590–606; and Marco Solimene, " 'I Go for Iron': Xoraxané Romá Collecting Scrap Metal in Rome," in *Gypsy Economy: Romani Livelihoods and Notions of Worth in the Twenty-First Century*, ed. Micol Brazzabeni, Manuela Ivone Cunha, and Martin Fotta (London: Berghahn, 2015), 107–26.

41. See Isabella Clough Marinaro, "Between Surveillance and Exile: Biopolitics and the Roma in Italy," *Bulletin of Italian Studies* 1, no. 2 (2009): 265–87; Giovanni Picker, *Racial Cities: Governance and the Segregation of Romani People in Urban Europe* (New York: Routledge, 2017); Nando Sigona, "Locating 'The Gypsy Problem' "; and Huub van Baar, "Socio-economic Mobility and Neoliberal Governmentality in Post-socialist Europe: Activation and the Dehumanization of the Roma," *Journal of Ethnic and Migration Studies* 38, no. 8 (2012): 1289–304.

42. Michel Foucault, *The History of Sexuality*, vol. 1, *An Introduction* (New York: Vintage Books, 1976), 133–59.

43. Michel Foucault, *Society Must Be Defended*, trans. D. Macey (London: Penguin, 1997), 256.

44. Giorgio Agamben, *Homo Sacer: Sovereign Power and Bare Life* (Stanford, CA: Stanford University Press, 1998), 175. See also Giorgio Agamben, *State of Exception* (Chicago: University of Chicago Press, 2005).

45. Zlata Vuksanović-Macura, "The Mapping and Enumeration of Informal Roma Settlements in Serbia," *Environment & Urbanization* 24, no. 2 (2012): 693.

46. Eva Schwab, "Construction and Governance of 'Unhygienic Roma Settlements' in Belgrade: An Anthropological Investigation in Urban Citizenship Rights" (MA thesis, University of Vienna, Vienna, 2013), 1.

47. Sasha Tsenkova, "Informal Settlements in Post-communist Cities: Diversity Factors and Patterns," *Urbani Izziv* 21, no. 2 (2010): 75.

48. Vladimir Macura, *Roma Settlements in Serbia: Current State of Affairs and Future Goals* (Belgrade: Society for the Improvement of Local Roma Communities, 2009), 6.

49. Caroline Humphrey, "Sovereignty," in *A Companian to the Anthropology of Politics*, ed. David Nugent and Joan Vincent (Malden, MA: Blackwell, 2007), 418-63.

50. Humphrey, "Sovereignty," 433.

51. Data on informal recycling is imprecise in part because scavenging is considered to be detached from the formal economy and therefore absent from official statistics. Furthermore, many scavengers reside in settlements, whose populations are in flux and often uncounted. Mayling Simpson-Hebert, Aleksandra Mitrović, Gradamir Zajić, and Miloš Petrović, *A Paper Life: Belgrade's Roma in the Underworld of Waste Scavenging and Recycling* (New York: WEDC, 2005), 3.

52. Like Ashkali scavengers, some Serbs also relied on salvaged items when money was in short supply. However, their economic strategies and circumstances were very different. Although Serbs repurposed commodities and even purchased recycled items at street markets, they would almost never procure goods directly from dumpsters. Aside from homeless individuals and others facing extreme insecurity, this task was left to *cigani*. Furthermore, unlike a Serbian household seeking to save money by using recycled products, Ashkali and Romani scavengers acted as middlemen, gathering refuse and selling it to market shoppers, junkyards, or paper consolidators. Finally, Serbs typically enjoyed much greater access to resources while Ashkali were largely confined to trash.

53. Working in Bulgaria primarily among Roma employed by urban waste management companies, Resnick argues that while reclaimed materials are transformed, humans are not. Recycled objects may take on new lives as they transition from trash to income, but individuals remain stigmatized and in poverty. Elana Resnick, "Nothing Ever Perishes: Waste, Race, and Transformation in an Expanding European Union" (PhD diss., University of Michigan, Ann Arbor, 2016). Polje's residents, however, took a different view. Trash signified economic advancement and therefore transformation, albeit one that was inevitably constrained.

54. See Mary Downs, "A Short History of Scavenging," *Comparative Civilizations Review* 42 (2000): 23-45; and Susan Strasser, *Waste and Want: A Social History of Trash* (New York: Holt Paperbacks, 2000).

55. Martin O'Brien, *A Crisis of Waste? Understanding the Rubbish Society* (Routledge: London, 2007), 58.

56. Peter Stallybrass and Allon White, *The Politics and Poetics of Transgression* (Ithaca, NY: Cornell University Press, 1986).

57. Strasser, *Waste and Want*, 15.

58. See Krisztina Fehérváry, "Goods and States: The Political Logic of State-Socialist Material Culture," *Comparative Studies in Society and History* 51, no. 2 (2009): 426–59; Liviu Chelcea, "The Culture of Shortage during State-Socialism: Consumption Practices in a Romanian Village in the 1980s," *Cultural Studies* 16, no. 1 (2002): 16–43; and Zsusza Gille, *From the Cult of Waste to the Trash Heap of History: The Politics of Waste in Socialist and Postsocialist Hungary* (Bloomington: Indiana University Press, 2007).

59. Gille, *From the Cult of Waste to the Trash Heap of History*, 209.

60. Katherine Verdery, *What Was Socialism, and What Comes Next?* (Princeton, NJ: Princeton University Press, 1996), 98.

61. Verdery, *What Was Socialism*, 98.

62. Catherine Alexander and Joshua Reno, "Introduction," in *Economies of Recycling: The Global Transformation of Materials, Values and Social Relations*, ed. Catherine Alexander and Joshua Reno (London: Zed Books, 2012), 7; Kathleen Millar, *Reclaiming the Discarded: Life and Labor on Rio's Garbage Dump* (Durham, NC: Duke University Press, 2018), 8; and Joshua Reno "Your Trash Is Someone's Treasure: The Politics of Value at a Michigan Landfill," *Journal of Material Culture* 14, no. 1 (2009): 32.

63. Joshua Reno, "Waste and Waste Management," *Annual Review of Anthropology* 44, no. 1 (2015): 558.

64. See Vinay Gidwani and Rajyashree Reddy, "The Afterlives of 'Waste': Notes from India for a Minor History of Capitalist Surplus," *Antipode* 43, no. 5 (2011): 1625–58; Gille, *From the Cult of Waste to the Trash Heap of History*; Minh Nguyen, "Trading in Broken Things: Gendered Performances and Spatial Practices in a Northern Vietnamese Rural-Urban Waste Economy," *American Ethnologist* 43, no. 1 (2016): 116–29; and Trang Ta, "A Space for Secondhand Goods: Trading the Remnants of Material Life in Hong Kong," *Economic Anthropology* 4 (2017): 120–31.

65. See Mike Crang, Alex Hughes, Nicky Gregson, Lucy Norris, and Farid Ahamed, "Rethinking Governance and Value in Commodity Chains through Global Recycling Networks," *Transactions of the Institute of British Geographers* 38, no. 1 (2013): 12–24; Anna Davies, "Geography and the Matter of Waste Mobilities," *Transactions of the Institute of British Geographers* 37 (2012): 191–96; and Downs, "Short History."

66. Kathleen Millar, "Trash Ties: Urban Politics, Economic Crisis and Rio de Janeiro's Garbage Dump," in *Economies of Recycling: The Global Transformation of Materials, Values, and Social Relations,* ed. Catherine Alexander and Joshua Reno (London: Zed Books, 2012), 182.

67. Micol Brazzabeni, Manuela Ivone Cunha, and Martin Fotta, "Introduction: Gypsy Economy," in *Gypsy Economy: Romani Livelihoods and Notions of Worth in the 21st Century,* ed. Micol Brazzabeni, Manuela Ivone Cunha, and Martin Fotta (London: Berghahn, 2015), 7.

68. Brazzabeni et al., "Introduction," 1.

69. Arjun Appadurai, "Introduction: Commodities and the Politics of Value," in *The Social Life of Things*, ed. Arjun Appadurai (Cambridge: Cambridge University Press, 1986), 4.

70. Igor Kopytoff, "The Cultural Biography of Things: Commoditization as a Process," in *The Social Life of Things*, ed. Arjun Appadurai (Cambridge: Cambridge University Press, 1986), 66.

71. Pierre Bourdieu, *Distinction: A Social Critique of the Judgement of Taste*, trans. Richard Nice (Cambridge, MA: Harvard University Press, 1984).

72. Martin Heidegger, *Being and Time* (London: SCM Press, 1962).

73. Millar, *Reclaiming the Discarded*, 9.

74. Vuksanović-Macura, "Mapping and Enumeration," 689.

75. See Patrice McMahon, *The NGO Game: Post-conflict Peacebuilding in the Balkans and Beyond* (Ithaca, NY: Cornell University Press, 2017); and Nidhi Trehan, "The Romani Subaltern within Neoliberal European Civil Society: NGOization of Human Rights and Silent Voices," in *Romani Politics in Contemporary Europe: Poverty, Ethnic Mobilization, and the Neoliberal Order*, ed. Nando Sigona and Nidhi Trehan (London: Palgrave Macmillan, 2009), 51–71.

76. For an analysis of how statistics of suffering are transformed into commercial artifacts, see Susan Erikson, "Global Health Business: The Production and Performativity of Statistics in Sierra Leone and Germany," *Medical Anthropology* 31, no. 4 (2012): 367–84; and Sally Engle Merry, *The Seductions of Quantification: Measuring Human Rights, Gender Violence, and Sex Trafficking* (Chicago: University of Chicago Press, 2016).

77. Tess Lea, *Bureaucrats and Bleeding Hearts: Indigenous Health in Northern Australia* (Sydney: University of New South Wales Press, 2008), 178.

78. See Andria Timmer, "Constructing the 'Needy Subject': NGO Discourses of Roma Need," *Political and Legal Anthropology Review* 33, no. 2 (2010): 264–81; and Trehan, "Romani Subaltern," 51–71.

79. Mihai Surdu and Martin Kovats, "Roma Identity as an Expert-Political Construction," *Social Inclusion* 3, no. 5 (2015): 7.

80. Amnesty International, *Serbia: Submission to the U.N. Committee on Economic, Social, and Cultural Rights, 52nd Session, May 2014* (London: Amnesty International, 2014), 9–15; and Praxis, *Analysis of the Main Obstacles and Problems in Access of Roma to the Right to Adequate Housing* (Belgrade: Praxis, 2013), 8.

81. Aihwa Ong, *Neoliberalism as Exception: Mutations in Citizenship and Sovereignty* (Durham, NC: Duke University Press, 2006), 78.

82. Sreten Vujović and Mina Petrović, "Belgrade's Post-socialist Development," in *The Post-socialist City*, ed. Kiril Stanilov (London: Springer, 2007), 375.

83. Aihwa Ong, "Graduated Sovereignty in South-East Asia," *Theory, Culture & Society* 17, no. 4 (2000): 55–75.

84. For recent debates regarding the role of scholars, academic journals, and professional organizations in disseminating stereotypes of Roma, see Yaron Matras, "Letter from the Outgoing Editor: From *Journal of the Gypsy Lore Society* to *Romani Studies:* Purpose and Essence of a Modern Academic Platform," *Romani Studies* 27, no. 2 (2017): 113–23; Anna Mirga-Kruszelnicka, "Challenging Anti-gypsyism in Academic: The Role of Romani Scholars," *Critical Romani Studies* 1, no. 1 (2018): 8–28; Selling, "Assessing the Historical Irresponsibility of the Gypsy Lore Society"; and Andrew Richard Ryder, "Game of Thrones: Power Struggles and Contestation in Romani Studies," *International Journal of Romani Studies* 1, no. 2 (2019): 120–43.

85. Primary fieldwork was conducted from 2013 to 2015 and a follow-up visit was made in 2017.

86. Clifford Geertz, "Deep Hanging Out," *New York Review of Books*, October 22, 1998.

87. At his request, I have not disguised Slobodan's identity. Due to the limited amount of time Slobodan spent with me in Polje, he was absent for most of the events described in this book.

88. For discussions of race, whiteness, and their relationship to socialist and postsocialist ideology in the Balkans, see Catherine Baker, *Race and the Yugoslav Region: Postsocialist, Post-conflict, Postcolonial?* (Manchester: Manchester University Press, 2018); Dušan Bjelić, "Toward a Genealogy of the Balkan Discourses on Race," *Interventions* 20, no. 6 (2018): 906–29; and Imre, "Whiteness in Post-socialist Eastern Europe."

89. Everything I collected from the dumpsters was given to others.

90. To ensure the accuracy of my knowledge, Rajim occasionally quizzed me on the specifics of people's backgrounds. In each instance, he deemed my responses to be sufficient and appropriate.

91. See Judith Butler, *Frames of War: When Is Life Grievable?* (London: Verso, 2010); Veena Das, *Affliction: Health, Disease, Poverty* (New York: Fordham University Press, 2015); Clara Han, *Life in Debt: Times of Care and Violence in Neoliberal Chile* (Berkeley: University of California Press, 2012); and Elizabeth Povenelli, *Economies of Abandonment: Social Belonging and Endurance in Late Liberalism* (Durham, NC: Duke University Press, 2011).

92. Anne Allison, "Precarity: Commentary by Anne Allison," *Cultural Anthropology,* https://journal.culanth.org/index.php/ca/precarity-commentary-by-anne-allison (accessed September 30, 2019).

93. See Patrick O'Hare, " 'The Landfill Has Always Borne Fruit': Precarity, Formalisation, and Dispossession among Uruguay's Waste Pickers," *Dialectical Anthropology* 43, no. 1 (2019): 31–44; Elana Resnick, "Durable Remains: Glass

Reuse, Material Citizenship and Precarity in EU-era Bulgaria," *Journal of Contemporary Archaeology* 5, no. 1 (2018): 103–15; and Risa Whitson, "Negotiating Place and Value: Geographies of Waste and Scavenging in Buenos Aires," *Antipode* 43, no. 4 (2011): 1404–33.

94. See João Biehl, *Vita: Life in a Zone of Social Abandonment* (Berkeley: University of California Press, 2005); Seth Holmes, *Fresh Fruit, Broken Bodies: Migrant Farmworkers in the United States* (Berkeley: University of California Press, 2013); and Nancy Scheper-Hughes and Philippe Bourgois, "Introduction: Making Sense of Violence," in *Violence in War and Peace: An Anthology*, ed. Nancy Scheper-Hughes and Philippe Bourgois (New York: Wiley-Blackwell, 2003), 1–31.

95. Arthur Kleinman, Veena Das, and Margaret Lock, "Introduction," in *Social Suffering*, ed. Arthur Kleinman, Veena Das, and Margaret Lock (Berkeley: University of California Press, 1997), ix.

96. Robert Desjarlais, "Struggling Along," in *Things as They Are: New Directions in Phenomenological Anthropology*, ed. Michael Jackson (Bloomington: Indiana University Press, 1996), 74.

97. Das, *Affliction*, 17.

98. Das, *Affliction*, 1.

99. Kathleen Stewart, *Ordinary Affects* (Durham, NC: Duke University Press, 2007).

100. Giorgio Agamben, *The Open: Man and Animal* (Stanford, CA: Stanford University Press, 2003), 66.

101. Bruce O'Neill, "Cast Aside: Boredom, Downward Mobility, and Homelessness in Post-communist Bucharest," *Cultural Anthropology* 29, no. 1 (2014): 11. See also Bruce O'Neill, *The Space of Boredom: Homelessness in the Slowing Global Order* (Durham, NC: Duke University Press, 2017).

102. See Myall, *Gypsy Identities*.

CHAPTER ONE. THE SOCIALITY OF EXCEPTION

1. See Fraser, *The Gypsies;* Myall, *Gypsy Identities;* Okely, "Recycled (Mis) representations"; and Stewart, "Roma and Gypsy 'Ethnicity'."

2. Thomas Acton, *Gypsy Politics and Social Change* (London: Routledge & Kegan Paul Books, 1974), 54.

3. While Ashkali and Bayash are categories recognized by scholars, I have introduced the phrase "Yugoslav Roma" to denote individuals who broadly define themselves as Roma but assert no further affiliation aside from situating their heritage within the former Yugoslavia.

4. See David Scheffel, *Svinia in Black and White: Slovak Roma and Their Neighbours* (Toronto: University of Toronto Press, 2005); and Michael Stewart, *The Time of the Gypsies* (London: Westview Press, 1999).

5. Diana Allan, *Refugees of the Revolution: Experiences of Palestinian Exile* (Stanford, CA: Stanford University Press, 2013).

6. Allan, *Refugees of the Revolution*, 73.

7. Bourgois and Schonberg also examine how exclusion and need intersect to create relatedness in excepted spaces. Reflecting on the lives of heroin addicts in San Francisco, they write, "We realized that cooperating to purchase bags is not simply a pragmatic, economic, or logistical necessity; it is the basis for sociality and establishes the boundaries of networks that provide companionship and also facilitate material survival." Philippe Bourgois and Jeff Schonberg, *Righteous Dopefiend* (Berkeley: University of California Press, 2009), 106. Furthermore, these individuals were forced to interact across hostile racial boundaries. While ethnic differences were similarly transcended in Polje, these divisions—between Ashkali, Bayash Roma, and Yugoslav Roma—were invisible to Serbs. Consequently, Polje's residents negotiated two ethnic registers: one outside of Polje (between Serbs and *cigani*) and another inside.

8. Statements detailing one's struggles provided a shared discourse for Polje's residents. Examining the experiences of Russians in the 1990s, Shevchenko notes that narratives of a chronic crisis were "a rhetorical resource that could be strategically used for building rapport, creating solidarities, and asserting one's practical competence in everyday interactions." Olga Shevchenko, *Crisis and the Everyday in Postsocialist Moscow* (Bloomington: University of Indiana Press, 2008), 62.

9. The behavior of some Ashkali residents occasionally confirmed this reputation. During an ongoing dispute, Bekim burst into the home of his Romani neighbor and threatened to burn the man alive. Bekim yelled that because he was "Albanian," killing the man would be easy for him. However, this type of open conflict was rare.

10. See Fraser, *The Gypsies;* and Ian Hancock, "Three-fold Identity? The Ethnical and National Identity of the Hungarian Boyash Gypsies," in *Nations and National Minorities in the European Union*, ed. Barna Bodó and Márton Tonk (Cluj-Napoca: Scientia, 1991), 91–102.

11. Snezana Bjelotomić, *Average Salary in Serbia: Gap between Data and Reality*, December 23, 2016, http://serbianmonitor.com/en/economy/28266/average-salary-serbia/ (accessed March 29, 2018).

12. I believe that Bayash residents built homes in their village as a marker of personhood and belonging. Cortorari Romani houses in Romania have similarly been understood as a proclamation of identity. Home décor and architecture marked a family as both civilized and worldly even though some items, such as ashtrays and forks, were never utilized. See Cătălina Tesăr, "Houses under Construction: Conspicuous Consumption and the Values of Youth among Romanian Cortorari Gypsies," in *Gypsy Economy: Romani Livelihoods and Notions of Worth in the 21st Century*, ed. Micol Brazzabeni, Manuela Ivone Cunha, and Martin Fotta (London: Berghahn, 2015), 181–200.

13. Bartering, buying, and selling were largely the domain of men. Occasionally, a woman would participate but this was rare.

14. Throughout postsocialist Europe, rising levels of unemployment coupled with unstable economies have resulted in the continuation of informal exchange networks that were often relied upon during the socialist era. See Ivana Bajić-Hajduković, "Remembering the 'Embargo Cake': The Legacy of Hyperinflation and the UN Sanctions in Serbia," *Contemporary Southeastern Europe* 1, no. 2 (2014): 61–79; Marija Đekić, Miloš Nikolić, and Raica Milićević, "Causes, Manifestations, and Representation of the Shadow Economy with Reference to Serbia," *Ekonomika* 65, no. 3 (2019): 103–14; Alena Ledeneva, *How Russia Really Works: The Informal Practices That Shaped Post-Soviet Politics and Business* (Ithaca, NY: Cornell University Press, 2013); and Olga Shevchenko, *Crisis and the Everyday*. While Polje's economic networks may appear to resemble these, I believe they were distinct. Serbs may face economic hardship but they were nevertheless full members of the national project. Because Ashkali and Roma were systematically excluded, their activities were far more constrained and their reliance on one another was far more essential.

15. See Judit Durst, "New Redistributors in Times of Insecurity: Different Types of Informal Lending in Hungary," in *Gypsy Economy: Romani Livelihoods and Notions of Worth in the 21st Century*, ed. Micol Brazzabeni, Manuela Ivone Cunha, and Martin Fotta (London: Berghahn, 2015), 49–67; Tomáš Hrustič, "Usury among the Slovak Roma: Notes on Relations between Lenders and Borrowers in a Segregated Taboris," in *Gypsy Economy: Romani Livelihoods and Notions of Worth in the 21st Century*, ed. Micol Brazzabeni, Manuela Ivone Cunha, and Martin Fotta (London: Berghahn, 2015), 31–48; and Scheffel, *Svinia in Black and White*.

16. As in this interaction, I often remained silent because I felt uncomfortable participating in these jokes. On one occasion when Dragomir saw my anxiety, he assured me that everything said was in jest. Nevertheless, I did not want to position myself as an individual who, even jokingly, sexualized Ashkali and Romani women. Furthermore, as a queer man, I could not adopt a fully heteronormative sexuality, but neither did I want to publicly identify as gay, given the prevalence of homophobia throughout Serbia. Consequently, I found excuses to situate myself on the periphery of these jests rather than become the subject of them.

17. Michel Agier, "Camps, Encampments, and Occupations: From the Heterotopia to the Urban Subject," *Ethnos* 84, no. 1 (2019): 24.

CHAPTER TWO. PRECARIOUS DOMESTICITY

1. Most flat tires were repaired by locating the puncture and tying if off with a string. But eventually there came a point at which an inner tube could no longer

be effectively patched. When this occurred, the cost of a replacement could require all of a family's daily earnings.

2. Moving to a new community entailed a number of potentially disastrous unknowns: larcenous neighbors, aggressive police, and a lack of good trash.

3. A parallel can be found in Biehl's work: both Vita and Polje were sites where residents were dehumanized and forsaken but, in each instance, inhabitants sought to maintain social connections. Biehl asserts that Catarina's narratives, while often dismissed as the rantings of a madwoman, were an effort to hold onto the real. See Biehl, *Vita,* 88. In Polje, where people's lives were far less regulated and the materiality of trash provided ever-changing raw materials, inhabitants could create relatedness through décor.

4. See Elizabeth Cullen Dunn, *No Path Home: Humanitarian Camps and the Grief of Displacement* (Ithaca, NY: Cornell University Press, 2018); and Elizabeth Cullen Dunn and Jason Cons, "Aleatory Sovereignty and the Rule of Sensitive Spaces," *Antipode* 46, no. 1 (2014): 98–99.

5. I was not expected to pay rent and doing so would have been considered inappropriate given that I was godfather to Bekim's child. However, I did provide cash for the household's food and other essentials. This money was referred to as a loan although I never expected repayment and it was never offered. I also contributed my labor by fetching water, tacking up horses, watching children, and scavenging.

6. While dumpsters were the most common source of scavenged foods, there were occasionally others. Aleksander, for instance, commented that he always enjoyed Easter because he could feed his family by collecting the dyed eggs Serbs placed on the gravestones of loved ones.

7. Gender roles around the domestic sphere were clearly defined and always enforced. Men never cooked, set out, or served the meal.

8. Fueled with wood gathered from the dumpsters, these stoves were essential features of settlement life and provided a shack's only source of heat in winter. In summer, when homes became oppressively hot, families moved their stoves outside.

9. Because I was a foreigner and hence deemed vulnerable to Serbs and the Serbian authorities, the men were especially concerned to protect me from arrest (as, in other contexts, they sought to protect me from assault). As a result, I was forbidden from touching the cable and only allowed to closely observe the procedure twice.

10. Allan, *Refugees of the Revolution,* 104.

11. Allan, *Refugees of the Revolution,* 134.

12. Republic of Serbia, *Serbia Floods 2014* (Belgrade: Ministry of Environmental Protection, 2014), 8.

13. Republic of Serbia, *Serbia Floods 2014,* 107.

CHAPTER THREE. ABJECT ECONOMIES

1. Millar, *Reclaiming the Discarded,* 9.

2. Franco Barchiesi, *Precarious Liberation: Workers, the State, and Contested Social Citizenship in Postapartheid South Africa* (Albany: SUNY Press, 2011), 24.

3. Julia Kristeva, *Powers of Horror: An Essay on Abjection* (New York: Columbia University Press, 1982).

4. Kristeva, *Powers of Horror,* 4.

5. David Boarder Giles, "The Anatomy of a Dumpster: Abject Capital and the Looking Glass of Value," *Social Text* 32, no. 1 (2014): 108.

6. Marcel Mauss, *The Gift: Forms and Functions of Exchange in Archaic Societies,* trans. Ian Cunnison (New York: Martino Fine Books, 2011).

7. When scavenging with Ashkali, my appearance and accent clearly marked me as different. Initially, I wondered if this would elicit a response from Serbs such as curiosity or opprobrium, but it did not. As far as I could tell, I was treated similarly to the Ashkali whom I was accompanying.

8. Examining sovereignty within excepted spaces, Dunn and Cons note, "Sometimes acting within the constraints of burdened agency is transgressive because it entails criminality. Prostitution, drug trafficking, smuggling, theft, and other forms of petty crime are strategic responses to the insufficiency of life in camps and border zones that provide employment, income, and the ability to govern one's own life, at least to some degree." This was certainly the case in Polje. Dunn and Cons, "Aleatory Sovereignty and the Rule of Sensitive Spaces," 100.

9. Craig Hempfling, *Secondary Materials and Waste Recycling Commercialization in Serbia, Part I: Assessment* (Belgrade: US AID, 2010), 19.

10. Boasting five hundred shops, this was the largest wholesale facility in the Balkans. See Maja Korać, "Transnational Pathways to Integration: Chinese Traders in Serbia," *Sociologija* 55, no. 2 (2013): 248.

11. Republic of Serbia, *Action Plan for the Implementation of the Strategy of Social Inclusion of the Roma in the Republic of Serbia for the Period 2016-2025* (Belgrade: Republic of Serbia, 2017), 42.

12. European Union Agency for Fundamental Rights, *Poverty and Employment: The Situation of Roma in 11 EU Member States* (Vienna: FRA, 2014), 7.

13. Citing evidence that Roma have been posing as mendicants since at least the fourteenth century, some scholars argue that begging is an integral aspect of Romani culture. See Fraser, *The Gypsies,* 60-84; and Ilenia Ruggiu, "Is Begging a Roma Cultural Practice? Answers from the Italian Legal System and Anthropology," *Romani Studies* 26, no. 1 (2016): 31-61. My experience in Polje was the opposite: begging was a response to newfound economic marginalization, not the result of long-standing cultural norms.

14. In Uruguay, landfills could provide a more secure income than did wage labor because the latter required establishing an unpredictable relationship with the state. See O'Hare, "The Landfill Has Always Borne Fruit."

CHAPTER FOUR. CONSTRAINED ASPIRATIONS

1. The amount varied based on the number of minors in a household and type of benefits awarded.

2. Veena Das, "State, Citizenship, and the Urban Poor," *Citizenship Studies* 15, nos. 3–4 (2011): 321.

3. Many favored a horse and cart because they could be driven without a license, which required identification documents, literacy, and a substantial monetary investment. Nevertheless, laws forbade horse carts in the city center, confining scavengers to the periphery.

4. See Fraser, *The Gypsies;* Elena Marushiakova and Vesselin Popov, *Gypsies in the Ottoman Empire* (Hatfield: University of Hertfordshire Press, 2001); and Evelyn Urech and Wilco van den Heuvel, "A Sociolinguistic Perspective on Roma Group Names in Transylvania," *Romani Studies* 21, no. 2 (2011): 145–60.

5. Elena Marushiakova and Vesselin Popov, " 'Gypsy' Groups in Eastern Europe: Ethnonyms vs. Professionyms," *Romani Studies* 23, no. 1 (2013): 62.

6. See Gaja Maestri, "Struggles and Ambiguities over Political Subjectivities in the Camp: Roma Camp Dwellers between Neoliberal and Urban Citizenship in Italy," *Citizenship Studies* 21, no. 6 (2017): 640–56; Helen O'Nions, "How Citizenship Laws Leave the Roma in Europe's Hinterland," in *The Human Right to Citizenship: A Slippery Concept,* ed. Rhonda Howard-Hassmann and Margaret Walton-Roberts (Philadelphia: University of Pennsylvania Press, 2015), 209–31; and van Baar, "Socio-economic Mobility."

7. A Belgrade-based NGO notes, "In Serbia also, due to the unresolved issue of citizenship, thousands of individuals are deprived of exercising their fundamental human rights. Unlike *de jure* stateless persons—those not considered citizens by any state under the operation of their laws, the majority of persons who do not manage to resolve the issue of citizenship in Serbia do have legal basis for the acquisition of Serbian citizenship. However, the fact that many of them have for years been unsuccessful in proving their identity or citizenship and that in some families this problem is transgenerational, represents a serious challenge and leaves these persons in a state of uncertainty that is sometimes almost equal to the absence of citizenship." Praxis, *Persons at Risk of Statelessness in Serbia* (Belgrade: Praxis, 2011), 7.

8. Julija Sardelić, "Romani Minorities and Uneven Citizenship Access in the Post-Yugoslav Space," *Ethnopolitics* 14, no. 2 (2015): 166–67.

9. UNHCR, *Assessment of the Needs of Internally Displaced Persons in the Republic of Serbia* (Belgrade: UNHCR, 2011), 89.

10. As more and more Roma, Ashkali, and Egyptians crossed the border, the Serbian government made it increasingly difficult for these individuals to obtain IDP status. Consequently, only half of Roma, Ashkali, and Egyptian IDPs were registered. See UNHCR, *Assessment of the Needs*, 89.

11. In 2011 it was estimated that 17.6 percent of Romani IDPs in Serbia lacked basic identification documents while 43 percent of Romani IDPs in need did not receive state aid for their dependent children. See UNHCR, *Assessment of the Needs*, 4, 31.

12. While identity documents were a vital aspect of socialist states throughout the region, they assumed new significance during the breakup of Yugoslavia as newly independent nations sought to concretize, and link, ethnic identity and citizenship through formal documentation. See Tone Bringa, "National Categories, National Identification, and Identity Formation in 'Multinational' Bosnia," *Anthropology of East Europe Review* 11, nos. 1 and 2 (1993): 80–88; Robert Hayden, "Constitutional Nationalism in the Formerly Yugoslav Republics," *Slavic Review* 51, no. 4 (1992): 654–73; and Jelena Vasiljević, "Citizenship as Lived Experience: Belonging and Documentality after the Breakup of Yugoslavia," *CITSEE Working Paper Series* 36 (2014): 1–29.

13. The costs for identity documents were as follows: birth certificate—720 dinars ($7.60); citizenship certificate—770 dinars ($8); and national identity card—1,154 dinars ($12.10). It was possible to obtain a free version of birth and citizenship documents but presenting these to the police or other officials could elicit discrimination. Furthermore, no-cost documents were not valid when applying for identity cards.

14. While Roma and Ashkali were routinely the subject of bureaucratic marginalization, homeless people, alcoholics, former prisoners, migrants, and members of other groups deemed to be unproductive also faced similar barriers.

15. While Ashkali believed that their activities put me at risk, my presence could also endanger them. An anti-American sentiment pervaded Serbia as a result of the NATO bombing campaign in 1999. Ashkali worried that if my nationality was discovered by police or security guards, it could elicit retribution against everyone present. When we were confronted at the market, Bekim whispered that I should remain silent, lest the guards recognize my accent. On such occasions I was circumspect and my identity was never revealed.

16. See Gordana Blagojević, "The Chinese Baptists: An Example of a Twofold Minority in Serbia Today," *Glasnik Etnografskog Instituta SANU* 59, no. 1 (2011): 106–14; Maja Korać-Sanderson, "Chinese Traders in Serbia: Gender Opportunities, Translocal Family Strategies, and Transnational Mobility," *Ars & Humanitas* 7, no. 2 (2013): 86–98; and Svetlana Milutinović, "Chinese Transnational Entrepreneurs in Budapest and Belgrade: Seeking Markets, Carrying Glo-

balization," in *Transnational Ties: Cities, Migrations, and Identities,* ed. Richard Brail (New York: Taylor & Francis, 2008), 90–106.

17. Korać, "Transnational Pathways," 251.

18. Pal Nyiri, *Chinese in Eastern Europe and Russia: A Middleman Minority in a Transnational Era* (New York: Routledge, 2007), 139.

19. Felix Chang, "The Chinese under Serbian Laws," in *Chinese Migrants in Russia, Central Asia, and Eastern Europe,* ed. Felix Chang and Sunnie Rucker-Change (New York: Routledge, 2012).

20. See Ong, "Graduated Sovereignty."

21. Researchers have noted that Roma alternatively hide and perform their identity as an economic strategy. For example, voluble exhortations by market traders serve to demonstrate agency and create legitimacy. See Micol Brazzabeni, "Sounds of the Markets: Portuguese Cigano Vendors in Open-Air Markets in the Lisbon Metropolitan Area," in *Informal Urban Street Markets: International Perspectives,* ed. Clifton Evers and Kirsten Seale (New York: Routledge, 2015), 51–61; and Judith Okely, "Trading Stereotypes: The Case of English Gypsies," in *Ethnicity at Work,* ed. Sandra Wallman (London: MacMillan, 1979), 16–33. Consequently, for men like Miloš, an expert identity was formed through enacting the trope of the loud Gypsy metal collector.

22. Women were much more vulnerable to reprisals when accused of wrongdoing. While men occasionally came to blows with one another, it was rare. However, husbands could emotionally, verbally, and physically assault their wives with few consequences. These events often took place in the privacy of a family's home, thus concealing their severity from other settlement residents.

CHAPTER FIVE. RELOCATIONS

1. See Konstantin Kilibarda, "Clearing Space: An Anatomy of Urban Renewal, Social Cleansing, and Everyday Life in a Belgrade Mahala," *Cambridge Review of International Affairs* 24, no. 4 (2011): 593–612; Gezim Krasniqi, "Equal Citizens, Uneven Communities: Differentiated and Hierarchical Citizenship in Kosovo," *Ethnopolitics* 14, no. 2 (2015): 197–217; and van Baar, "Socio-Economic Mobility."

2. See Dragos Ciulinaru, "When 'Inclusion' Means 'Exclusion': Discourses on the Eviction and Repatriation of Roma Migrants, at National and European Union Level," *Journal of International Migration & Integration* 19, no. 4 (2018): 1059–73; Angela Kóczé, "Roma Migration and Neoliberalism: Distorted Notions of Romani Migration in European Public Discourses," *Social Identities* 24, no. 4 (2018): 459–73; and Huub van Baar, "The Perpetual Mobile Machine of Forced Mobility: Europe's Roma and the Institutionalization of Rootlessness," in *The Irregularization of Migration in Contemporary Europe: Detention, Deportation,*

Drowning, ed. Yolande Jansen, Robin Celikates, and Joost de Bloois (London: Rowman & Littlefield International, 2015), 71–86.

3. See Zlata Vuksanović-Macura and Vladimir Macura, *Existing Models of Housing Improvement for Roma: Social and Affordable Housing Solutions for Roma and Vulnerable Population in Serbia* (Belgrade: OSCE Mission to Serbia, 2014); and Zlata Vuksanović-Macura and Vladimir Macura, *Housing Models for Substandard Roma Settlements: Guidelines for Local Self-Governments, Civil Society Organizations and Roma Communities* (Belgrade: OSCE Mission to Serbia, 2014).

4. Amnesty International, *Serbia: Submission to the U.N.,* 9.

5. See Praxis, *Eviction from the Informal Settlement in Block 72, New Belgrade* (Belgrade: Praxis, 2012); and Laura Renzi, "Roma People in Europe: A Long History of Discrimination," *European Social Watch Report,* 2010, 40–43.

6. Goran Bašić, *Report with Recommendations on the Resettlement of the Informal Roma Settlement near Belville* (Belgrade: Protector of Citizens of the Republic of Serbia, 2012), 9.

7. Amnesty International, *Serbia: How the EBRD's Funding Contributed to a Forced Eviction in Belgrade, Serbia* (London: Amnesty International, 2014), 1.

8. Reported in Gordana Andric, "Belgrade Shuns Plight of Kosovo Roma Refugees," *Balkan Transnational Justice,* April 9, 2012, https://balkaninsight.com/2012/04/09/belgrade-shuns-plight-of-kosovo-roma-refugees/ (accessed March 28, 2020); and Bašić, *Report with Recommendations,* 9.

9. See Amnesty International, *Serbia: Roma Still Waiting for Adequate Housing* (London: Amnesty International, 2015); and Amnesty International, *Serbia: Submission to the U.N.;* and Praxis, *Analysis of the Main Obstacles.*

10. Kilibarda, "Clearing Space."

11. Kilibarda, "Clearing Space," 605.

12. Praxis, *Analysis of the Main Obstacles,* 2.

13. Uros Vesic, Tatijana Kosic, and Aleksandra Krstic-Furundzic, "Social Housing in Serbia: Dual Approach," in *Proceedings of Real Corp 2013: Planning Times,* ed. Manfred Schrenk, Vasily Popovich, and Peter Zeile (Rome: Real Corp, 2013), 801–9.

14. See Amnesty International, *Serbia: Roma Still Waiting;* and Schwab, "Construction and Governance."

15. While the manufacturer, Euromodul, has created and marketed a range of high-tech modular buildings including post offices, cafés, laboratories, and homes, the containers at the center were the most basic available.

16. The complete list can be found at www.gcsrbg.org/index.php?option = com_content&view = article&id = 128&catid = 85&Itemid = 524.

17. OSCE, *Municipal Responses to Displacement and Returns in Kosovo* (Pristina: OSCE, 2010), 2.

18. UNHCR, *Assessment of the Needs,* 33.

19. To qualify, individuals must be registered IDPs, have lost their domiciles in the conflict, and not own a home in Kosovo. See OSCE, *Eight Years After: Minority Returns and Housing and Property Restitution in Kosovo* (Pristina: OSCE, 2007).

20. Republic of Kosovo, *Strategy for Inclusion of Roma and Ashkali Communities in the Kosovo Society 2017–2021* (Pristina: Republic of Kosovo, 2017), 28.

21. For details, see UNDP, *SPARK: Sustainable Partnerships for Assistance to Minority Returns to Kosovo, Bi-Monthly Report July–August 2009* (Pristina: UNDP, 2009).

22. For a further discussion of postwar NGOs in the former Yugoslavia, see McMahon, *NGO Game*.

23. Had Bekim possessed an identity card or passport, he could have taken a bus directly from Belgrade to Pristina. From there, it was only fifteen kilometers to Endrit's home.

24. Economic data shows that Kosovo has the highest poverty and unemployment rates in the Western Balkans, with 36 percent of Roma, Ashkali, and Egyptians living in extreme poverty and 60 percent unemployed. See Nando Sigona, "Between Competing Imaginaries of Statehood: Roma, Ashkali, and Egyptian (RAE) Leadership in Newly Independent Kosovo," *Journal of Ethnic and Migration Studies* 38, no. 8 (2012): 1219; and UNDP, *Kosovo Human Development Report* (Pristina: UNDP, 2016), 14.

25. For people such as Emine and Agim, who grew up in Serbia, this was unbearable. Polje might have been a circumscribed space but it was only a few hundred meters from a cityscape.

26. In Kosovo, Ashkali have been labeled "the most vulnerable" with regard to income levels, with almost half experiencing difficulty affording food and other basic needs. UNDP, *Community Vulnerability Assessment Report* (Pristina: UNDP, 2013), 8.

27. Sigona, "Between Competing Imaginaries," 1223.

28. Despite efforts to ensure minority rights in Kosovo, Roma, Ashkali, and Egyptians continue to face prejudice, exclusion, and segregation, with safety and security remaining a primary concern. See Adem Beha, "Minority Rights: An Opportunity for Adjustment of Ethnic Relations in Kosovo?" *Journal on Ethnopolitics and Minority Issues in Europe* 13, no. 4 (2014): 85–110; Krasniqi, "Equal Citizens, Uneven Communities"; Angela Mattli and Stephan Müller, *Lost in Transition: The Forced Migration Circle of Roma, Ashkali, and Balkan Egyptians from Kosovo* (Bern: Society for Threatened Peoples, 2015); and Gezim Visoka and Oliver Richmond, "After Liberal Peace? From Failed State-Building to an Emancipatory Peace in Kosovo," *International Studies Perspectives* 18, no. 1 (2017): 110–29.

29. Throughout much of Europe, Roma, Ashkali, and Egyptians are commonly referred to as black people. After a store clerk called Bekim black, he

responded that he was not from Africa. But as scholars note, blackness is not about skin hue but is rather a culturally constructed category that embeds notions of race and nation. See Catherine Baker, "Postcoloniality without Race? Racial Exceptionalism and Southeast European Cultural Studies," *Interventions: International Journal of Postcolonial Studies* 20, no. 6 (2018): 759–84; and Alaina Lemon, " 'What Are They Writing about Us Blacks?' Roma and 'Race' in Russia," *Anthropology of East Europe Review* 13, no. 2 (1995): 35.

30. Julija Sardelić, "Romani Minorities and the Variety of Migration Patterns in the Post-Yugoslav Space," *Roma Rights* 1 (2014): 16.

31. Florian Trauner and Emanule Manigrassi, "When Visa-Free Travel Becomes Difficult to Achieve and Easy to Lose: The EU Visa Free Dialogues after the EU's Experience with the Western Balkans," *European Journal of Migration and Law* 16, no. 1 (2014): 124, 132.

32. European Stability Initiative, *New Facts and Figures on Western Balkan Asylum Seekers* (Berlin: European Stability Initiative, 2015), 2.

33. Mattli and Müller, *Lost in Transition,* 24

34. See Herbert Adam, "Xenophobia, Asylum Seekers, and Immigration Policies in Germany," *Nationalism and Ethnic Politics* 21, no. 4 (2015): 446–64; Heide Castañeda, "European Mobilities or Poverty Migration? Discourses on Roma in Germany," *International Migration* 53, no. 3 (2015): 87–99; Christina Lee, "Counting on Confusion: Romani Asylum-Seekers in the German Media, 2012–2013," *Roma Rights* 1 (2014): 79–86; and Jure Leko, "Migration Regimes and the Translation of Human Rights: On the Struggles for Recognition of Romani Migrants in Germany," *Social Inclusion* 5, no. 3 (2017): 77–88.

35. See Ciulinaru, "When 'Inclusion' Means 'Exclusion' "; Kóczé, "Roma Migration and Neoliberalism"; and van Baar, "Perpetual Mobile Machine."

36. Trauner and Manigrassi, "When Visa-Free Travel Becomes Difficult," 137.

37. While I conducted fieldwork in container settlements, social housing complexes, and throughout Kosovo, I was unable to travel to the EU with migrants or visit them during their bid to claim asylum. I did have several video calls with people while they were in Germany but relied solely on their representations of events.

38. Barbara Laubenthal, "Refugees Welcome? Federalism and Asylum Policies in Germany," *Fieri Working Papers,* September 2015, 11.

39. Asylum applicants received €135 ($169) per month for an adult in shared accommodation and €354 ($443) in single accommodation. This is about €70 ($88) less than what is paid to German welfare recipients. Married couples were eligible for €636 ($795) plus €276 ($345) to €214 ($268) for each child under the age of eighteen. *Deutsche Welle,* "Asylum Benefits in the EU: How Member States Compare," June 19, 2018, www.dw.com/en/asylum-benefits-in-the-eu-how-member-states-compare/a-44298599 (accessed February 2, 2019); and Marion MacGregor, *The Asylum Seeker's Benefits Act,* May 30, 2018, www.info-

migrants.net/en/post/9560/the-asylum-seekers-benefits-act (accessed February 2, 2019).

40. This expedited procedure has been criticized for ignoring refugee rights, failing to collect detailed and accurate information, and assuming that these applications were futile. See Helene Heuser, "Blitzverfahren—German Asylum Procedures for Roma from Western Balkan Countries," in *Going Nowhere? Western Balkan Roma and EU Liberalisation,* ed. Elspeth Guild, Kieran O'Reilly, and Marek Szilvas (Budapest: European Roma Rights Centre, 2014), 71–78.

41. European Stability Initiative, *New Facts,* 5.

42. European Stability Initiative, *New Facts,* 5.

43. Jelena Čvorović and Kathryn Coe, "'Visiting' Close Kin Abroad: Migration Strategies of Serbian Roma," *Journal of Gypsy Studies* 1, no. 1 (2017): 19; and Milena Tmava and Adem Beha, *Helplessness: Roma, Ashkali, and Egyptian Forced Returnees in Kosovo* (Pristina: RAD Centre, 2009), 8.

44. See Mattli and Müller, *Lost in Translation;* OSCE, *Municipal Responses;* Tmava and Beha, *Helplessness;* and Gezim Visoka and Adem Beha, *Repatriation without Responsibility: The Nature and Implications of Roma, Ashkali and Egyptian Forced Repatriation to Kosovo* (Pristina: FORUM, 2015).

CONCLUSION

1. This was the only instance of gendered violence that I witnessed, although I did occasionally hear rumors of such acts. However, my position as a male restricted the type of information I was given. Consequently, I am unable to estimate the true rate at which intimate partner violence occurred.

2. Concerned that I could be arrested and prosecuted, Polje's residents never invited me to participate in theft.

Bibliography

Acton, Thomas. *Gypsy Politics and Social Change*. London: Routledge & Kegan Paul Books, 1974.

———. "Modernity, Culture, and 'Gypsies': Is There a Meta-Scientific Method for Understanding the Representation of 'Gypsies'? And Do the Dutch Really Exist?" In *The Role of the Romanies: Images and Counter-Images of "Gypsies"/Romanies in European Cultures,* edited by Nicholas Saul and Susan Tebbutt, 98–117. Liverpool: Liverpool University Press, 2004.

Adam, Herbert. "Xenophobia, Asylum Seekers, and Immigration Policies in Germany." *Nationalism and Ethnic Politics* 21, no. 4 (2015): 446–64.

Agamben, Giorgio. *Homo Sacer: Sovereign Power and Bare Life*. Stanford, CA: Stanford University Press, 1998.

———. *The Open: Man and Animal*. Stanford, CA: Stanford University Press, 2003.

———. *State of Exception*. Chicago: University of Chicago Press, 2005.

Agier, Michel. "Camps, Encampments, and Occupations: From the Heterotopia to the Urban Subject." *Ethnos* 84, no. 1 (2019): 14–26.

Alexander, Catherine, and Joshua Reno. "Introduction." In *Economies of Recycling: The Global Transformation of Materials, Values and Social Relations,* edited by Catherine Alexander and Joshua Reno, 1–33. London: Zed Books, 2012.

Allan, Diana. *Refugees of the Revolution: Experiences of Palestinian Exile*. Stanford, CA: Stanford University Press, 2013.

Allison, Anne. "Precarity: Commentary by Anne Allison." *Cultural Anthropology.* Accessed September 30, 2019. https://journal.culanth.org/index.php /ca/precarity-commentary-by-anne-allison.

Amnesty International. *Serbia: How the EBRD's Funding Contributed to a Forced Eviction in Belgrade, Serbia.* London: Amnesty International, 2014.

———. *Serbia: Submission to the U.N. Committee on Economic, Social, and Cultural Rights, 52nd Session, May 2014.* London: Amnesty International, 2014.

———. *Serbia: Roma Still Waiting for Adequate Housing.* London: Amnesty International, 2015.

Andric, Gordana. "Belgrade Shuns Plight of Kosovo Roma Refugees." *Balkan Transnational Justice,* April 9, 2012. Accessed March 11, 2020. https:// balkaninsight.com/2012/04/09/belgrade-shuns-plight-of-kosovo-roma-refugees/.

Appadurai, Arjun. "Introduction: Commodities and the Politics of Value." In *The Social Life of Things,* edited by Arjun Appadurai, 3–63. Cambridge: Cambridge University Press, 1986.

Bajić-Hajduković, Ivana, "Remembering the 'Embargo Cake': The Legacy of Hyperinflation and the UN Sanctions in Serbia." *Contemporary Southeastern Europe* 1, no. 2 (2014): 61–79.

Baker, Catherine. "Postcoloniality without Race? Racial Exceptionalism and Southeast European Cultural Studies." *Interventions: International Journal of Postcolonial Studies* 20, no. 6 (2018): 759–84.

———. *Race and the Yugoslav Region: Postsocialist, Post-conflict, Postcolonial?* Manchester: Manchester University Press, 2018.

Balcer, Adam. "The Development of Identities among the Population of Gypsy Origin in Kosovo: Ashkali, Egyptians, and Roma." *Sprawy Narodowos'ciowe* 31 (2007): 247–62.

Barchiesi, Franco. *Precarious Liberation: Workers, the State, and Contested Social Citizenship in Postapartheid South Africa.* Albany: SUNY Press, 2011.

Bašić, Goran. *Report with Recommendations on the Resettlement of the Informal Roma Settlement near Belville.* Belgrade: Protector of Citizens of the Republic of Serbia, 2012.

Beha, Adem. "Minority Rights: An Opportunity for Adjustment of Ethnic Relations in Kosovo?" *Journal on Ethnopolitics and Minority Issues in Europe* 13, no. 4 (2014): 85–110.

Bhopal, Kalwant, and Martin Myers. *Insiders, Outsiders, and Others: Gypsies and Identity.* Hatfield: University of Hertfordshire Press, 2008.

Biehl, João. *Vita: Life in a Zone of Social Abandonment.* Berkeley: University of California Press, 2005.

Bjelić, Dušan. "Toward a Genealogy of the Balkan Discourses on Race." *Interventions* 20, no. 6 (2018): 906–29.

Bjelotomić, Snezana. *Average Salary in Serbia: Gap between Data and Reality.* December 23, 2016. Accessed March 29, 2018. http://serbianmonitor.com /en/economy/28266/average-salary-serbia/.

Blagojević, Gordana. "The Chinese Baptists: An Example of a Twofold Minority in Serbia Today." *Glasnik Etnografskog Instituta SANU* 59, no. 1 (2011): 106–14.

Bloom, Carol, Sunil Sharma, and Ann Neel. *The Current Plight of the Kosovo Roma.* Sebastopol, CA: Voice of Roma, 2002.

Bourdieu, Pierre. *Distinction: A Social Critique of the Judgement of Taste.* Translated by Richard Nice. Cambridge, MA: Harvard University Press, 1984.

Bourgois, Philippe, and Jeff Schonberg. *Righteous Dopefiend.* Berkeley: University of California Press, 2009.

Brazzabeni, Micol. "Sounds of the Markets: Portuguese Cigano Vendors in Open-Air Markets in the Lisbon Metropolitan Area." In *Informal Urban Street Markets: International Perspectives,* edited by Clifton Evers and Kirsten Seale, 51–61. New York: Routledge, 2015.

Brazzabeni, Micol, Manuela Ivone Cunha, and Martin Fotta. "Introduction: Gypsy Economy." In *Gypsy Economy: Romani Livelihoods and Notions of Worth in the 21st Century,* edited by Micol Brazzabeni, Manuela Ivone Cunha, and Martin Fotta, 1–29. London: Berghahn, 2015.

Bringa, Tone. "National Categories, National Identification, and Identity Formation in 'Multinational' Bosnia," *Anthropology of East Europe Review* 11, nos. 1 and 2 (1993): 80–88.

Brown, Mary Jean, et al. "Lead Poisoning among Internally Displaced Roma, Ashkali and Egyptian Children in the United Nations-Administered Province of Kosovo." *European Journal of Public Health* 20, no. 3 (2010): 288–92.

Brüggemann, Christian, and Eben Friedman. "The Decade of Roma Inclusion: Origins, Actors, and Legacies." *European Education* 49 (2017): 1–9.

Butler, Judith. *Frames of War: When Is Life Grievable?* London: Verso, 2010.

Cahn, Claude, and Tatjana Peric. *Roma and the Kosovo Conflict.* Budapest: European Roma Rights Centre, 1999. Accessed February 2, 2019. www.errc .org/cikk.php?cikk = 798.

Castañeda, Heide. "European Mobilities or Poverty Migration? Discourses on Roma in Germany." *International Migration* 53, no. 3 (2015): 87–99.

Chang, Felix. "The Chinese under Serbian Laws." In *Chinese Migrants in Russia, Central Asia, and Eastern Europe,* edited by Felix Chang and Sunnie Rucker-Change. New York: Routledge, 2012.

Chelcea, Liviu. "The Culture of Shortage during State-Socialism: Consumption Practices in a Romanian Village in the 1980s." *Cultural Studies* 16, no. 1 (2002): 16–43.

Ciulinaru, Dragos. "When 'Inclusion' Means 'Exclusion': Discourses on the Eviction and Repatriation of Roma Migrants, at National and European Union Level." *Journal of International Migration & Integration* 19, no. 4 (2018): 1059–73.

Clough Marinaro, Isabella. "Between Surveillance and Exile: Biopolitics and the Roma in Italy." *Bulletin of Italian Studies* 1, no. 2 (2009): 265–87.

Clough Mariano, Isabella, and Ulderico Daniele. "Roma and Humanitarianism in the Eternal City." *Journal of Modern Italian Studies* 16, no. 5 (2011): 621–36.

Crang, Mike, Alex Hughes, Nicky Gregson, Lucy Norris, and Farid Ahamed. "Rethinking Governance and Value in Commodity Chains through Global Recycling Networks." *Transactions of the Institute of British Geographers* 38, no. 1 (2013): 12–24.

Csepeli, Gyorgy, and David Simon. "Construction of Roma Identity in Eastern and Central Europe: Perception and Self-Identification." *Journal of Ethnic and Migration Studies* 30, no. 1 (2004): 129–50.

Čvorović, Jelena, and Kathryn Coe. "'Visiting' Close Kin Abroad: Migration Strategies of Serbian Roma." *Journal of Gypsy Studies* 1, no. 1 (2017): 17–29.

Das, Veena. "State, Citizenship, and the Urban Poor." *Citizenship Studies* 15, nos. 3–4 (2011): 319–33.

———. *Affliction: Health, Disease, Poverty.* New York: Fordham University Press, 2015.

Davies, Anna. "Geography and the Matter of Waste Mobilities." *Transactions of the Institute of British Geographers* 37 (2012): 191–96.

Desjarlais, Robert. "Struggling Along." In *Things as They Are: New Directions in Phenomenological Anthropology,* edited by Michael Jackson, 70–93. Bloomington: Indiana University Press, 1996.

Deutsche Welle. "Asylum Benefits in the EU: How Member States Compare." June 19, 2018. Accessed February 2, 2019. www.dw.com/en/asylum-benefits-in-the-eu-how-member-states-compare/a-44298599.

Downs, Mary. "A Short History of Scavenging." *Comparative Civilizations Review* 42 (2000): 23–45.

Dunn, Elizabeth Cullen. *No Path Home: Humanitarian Camps and the Grief of Displacement.* Ithaca, NY: Cornell University Press, 2018.

Dunn, Elizabeth Cullen, and Jason Cons. "Aleatory Sovereignty and the Rule of Sensitive Spaces." *Antipode* 46, no. 1 (2014): 92–109.

Durst, Judit. "New Redistributors in Times of Insecurity: Different Types of Informal Lending in Hungary." In *Gypsy Economy: Romani Livelihoods and Notions of Worth in the 21st Century,* edited by Micol Brazzabeni, Manuela Ivone Cunha, and Martin Fotta, 49–67. London: Berghahn, 2015.

Đekić, Marija, Miloš Nikolić, and Raica Milićević. "Causes, Manifestations, and Representation of the Shadow Economy with Reference to Serbia." *Ekonomika* 65, no. 3 (2019): 103–14.

Đurđević, Snežana. "Obstacles for the Integration of the Ashkali Community into the Serbian Society." *Facta Universitatis* 12, no. 1 (2014): 43–51.

Erikson, Susan. "Global Health Business: The Production and Performativity of Statistics in Sierra Leone and Germany." *Medical Anthropology* 31, no. 4 (2012): 367–84.

European Roma Rights Centre. *Abandoned Minority*. Budapest: European Roma Rights Centre, 2011.

European Stability Initiative. *New Facts and Figures on Western Balkan Asylum Seekers*. Berlin: European Stability Initiative, 2015.

European Union Agency for Fundamental Human Rights. *Poverty and Employment: The Situation of Roma in 11 EU Member States*. Vienna: FRA, 2014.

Fehérváry, Krisztina. "Goods and States: The Political Logic of State-Socialist Material Culture." *Comparative Studies in Society and History* 51, no. 2 (2009): 426–59.

Fings, Karola, Herbert Heuss, and Frank Sparing. *The Gypsies during the Second World War: From "Race Science" to the Camps*. Hatfield: University of Hertfordshire Press, 1997.

Foucault, Michel. *The History of Sexuality*, vol. 1, *An Introduction*. New York: Vintage Books, 1976.

———. *Society Must Be Defended*. London: Penguin, 1997.

Fraser, Angus. *The Gypsies*. London: Blackwell, 1995.

Friedman, Eben. *Roma in the Yugoslav Successor States*. European Centre for Minority Issues. Working Paper #82, December 2014.

Geertz, Clifford. "Deep Hanging Out." *New York Review of Books*, October 22, 1998.

Gidwani, Vinay, and Rajyashree Reddy. "The Afterlives of 'Waste': Notes from India for a Minor History of Capitalist Surplus." *Antipode* 43, no. 5 (2011): 1625–58.

Giles, David Boarder. "The Anatomy of a Dumpster: Abject Capital and the Looking Glass of Value." *Social Text* 32, no. 1 (2014): 93–113.

Gille, Zsusza. *From the Cult of Waste to the Trash Heap of History: The Politics of Waste in Socialist and Postsocialist Hungary*. Bloomington: Indiana University Press, 2007.

Han, Clara. *Life in Debt: Times of Care and Violence in Neoliberal Chile*. Berkeley: University of California Press, 2012.

Hancock, Ian. "Three-fold Identity? The Ethnical and National Identity of the Hungarian Boyash Gypsies." In *Nations and National Minorities in the*

European Union, edited by Barna Bodó and Márton Tonk, 91–102. Cluj-Napoca: Scientia, 1991.

———. *We Are the Romani People.* London: Hertfordshire Press, 2002.

———. "Romanies and the Holocaust: A Re-evaluation and Overview." In *The Historiography of the Holocaust,* edited by Dan Stone, 383–96. London: Palgrave Macmillan, 2004.

Hayden, Robert. "Constitutional Nationalism in the Formerly Yugoslav Republics." *Slavic Review* 51, no. 4 (1992): 654–73.

Heidegger, Martin. *Being and Time.* London: SCM Press, 1962.

Hempfling, Craig. *Secondary Materials and Waste Recycling Commercialization in Serbia, Part I: Assessment.* Belgrade: US AID, 2010.

Heuser, Helene. "Blitzverfahren—German Asylum Procedures for Roma from Western Balkan Countries." In *Going Nowhere? Western Balkan Roma and EU Liberalisation,* edited by Elspeth Guild, Kieran O'Reilly, and Marek Szilvas, 71–78. Budapest: European Roma Rights Centre, 2014.

Holmes, Seth. *Fresh Fruit, Broken Bodies: Migrant Farmworkers in the United States.* Berkeley: University of California Press, 2013.

Hrustič, Tomáš. "Usury among the Slovak Roma: Notes on Relations between Lenders and Borrowers in a Segregated Taboris." In *Gypsy Economy: Romani Livelihoods and Notions of Worth in the 21st Century,* edited by Micol Brazzabeni, Manuela Ivone Cunha, and Martin Fotta, 31–48. London: Berghahn, 2015.

Human Rights Watch. *Kosovo: Poisoned by Lead.* New York: Human Rights Watch, 2009.

Humphrey, Caroline. "Sovereignty." In *A Companion to the Anthropology of Politics,* edited by David Nugent and Joan Vincent, 418–63. Malden, MA: Blackwell, 2007.

Imre, Aniko. "Whiteness in Post-socialist Eastern Europe: The Time of the Gypsies, the End of Race." In *Postcolonial Whiteness: A Critical Reader on Race and Empire,* edited by Alfred Lopez, 79–102. Albany: State University of New York Press, 2005.

Internal Displacement Monitoring Centre. *Kosovo: Durable Solutions Still Elusive 13 Years after Conflict.* Geneva: Internal Displacement Monitoring Centre, 2012.

International Crisis Group. *Violence in Kosovo: Who's Killing Whom?* Pristina: ICG Balkans, 1999.

Kenrick, Donald, and Grattan Puxon. *Gypsies under the Swastika.* Hatfield: University of Hertfordshire Press, 2009.

Kilibarda, Konstantin. "Clearing Space: An Anatomy of Urban Renewal, Social Cleansing, and Everyday Life in a Belgrade Mahala." *Cambridge Review of International Affairs* 24, no. 4 (2011): 593–612.

Kleinman, Arthur, Veena Das, and Margaret Lock. "Introduction." In *Social Suffering*, edited by Arthur Kleinman, Veena Das and Margaret Lock, ix–xxvii. Berkeley: University of California Press, 1997.

Kóczé, Angela. "Roma Migration and Neoliberalism: Distorted Notions of Romani Migration in European Public Discourses." *Social Identities* 24, no. 4 (2018): 459–73.

Kopytoff, Igor. "The Cultural Biography of Things: Commoditization as a Process." In *The Social Life of Things*, edited by Arjun Appadurai, 64–91. Cambridge: Cambridge University Press, 1986.

Korać, Maja. "Transnational Pathways to Integration: Chinese Traders in Serbia." *Sociologija* 55, no. 2 (2013): 245–60.

Korać-Sanderson, Maja. "Chinese Traders in Serbia: Gender Opportunities, Translocal Family Strategies, and Transnational Mobility." *Ars & Humanitas* 7, no. 2 (2013): 86–98.

Krasniqi, Gezim. "Equal Citizens, Uneven Communities: Differentiated and Hierarchical Citizenship in Kosovo." *Ethnopolitics* 14, no. 2 (2015): 197–217.

Kristeva, Julia. *Powers of Horror: An Essay on Abjection*. New York: Columbia University Press, 1982.

Laubenthal, Barbara. "Refugees Welcome? Federalism and Asylum Policies in Germany." *Fieri Working Papers*. September 2015.

Lea, Tess. *Bureaucrats and Bleeding Hearts: Indigenous Health in Northern Australia*. Sydney: University of New South Wales Press, 2008.

Ledeneva, Alena. *How Russia Really Works: The Informal Practices That Shaped Post-Soviet Politics and Business*. Ithaca, NY: Cornell University Press, 2013.

Lee, Christina. "Counting on Confusion: Romani Asylum-Seekers in the German Media, 2012–2013." *Roma Rights* 1 (2014): 79–86.

Leko, Jure. "Migration Regimes and the Translation of Human Rights: On the Struggles for Recognition of Romani Migrants in Germany." *Social Inclusion* 5, no. 3 (2017): 77–88.

Lemon, Alaina. *Between Two Fires: Gypsy Performance and Romani Memory from Pushkin to Post-socialism*. Durham NC: Duke University Press, 2000,
———. "'What Are They Writing about Us Blacks?' Roma and 'Race' in Russia." *Anthropology of East Europe Review* 13, no. 2 (1995): 34–40.

Lewy, Guenter. *The Nazi Persecution of the Gypsies*. Oxford: Oxford University Press, 2000.

Lichnofsky, Claudia. "Ashkali and Egyptians in Kosovo: New Ethnic Identifications as a Result of Exclusion during Nationalist Violence from 1990 till 2010." *Romani Studies* 23, no. 1 (2013): 29–59.

MacGregor, Marion. *The Asylum Seeker's Benefits Act*. May 30, 2018. Accessed February 2, 2019. www.infomigrants.net/en/post/9560/the-asylum-seekers-benefits-act.

Macura, Vladimir. *Roma Settlements in Serbia: Current State of Affairs and Future Goals*. Belgrade: Society for the Improvement of Local Roma Communities, 2009.

Maestri, Gaja. "Struggles and Ambiguities over Political Subjectivities in the Camp: Roma Camp Dwellers between Neoliberal and Urban Citizenship in Italy." *Citizenship Studies* 21, no. 6 (2017): 640–56.

Malkki, Liisa. *Purity and Exile: Violence, Memory, and National Cosmology among Hutu Refugees in Tanzania*. Chicago: University of Chicago Press, 1995.

Marjanović, Miloš. "Encountering the Ethnic Stereotypes about the Romanies." *Facta Universitatis* 2, no. 8 (2001): 433–43.

Marushiakova, Elena, and Vesselin Popov. *Gypsies in the Ottoman Empire*. Hatfield: University of Hertfordshire Press, 2001.

———. "New Ethnic Identities in the Balkans: The Case of the Egyptians." *Facta Universitas* 2, no. 8 (2001): 465–77.

———. "'Gypsy' Groups in Eastern Europe: Ethnonyms vs. Professionyms." *Romani Studies* 23, no. 1 (2013): 61–82.

Marushiakova, Elena, et al. *Identity Formation among Minorities in the Balkans: The Cases of Roms, Egyptians, and Ashkali in Kosovo*. Sofia: Minority Studies Society, 2001.

Matras, Yaron. "Letter from the Outgoing Editor: From *Journal of the Gypsy Lore Society* to *Romani Studies:* Purpose and Essence of a Modern Academic Platform." *Romani Studies* 27, no. 2 (2017): 113–23.

Mattli, Angela, and Stephan Müller. *Lost in Transition: The Forced Migration Circle of Roma, Ashkali, and Balkan Egyptians from Kosovo*. Bern: Society for Threatened Peoples, 2015.

Mauss, Marcel. *The Gift: Forms and Functions of Exchange in Archaic Societies*. Translated by Ian Cunnison. New York: Martino Fine Books, 2011.

McGarry, Aidan. "Roma as a Political Identity: Exploring Representations of Roma in Europe." *Ethnicities* 14, no. 6 (2014): 756–74.

McMahon, Patrice. *The NGO Game: Post-conflict Peacebuilding in the Balkans and Beyond*. Ithaca, NY: Cornell University Press, 2017.

Merry, Sally Engle. *The Seductions of Quantification: Measuring Human Rights, Gender Violence, and Sex Trafficking*. Chicago: University of Chicago Press, 2016.

Millar, Kathleen. "Trash Ties: Urban Politics, Economic Crisis and Rio de Janeiro's Garbage Dump." In *Economies of Recycling: The Global Transformation of Materials, Values, and Social Relations*, edited by Catherine Alexander and Joshua Reno, 164–84. London: Zed Books, 2012.

———. *Reclaiming the Discarded: Life and Labor on Rio's Garbage Dump*. Durham, NC: Duke University Press, 2018.

Milutinović, Svetlana. "Chinese Transnational Entrepreneurs in Budapest and Belgrade: Seeking Markets, Carrying Globalization." In *Transnational Ties: Cities, Migrations, and Identities*, edited by Richard Brail, 90–106. New York: Taylor & Francis, 2008.

Mirga-Kruszelnicka, Anna. "Challenging Anti-Gypsyism in Academic: The Role of Romani Scholars." *Critical Romani Studies* 1, no. 1 (2018): 8–28.

Myall, David. *Gypsy Identities 1500–2000: From Egipcyans and Moon-Men to Ethnic Romany*. London: Routledge, 2004.

Nguyen, Minh. "Trading in Broken Things: Gendered Performances and Spatial Practices in a Northern Vietnamese Rural-Urban Waste Economy." *American Ethnologist* 43, no. 1 (2016): 116–29.

Nyiri, Pal. *Chinese in Eastern Europe and Russia: A Middleman Minority in a Transnational Era*. New York: Routledge, 2007.

O'Brien, Martin. *A Crisis of Waste? Understanding the Rubbish Society*. Routledge: London, 2007.

O'Hare, Patrick. " 'The Landfill Has Always Borne Fruit': Precarity, Formalisation, and Dispossession among Uruguay's Waste Pickers." *Dialectical Anthropology* 43, no. 1 (2019): 31–44.

Okely, Judith. "Trading Stereotypes: The Case of English Gypsies." In *Ethnicity at Work*, edited by Sandra Wallman, 16–33. London: MacMillan, 1979.

———. "Recycled (Mis)representations: Gypsies, Travellers or Roma Treated as Objects, Rarely Subjects." *People, Place & Policy* 8, no. 1 (2014): 65–85.

O'Neill, Bruce. "Cast Aside: Boredom, Downward Mobility, and Homelessness in Post-Communist Bucharest." *Cultural Anthropology* 29, no. 1 (2014): 8–31.

———. *The Space of Boredom: Homelessness in the Slowing Global Order*. Durham, NC: Duke University Press, 2017.

Ong, Aihwa. "Graduated Sovereignty in South-East Asia." *Theory, Culture & Society* 17, no. 4 (2000): 55–75.

———. *Neoliberalism as Exception: Mutations in Citizenship and Sovereignty*. Durham, NC: Duke University Press, 2006.

O'Nions, Helen. "How Citizenship Laws Leave the Roma in Europe's Hinterland." In *The Human Right to Citizenship: A Slippery Concept*, edited by Rhonda Howard-Hassmann and Margaret Walton-Roberts, 209–31. Philadelphia: University of Pennsylvania Press, 2015.

OSCE (Organization for Security and Cooperation in Europe). *Eight Years After: Minority Returns and Housing and Property Restitution in Kosovo*. Pristina: OSCE, 2007.

———. *Municipal Responses to Displacement and Returns in Kosovo*. Pristina: OSCE, 2010.

———. *Sustainable Solutions for Displaced Roma, Ashkali and Egyptians and Policies to Improve the Reintegration of Repatriated Roma*. Belgrade: Office for Democratic Institutions and Human Rights, Organization for Security and Cooperation in Europe, 2010.

Picker, Giovanni. *Racial Cities: Governance and the Segregation of Romani People in Urban Europe*. New York: Routledge, 2017.

Povinelli, Elizabeth. *Economies of Abandonment: Social Belonging and Endurance in Late Liberalism*. Durham, NC: Duke University Press, 2011.

Praxis. *Persons at Risk of Statelessness in Serbia*. Belgrade: Praxis, 2011.

———. *Eviction from the Informal Settlement in Block 72, New Belgrade*. Belgrade: Praxis, 2012.

———. *Analysis of the Main Obstacles and Problems in Access of Roma to the Right to Adequate Housing*. Belgrade: Praxis, 2013.

Reno, Joshua. "Your Trash Is Someone's Treasure: The Politics of Value at a Michigan Landfill." *Journal of Material Culture* 14, no. 1 (2009): 29–46.

———. "Waste and Waste Management." *Annual Review of Anthropology* 44, no. 1 (2015): 557–72.

Renzi, Laura. "Roma People in Europe: A Long History of Discrimination." *European Social Watch Report*, 2010, 40–43.

Republic of Kosovo. *Strategy for Inclusion of Roma and Ashkali Communities in the Kosovo Society 2017–2021*. Pristina: Republic of Kosovo, 2017.

Republic of Serbia. *Serbia Floods 2014*. Belgrade: Ministry of Environmental Protection, 2014.

———. *Action Plan for the Implementation of the Strategy of Social Inclusion of the Roma in the Republic of Serbia for the Period 2016–2025*. Belgrade: Republic of Serbia, 2017.

Resnick, Elana. "Nothing Ever Parishes: Waste, Race, and Transformation in an Expanding European Union." PhD diss., University of Michigan, Ann Arbor, 2016.

———. "Durable Remains: Glass Reuse, Material Citizenship and Precarity in EU-era Bulgaria." *Journal of Contemporary Archaeology* 5, no. 1 (2018): 103–15.

Ruggiu, Ilenia. "Is Begging a Roma Cultural Practice? Answers from the Italian Legal System and Anthropology." *Romani Studies* 26, no. 1 (2016): 31–61.

Ryder, Andrew Richard. "Game of Thrones: Power Struggles and Contestation in Romani Studies." *International Journal of Romani Studies* 1, no. 2 (2019): 120–43.

Said, Edward. *Orientalism*. New York: Vintage Books, 1979.

Sardelić, Julija. "Romani Minorities and the Variety of Migration Patterns in the Post-Yugoslav Space." *Roma Rights* 1 (2014): 15–22.

———. "Romani Minorities and Uneven Citizenship Access in the Post-Yugoslav Space." *Ethnopolitics* 14, no. 2 (2015): 159–79.

Scheffel, David. *Svinia in Black and White: Slovak Roma and Their Neighbours*. Toronto: University of Toronto Press, 2005.

Scheper-Hughes, Nancy, and Philippe Bourgois. "Introduction: Making Sense of Violence." In *Violence in War and Peace: An Anthology,* edited by Nancy Scheper-Hughes and Philippe Bourgois, 1–31. New York: Wiley-Blackwell, 2003.

Schwab, Eva. "Construction and Governance of 'Unhygienic Roma Settlements' in Belgrade: An Anthropological Investigation in Urban Citizenship Rights." MA thesis, University of Vienna, 2013.

Selling, Jan. "Assessing the Historical Irresponsibility of the Gypsy Lore Society in Light of Romani Subaltern Challenges." *Critical Romani Studies* 1, no. 1 (2018): 44–61.

Shevchenko, Olga. *Crisis and the Everyday in Postsocialist Moscow.* Bloomington: University of Indiana Press, 2008.

Sigona, Nando. "Locating 'The Gypsy Problem': The Roma in Italy—Stereotyping, Labelling and 'Nomad Camps'." *Journal of Ethnic and Migration Studies* 31, no. 4 (2005): 741–56.

———. "The Governance of Romani People in Italy: Discourse, Policy, and Practice." *Journal of Modern Italian Studies* 16, no. 5 (2011): 590–606.

———. "Between Competing Imaginaries of Statehood: Roma, Ashkali, and Egyptian (RAE) Leadership in Newly Independent Kosovo." *Journal of Ethnic and Migration Studies* 38, no. 8 (2012): 1213–32.

Silverman, Carol. "Negotiating 'Gypsiness': Strategy in Context." *Journal of American Folklore* 101, no. 401 (1988): 261–75.

Simpson-Hebert, Mayling, Aleksandra Mitrović, Gradamir Zajić, and Miloš Petrović. *A Paper Life: Belgrade's Roma in the Underworld of Waste Scavenging and Recycling.* New York: WEDC, 2005.

Solimene, Marco. "Undressing the Gağé Clad in State Garb: Bosnian Xoraxané Romá Face to Face with the Italian Authorities." *Romani Studies* 23, no. 2 (2013): 161–86.

———. " 'I Go for Iron': Xoraxané Romá Collecting Scrap Metal in Rome." In *Gypsy Economy: Romani Livelihoods and Notions of Worth in the Twenty-first Century,* edited by Micol Brazzabeni, Manuela Ivone Cunha, and Martin Fotta, 107–26. London: Berghahn, 2015.

Stallybrass, Peter, and Allon White. *The Politics and Poetics of Transgression.* Ithaca, NY: Cornell University Press, 1986.

Stewart, Kathleen. *Ordinary Affects.* Durham, NC: Duke University Press, 2007.

Stewart, Michael. *The Time of the Gypsies.* London: Westview Press, 1999.

———. "Roma and Gypsy 'Ethnicity' as a Subject of Anthropological Inquiry." *Annual Review of Anthropology* 42 (2013): 415–32.

Strasser, Susan. *Waste and Want: A Social History of Trash.* New York: Holt Paperbacks, 2000.

Surdu, Mihai, and Martin Kovats. "Roma Identity as an Expert-Political Construction." *Social Inclusion* 3, no. 5 (2015): 5–18.

Šabić, Dejan, Aleksandar Knežević, Snežana Vujadinović, Rajko Golić, Miroljub Milinčić, and Marko Joksimović. "Belgrade Slums: Life or Survival on the Margins of Serbian Society?" *Trames* 17, no. 1 (2013): 55–86.

Ta, Trang. "A Space for Secondhand Goods: Trading the Remnants of Material Life in Hong Kong." *Economic Anthropology* 4, no. 1 (2017): 120–31.

Tesăr, Cătălina. "Houses under Construction: Conspicuous Consumption and the Values of Youth among Romanian Cortorari Gypsies." In *Gypsy Economy: Romani Livelihoods and Notions of Worth in the 21st Century*, edited by Micol Brazzabeni, Manuela Ivone Cunha, and Martin Fotta, 181–200. London: Berghahn, 2015.

Timmer, Andria. "Constructing the 'Needy Subject': NGO Discourses of Roma Need." *Political and Legal Anthropology Review* 33, no. 2 (2010): 264–81.

Tmava, Milena, and Adem Beha. *Helplessness: Roma, Ashkali, and Egyptian Forced Returnees in Kosovo*. Pristina: RAD Centre, 2009.

Trauner, Florian, and Emanule Manigrassi. "When Visa-Free Travel Becomes Difficult to Achieve and Easy to Lose: The EU Visa Free Dialogues after the EU's Experience with the Western Balkans." *European Journal of Migration and Law* 16, no. 1 (2014): 123–43.

Trehan, Nidhi. "The Romani Subaltern within Neoliberal European Civil Society: NGOization of Human Rights and Silent Voices." In *Romani Politics in Contemporary Europe: Poverty, Ethnic Mobilization, and the Neoliberal Order*, edited by Nando Sigona and Nidhi Trehan, 51–71. London: Palgrave Macmillan, 2009.

Trubeta, Sevasti. "Balkan Egyptians and Gypsy / Roma Discourse." *Nationalities Papers* 33, no. 1 (2005): 71–95.

Tsenkova, Sasha. "Informal Settlements in Post-Communist Cities: Diversity Factors and Patterns." *Urbani Izziv* 21, no. 2 (2010): 73–84.

UNDP (United Nations Development Programme). *SPARK: Sustainable Partnerships for Assistance to Minority Returns to Kosovo, Bi-Monthly Report July–August 2009*. Pristina: UNDP, 2009.

———. *Community Vulnerability Assessment Report*. Pristina: UNDP, 2013.

———. *Kosovo Human Development Report*. Pristina: UNDP, 2016.

UN-HABITAT. *State of the World's Cities 2006/2007*. New York: UN-HABITAT, 2006.

UNHCR (United Nations High Commissioner for Refugees). *Assessment of the Needs of Internally Displaced Persons in the Republic of Serbia*. Belgrade: UNHCR, 2011.

Urech, Evelyn, and Wilco van den Heuvel. "A Sociolinguistic Perspective on Roma Group Names in Transylvania." *Romani Studies* 21, no. 2 (2011): 145–60.

V. V. B. "The Plights of Europe's Roma." *The Economist,* May 25, 2012. Accessed on January 15, 2020. www.economist.com/eastern-approaches/2012/05/25/the-plight-of-europes-roma.

van Baar, Huub. "Socio-Economic Mobility and Neo-Liberal Governmentality in Post-Socialist Europe: Activation and the Dehumanization of the Roma." *Journal of Ethnic and Migration Studies* 38, no. 8 (2012): 1289–304.

———. "The Perpetual Mobile Machine of Forced Mobility: Europe's Roma and the Institutionalization of Rootlessness." In *The Irregularization of Migration in Contemporary Europe: Detention, Deportation, Drowning,* edited by Yolande Jansen, Robin Celikates, and Joost de Bloois, 71–86. London: Rowman & Littlefield International, 2015.

Vasiljević, Jelena. "Imagining and Managing the Nation: Tracing Citizenship Policies in Serbia." *Citizenship Studies* 16, nos. 3–4 (2012): 323–36.

———. "Citizenship as Lived Experience: Belonging and Documentality after the Breakup of Yugoslavia." *CITSEE Working Paper Series* 36 (2014): 1–29.

Verdery, Katherine. *What Was Socialism, and What Comes Next?.* Princeton, NJ: Princeton University Press, 1996.

Vesic, Uros, Tatijana Kosic, and Aleksandra Krstic-Furundzic. "Social Housing in Serbia: Dual Approach." In *Proceedings of Real Corp 2013: Planning Times,* edited by Manfred Schrenk, Vasily Popovich, and Peter Zeile, 801–9. Rome: Real Corp, 2013.

Visoka, Gezim, and Adem Beha. *Repatriation without Responsibility: The Nature and Implications of Roma, Ashkalia and Egyptian Forced Repatriation to Kosovo.* Pristina: FORUM, 2015.

Visoka, Gezim, and Oliver Richmond. "After Liberal Peace? From Failed State-Building to an Emancipatory Peace in Kosovo." *International Studies Perspectives* 18, no. 1 (2017): 110–29.

Vučković, Milan, and Goran Nikolić. *Stanovništvo Kosova u razdoblju 1918–1991.* Munich: Slavica Verlag, 1996.

Vujović, Sreten, and Mina Petrović. "Belgrade's Post-Socialist Development." In *The Post-Socialist City,* edited by Kiril Stanilov, 361–84. London: Springer, 2007.

Vuksanović-Macura, Zlata. "The Mapping and Enumeration of Informal Roma Settlements in Serbia." *Environment & Urbanization* 24, no. 2 (2012): 685–705.

Vuksanović-Macura, Zlata, and Vladimir Macura. *Existing Models of Housing Improvement for Roma: Social and Affordable Housing Solutions for Roma and Vulnerable Population in Serbia.* Belgrade: OSCE Mission to Serbia, 2014.

———. *Housing Models for Substandard Roma Settlements: Guidelines for Local Self-Governments, Civil Society Organizations and Roma Communities.* Belgrade: OSCE Mission to Serbia, 2014.

Whitson, Risa. "Negotiating Place and Value: Geographies of Waste and Scavenging in Buenos Aires." *Antipode* 43, no. 4 (2011): 1404–33.

Wolf, Eric. *Europe and the People without History.* Berkeley: University of California Press, 2010.

Zemon, Rubin. *History of Ashkali Identity.* Brussels: Council of Europe, 2010.

Živković, Ljiljana, and Aleksandar Đorđević. *General Characteristics of Substandard Roma Settlements in Serbia and a Proposal for Further Development Initiatives for the Improvement of the Living Conditions of the Roma Community.* Belgrade: OSCE Mission to Serbia, 2015.

Index

Founded in 1893,
UNIVERSITY OF CALIFORNIA PRESS
publishes bold, progressive books and journals
on topics in the arts, humanities, social sciences,
and natural sciences—with a focus on social
justice issues—that inspire thought and action
among readers worldwide.

The UC PRESS FOUNDATION
raises funds to uphold the press's vital role
as an independent, nonprofit publisher, and
receives philanthropic support from a wide
range of individuals and institutions—and from
committed readers like you. To learn more, visit
ucpress.edu/supportus.

CPSIA information can be obtained
at www.ICGtesting.com
Printed in the USA
FSHW011536180321
79632FS